W9-DBP-112

A Preface to Education

By M. R. Charles

This preface to education systematically reveals to the reader that the materials which comprise the contents of education are derived from the social sciences. Based on a social-scientific orientation, this volume not only accepts education as one of the newer learned disciplines but also tries to treat it with the respect a learned discipline deserves.

The author discusses in order the disciplines of anthropology, history, political science, economics, sociology, psychology, and philosophy. Their contributions to education are dealt with in detail. He demonstrates why people need to be educated and how various societies handle this matter. An interpretation of what has been happening in American education is given as well as a delineation of the governmental and financial issues that affect education. The relatedness of the larger encompassing society to its schools and the learners themselves in the educational setting are treated in detail. Finally, the themes, goals, varying viewpoints, vocation, and changing status of education are presented for the enlightenment of all interested in today's schools.

There are discussion questions at the heads of the chapters and summaries at the ends, along with selected bibliographies. The text is amply illustrated.

About the Author

M. R. Charles is Professor of Social Science at Oregon College of Education, Monmouth, Oregon.

A PREFACE TO EDUCATION

A Preface to

EDUCATION

M. R. CHARLES

Professor of Social Science
Oregon College of Education

THE MACMILLAN COMPANY, NEW YORK

COLLIER-MACMILLAN LIMITED, LONDON

CARRIE RICH MEMORIAL LIBRARY
CAMPBELL COLLEGE
BUIES CREEK, N. C.

© Copyright, Milton R. Charles, 1965

All rights reserved. No part of this book may be reproduced in any form without permission in writing from the publisher, except by a reviewer who wishes to quote brief passages in connection with a review written for inclusion in a magazine or newspaper.

First Printing

Library of Congress catalog card number: 64–22598

THE MACMILLAN COMPANY, NEW YORK
COLLIER-MACMILLAN CANADA, LTD., TORONTO, ONTARIO

Printed in the United States of America

To BARBARA

PAMELA

and VINCENT

92819

Foreword

My *apologia pro libro meo* rests upon two contributions that I have attempted to make. First, this preface to education is organized in what I believe to be a unique fashion. The reader is shown that the materials which comprise the discipline of education derive from the social sciences. The organization of the book centers around this social-scientific orientation of education. Second, this volume not only accepts the view that education is one of the newer learned disciplines, but also tries to treat the field with the respect that a learned discipline deserves. The ensuing introduction makes no attempt to lure people into the field of education by offering a romanticized version of it. If education is, indeed, a learned discipline, those who study education must feel that they are receiving from their inquiry sturdy, academically reputable, important, meaningful information. Threadbare materials offered in the name of education can only contribute to the smug feeling of those pothunters who delight in using the study of education as their quarry.

This book is addressed to lower-division college students who have not enrolled for any previous academic work in the discipline of education. The book assumes that these students, in all probability, will have had but limited previous acquaintance with the social sciences. While this volume is introductory in nature, I have not thought of it as a primer. Some of the materials will be easy for the newcomer to grasp, but others may require effort on his part. I have not tried to protect my readers from all mentally taxing ideas; neither have I tried to inflate the book by making it falsely difficult. The student who begins his study of the learned field of education deserves to know that he will be able to master fairly quickly some of the basic concepts. He deserves to know, also, that an introduction to education is just an introduction. It does not guarantee complete mastery of the entire field.

Debates on education are becoming increasingly common nowadays. While I do not delude myself into thinking that my views on education are utterly absent from what I have written, this book is not intended to be either my credo or an addition to the rising quantity of polemical essays. The book is, rather, what its title suggests: a *preface* to education.

M. R. CHARLES

Monmouth, Oregon

Acknowledgments

Many individuals and groups have assisted in the preparation of this volume.

The College and Professional Division of The Macmillan Company and its readers have offered me much help.

Several individuals and organizations have granted me permission to reproduce illustrations and other materials belonging to them. While more specific credit lines appear elsewhere in this book, I wish to express my gratitude at this point as well.

Those sophomore students at Oregon College of Education who, between 1960 and 1963, enrolled in my experimental introductory course in education stimulated me to write this book.

I shall not attempt to list the names of all those people who have brought this volume into being, lest the imperfections of memory cause me to omit some names that deserve to be included. Nevertheless, I wish to pay special tribute to the efforts of four people, whom I shall use as symbols of the many other people who equally deserve mention. Two of my colleagues at Oregon College of Education, whose counsel I value, Dean Walter E. Snyder and Professor E. K. Dortmund, read the entire manuscript. Professor A. Kenneth Yost, of Oregon College of Education's Educational Media Center, was a source of advice concerning illustrative materials. And Mr. James Davis, of Central High School, Independence, Oregon, obtained the Volesky pictures for me. My hearty thanks to all of those people, named and unnamed.

M. R. C.

Contents

A PREFACE TO EDUCATION

1

Education and the Social Sciences

Today [education] is a principal instrument in awakening the child to cultural values, in preparing him for later profesional training, and in helping him to adjust normally to his environment. In these days, it is doubtful that any child may reasonably be expected to succeed in life if he is denied the opportunity of an education.

from *Brown* v. *Board of Education*, 347 U.S. 483 (1954).

Thinking It Over Beforehand

What would you want to know about the vocation of teaching before becoming a teacher?

What kinds of things do you learn in courses offered by a department of education?

The materials of which academic disciplines are most closely related to those taught in a department of education?

Does a person absolutely *have* to take courses in education in order to be a teacher? Explain your answer.

A person who has been trained in dentistry we call a dentist. One who has been trained in cosmetology we call a cosmetologist. What do you call a trained teacher in order to distinguish him from someone who tells you something that you had not known before and who, therefore, "teaches" you something?

The School and American Life

Education is an engrossing social structure. Daily, millions of students across the United States attend school. Tens of thousands of adults are employed to keep the schools of our nation in operation. Many people who earn their livelihood by teaching are dedicated to the occupation because they believe that education is crucial to human existence itself. Every day people discuss the nation's schools and the role of education in the lives of American citizens. Huge amounts of money are spent yearly for the ubiquitous enterprise of education. Legislative bodies, county groups, civic clubs, and school boards spend hours and hours deliberating the subject. Everybody in our civilized society is influenced by that institutional complex known as education in American life.

The Substructure of Education

You are invited to come along on a tour of inspection of education. This tour will be primarily behind the scenes. It will be one storey below the subflooring of education. We will examine the subterranean supports that form the foundations, bases, footings, and undergirdings upon which the superstructure rests, in order to determine how sturdy the building is.

Education is a specialized structure built on an ever increasing body of knowledge. In this chapter the relationship between education and the other specialized areas of man's knowledge will be delineated. The succeeding chapters will examine somewhat more closely the stones that form the substructure of education.

The Relationship of Education to Other Academic Disciplines

The subjects taught at a university may be classified, for the sake of convenience, into three major areas. The first is the humanities, the second is the sciences, and the third is the applied studies.

The humanities center attention on the evaluation of cultural products which human beings have developed for themselves, such as art, literature, music, or drama. In typical higher educational establishments, there are departments of study which offer series of courses in such subjects as music, art, English, and the like.

The sciences center attention on an objective classification of facts. The approach used is commonly called the scientific method. It involves carefully analyzing data acquired through one or more of the five senses—sight, taste, touch, smell, hearing—and reasoning from this analysis. It involves disregarding one's prejudices and biases as much as is humanly possible. It involves the cautious reporting of the activities and processes of the items being analyzed.

The sciences may be divided into three subareas: physical sciences, life sciences, and social sciences. The physical sciences, such as chemistry, physics, and astronomy, analyze the characteristics of the earth and the skies. The life sciences, such as botany, zoology, and anatomy, deal with plants and animals—flora and fauna. The social sciences, such as sociology, economics, and political science, inquire into human conduct.

The applied studies are vocationally oriented. These studies prepare the student to go directly from the university into some sort of job that is waiting to be filled. There are applied humanities. Journalism is one of the applied humanities; the newspaper is a literary medium. Dress designing is another of the applied humanities; it is a type of art work. There are applied physical sciences, such as chemical engineering, aeronautical engineering, and meteorology. There are applied life sciences, including medicine, veterinary medicine, and agriculture. There are applied social sciences; law, social work, personnel management, business administration, and education are a few.

Each applied study has grown out of one or more of the fields included in the humanities or sciences. Pharmacy is an example of a vocationally oriented study. A person with a college degree in pharmacy is prepared to qualify as a professional mixer and dispenser of prescriptions in that unique, unusual, yet ubiquitous type of American department store, the drug store. The applied study of pharmacy has grown out of knowledge gained through such sciences as chemistry, physiology, bacteriology, and parasitology.

Notice that education was classified above as an applied study. It, too, is vocationally oriented. A person with a degree in education is prepared, usually, to qualify for the occupation of schoolteaching. The applied study of education rests primarily on knowledge gained through various social sciences. Thus, it is an applied social science. The approach of this book will be to identify several social sciences out of which the field of education has developed, and to show how these bodies of scientific knowledge are basic to this vocational pursuit.

The Field of Education

A brief inquiry into the kinds of courses taught in a department of education will provide a vantage point from which to see more clearly the relationship between the social sciences and education. Education courses can be divided, more handily than accurately, into (1) foundational courses, sometimes called theory courses, and (2) courses in methodology, or educational techniques.

No attempt to establish rigid categories is ever entirely successful, as examples from the biological sciences will show. Since the days of Linnaeus, the Swedish naturalist who first tried to classify animals, there has never been total agreement as to how many species of animals belong within the primate order, the order to which human beings are assigned. Linnaeus himself placed bats in the primate order, an assignment not generally accepted today. The status of the lemur, another possible candidate for the primate order, is also disputed. Even a biological categorization of man creates difficulties. The story is told of the Greek philosophers, Plato and Diogenes, who attempted to agree upon a suitable description of man as an animal. Plato defined man as a two-legged animal without feathers. Diogenes then caught a chicken, removed its feathers, brought it to Plato's college, and said, "This is Plato's man!"

Examples showing the difficulty of classification are to be found in the realm of literature, as well. How shall we classify John Steinbeck's *The Grapes of Wrath?* Shall we call it an artistic work that belongs to the field of creative writing? Certainly it is that. Shall we say that it is a study of social disorganization and, even though fiction, therefore a sociological treatise? It is that, too. Shall we describe it as a fictitious description of population mobility and assign it to the field of demography? It is that, also. Shall we call it an economic essay in the form of a novel and include it under the discipline of economics? It is that, as well. And it is a discussion of geography, a discussion of psychology, and one of social ethics. No unpliable classification is adequate.

Thus, too, in the following discussion of courses in education, the two categories "foundational courses" and "methodology courses" are not meant to be inflexible divisions, nor can they be considered mutually exclusive. It is expedient, nevertheless, to use this tentative, though somewhat dubious, dichotomy in order to visualize better the subject matter of education.

A gross oversimplification, but a good starting point, is that foundational courses in education center around the question "why?" whereas methods courses concern themselves with "what?" and "how?". Foundational courses inquire into why human beings behave as they do, why they create schools, why schooling is significant. Courses in methodology inquire into what to teach and how to teach it, what to organize and how it should be organized, what to administer and how to go about administering it. Foundational courses bring social-scientific materials to bear on the field of education. Methodology courses examine theories and put them to work. Typically, a student planning to teach begins his study of education with foundational courses. Having become familiar with the foundations of education, he then studies techniques of education. Someday, with this type of background in the foundations and methods of education, the student will be ready to step into a school situation and use his vocational knowledge.[1]

This book is a beginning textbook of the "why to teach" variety. It is intended as an introduction to more advanced and specialized foundational materials in education. It offers a quick glimpse of the bases of education. Later, a person who plans to teach will want to study in more depth some of the particulars of educational theory.

The Social Sciences and Education

The social sciences that have been used most in the development of education as a vocation are anthropology, history, political science, economics, sociology, and psychology. There is another discipline that has made a crucial contribution to education: philosophy. Although, narrowly speaking, philosophy is not a social science, it has played too significant a role in education to be omitted or ignored. A discussion of philosophy will be included in this book also, even though its inclusion disrupts the neatness of the generalization that education is an applied social science.

Diagram I suggests, in idealized form, some of the relationships among the social sciences, foundational courses in education, and educational methodology.

The social sciences form the background from which the foundational courses in education have come. As can be seen in the diagram, methods courses spring directly from foundational materials in education and indirectly from the social sciences. For example, the diagram shows that from the science of psychology has come the foundational field of education known as educational psychology, and from knowledge about educational psychology have come numerous techniques used in the schools. The same generalization holds true for the other social sciences also.

A preliminary look at the materials labeled "Social-Scientific Disciplines" in the diagram will show more clearly how each of these social sciences, plus philosophy, are related to education.

Anthropology and Education

When one steps into the field of anthropology, one senses that it is vast. Anthropology forms a bridge between the life sciences and the social sciences. Life in its many forms is the concern of the life sciences, and

---

[1] This statement is not intended to underplay the importance of courses which the student will study in other disciplines. Assuredly, these noneducation courses are a *sine qua non* for the person who intends to teach.

there are two approaches to a study of any type of life. One approach is
to find out what the particular form of life looks like; thus the hours in the
biology laboratory that are devoted to taking apart worms and frogs and
cats to see how they are put together. The other approach is to study the
way of life of the particular life form. Where does it live? What does it eat?
How and where does it get its food? With what companions does it share
its days? How does it reproduce? How does it care for its young? The life
scientists use both of these approaches in their study of living matter. Finding out about the social ways of some creatures is a relatively easy task;
the phantomlike planaria, for example, behaves so simply that its way of
life may be described in a single paragraph. On the other hand, when it
comes to a study of human beings, the task of analyzing their way of life
is highly complex. Anthropology has taken upon itself this difficult
work.

The range of interests within the field of anthropology can be seen in
the kinds of investigations conducted by pioneer anthropologists. Some
of these pioneers sought ways to classify living human beings by their
physical characteristics, such as shape, size, color, complexion, and the like,
which vary greatly. Others sought to determine how the body of man has
changed physically through the ages. Others sought to discover, by searching for relics in the dust, how mankind lived in the long, dead past. Still
others sought to study the ways of existing cultures that had not become
civilized. These interests are still an integral part of anthropology; they
suggest in a rough way its two major divisions. On the one hand, anthropology is a study of the changed and changing physical appearance of
mankind. On the other hand, anthropology is a study of the changed and
changing ways of life of mankind. The label attached to the first division
is physical anthropology. For our purposes, we shall classify physical
anthropology as a life science rather than a social science and say no more
about it.

The second major division is much more difficult to categorize with a
single term. For the sake of simplicity, perhaps at the expense of accuracy,
we shall call it cultural anthropology. Technically, some cultural anthropologists specialize in reconstructing the ways of life of prehistoric or
precivilized human beings. These anthropologists who "go back of history"
are called archaeologists. A second group of cultural anthropologists are
ethnologists, whose main concern has been the behavior of contemporary
primitive people generally. A third group, ethnographers, make intensive
studies of individual cultures, such as those of Trobriand Islanders or
Dobuans or Hopi Indians. A fourth group, social anthropologists, study
the groupings of people into societies. A fifth group within this second main
division of anthropology are called, in a much more specialized sense, cul-

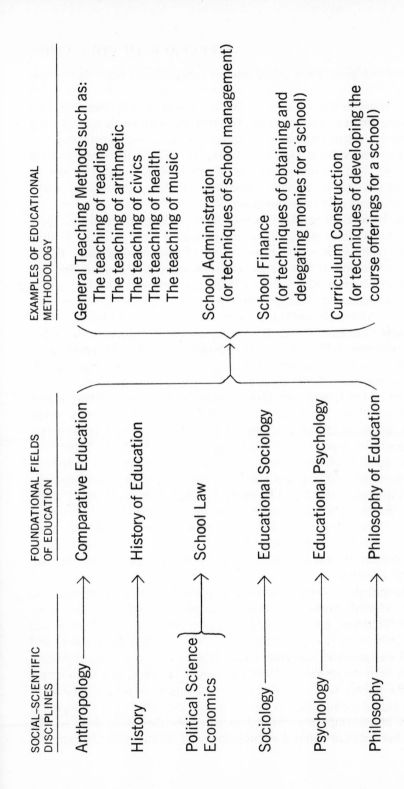

DIAGRAM I. THE SOCIAL SCIENCES AND THE SUBFIELDS OF EDUCATION.

[7]

tural anthropologists. Their prime interest is the human ways that people develop.

These subfields may seem confusing, because each of the five categories overlaps the others to a large extent. This difficulty with labels is a reminder of our earlier statement that rigid categories never are satisfactory. To escape from this anthropological confusion, we will use the term "cultural anthropology" (or, in some cases, just "anthropology" alone) in the remainder of this book to include archaeology, ethnlogy, ethnography, social anthropology, and cultural anthropology.

More, however, is involved than the mere seeking of simplicity. These five subfields of anthropology share in common a basic concept: culture. The term "culture" is so important to all of the social sciences that it deserves elaboration. It was the pioneer semi-sociologist, Herbert Spencer, who said that human beings live in three environments. The first is that of inanimate matter, of which the universe as we understand it is composed. Indeed, our bodies themselves illustrate the existence of this inanimate environment. The human body is 65% oxygen, 18% carbon, 10% hydrogen, 3% nitrogen, 1.5% calcium, 1% phosphorus, and 1.5% other chemicals. The second environment is that of living forms. Human beings could not survive without other forms of life on which to feed. And humans, too, are a form of life related somehow, apparently, to all other living matter which shares Planet Earth with mankind. The third environment, unlike the other two, is entirely of man's own making. It consists, first, of those tangible artifacts developed and modified by man to assist him in his living, such as chairs, tables, blackboards, crayons, erasers, and schoolrooms. It consists also of those intangible group habits, customs, traditions, and organizational arrangements developed by man to assist him in his living. The all-encompassing term to describe this man-made, artificial environment is "culture." Archaeologists, ethnologists, ethnographers, social anthropologists, and cultural anthropologists all study culture. Thus, broadly speaking, all of them are cultural anthropologists. By the same token they are also social scientists.

Anthropology is thought by some people to be both past-oriented and primitive-oriented. Archaeologists and some physical anthropologists study people of the remote past. And ethnographers, ethnologists, and social and cultural anthropologists have concentrated on reporting the manners and mores of our primitive contemporaries. While the past and the primitive may have been the emphasis of anthropology at one time, that is no longer true of the science today. Having developed highly useful scientific techniques, cultural anthropologists have begun to employ these techniques in the study of contemporary civilized societies. As they have done so, the dividing line between cultural anthropology and sociology has become too blurred for any cautious scholar to attempt to trace with accuracy. Anthropology recently has been merging with psychology, as anthropologists have become increasingly interested in the relationship between culture and the formation of personality. The close relationships that cultural anthropology has with sociology and psychology have led to a still embryonic attempt to merge the three disciplines into a single science of human relationships.

The vast and still growing social-scientific field of cultural anthropology presents many insights into education. Here are a few educational questions to which anthropology offers answers. How is culture perpetuated? Must children be educated? Can an adult with no education function effectively as a member of his social group? Can a person become educated if there are no schools? If so, how? Why are schools developed? Are school systems alike throughout the world? If school systems do differ from place to place and from time to time, how do they differ and why do they differ? A knowledge of the answers to the above questions gives the student of education a world view of the vocation. It makes him more sensitive to the educational system in his own society. It gives the educational planner a clearer perspective with which to improve his own educational system, when improvement is in order, because he has a wide basis for comparison.

College departments of education frequently offer course work in the anthropology of education. The term "anthropology," however, rarely appears in the course titles. Instead, they are likely to be termed "comparative education," reflecting the fact that comparisons are made between the educative techniques of different peoples, cultures, and societies.

History and Education

The question of the precise relationship of history to the other social sciences is debatable, as is the question of whether or not history should be classified as a social science. One basis for the controversy is the question of whether or not history can exist by itself, independent of the contents of other disciplines. History is viewed sometimes as a method of studying other disciplines. Historians describe political situations, which are the subject matter of political sicence. They describe economic conditions, which are the subject matter of economics. They describe social conditions, which are the subject matter of sociology and cultural anthropology. They describe revolts, riots, and mass hysteria, which are the subject matter of psychology and sociology. This pattern of thought leads to a common assertion that history is a handmaiden to the social sciences, just as mathematics is a handmaiden to the physical sciences. Social phenomena exist in a fourth dimension, time. History is a method that the social scientists can use to record and interpret the significance of the passing parade of human events, just as mathematics offers numbers, formulas, and equations to physical scientists for recording and interpreting the significance of the data with which they deal. According to this point of view, history is a technique or method to be employed by social scientists, instead of a social science in its own right.

A second basis for the controversy over the proper category for history may be seen readily if one translates the English word "history," into French. The French word is *histoire,* which, besides "history" in the English sense, means story, tale, narrative. Now, is history a tale, or is it, indeed, a social science? If it is but an anecdotal account of the past, if it is a "just-so story," if its purpose is to entertain, if it is designed to amuse, history is not a social science; it is factual, rather than fictitious, literature.

A third basis for the controversy over the place of history rests on the point, sometimes raised, that a discipline cannot be called a science unless the problems and phenomena investigated are repeated. While history, according to the proverb, repeats itself, it never does so in reality. Time can hardly rerun the Peloponnesian Wars or the raucous presidential campaign of William Henry Harrison or the coup d'état that brought Fidel Castro to power in Cuba. Since history deals with events that occur only once, it is said that the term "science" cannot be applied to history.

In rebuttal, one can point out that without history, science, social or otherwise, is impossible. Unless events are remembered, recorded, and reposited, there can be no science. History is more than a handmaiden to the social sciences; it is an indispensable ingredient. Only by understanding the past thoroughly can any social scientist hope to make sense of the present. As we have attempted to demonstrate already, rigid categories are never satisfactory. It is naive to think that any scholarly discipline exists in a vacuum. Every discipline cuts across other disciplines: biology invades the discipline of chemistry, and astronomy that of physics; the study of a national literature invades all of the social sciences; and the social sciences themselves overlap one another and rest, eventually, on a foundation of biology. In the convenient and necessary division of labor involved in the analysis of the human way of life, the historians are charged with the full-time task of separating facts about the human past from propaganda and myth, and of accurately and cautiously reporting these facts meaningfully. Sober historians are not content with merely giving a careful, accurate, and objective account of events which once upon a time took place. Through the use of temporal sequences, they attempt not only to identify and describe events, but also to interpret and explain these events in terms of cause-and-effect relationships. By this process they endeavor to establish historical principles based on probability, just as laws of physics are based on probability. When historians perform these important services, they can hardly be called littérateurs only. They are scientists of social phenomena.

Single events frequently are used by several branches of the sciences as the basis from which to interpret and explain phenomena. For example, in December, 1962, an unmanned, complex mechanical device known as Mariner II, which had been launched from the United States, visited the planet Venus and sent information about Venus to waiting physical scientists thirty-six million miles away on Earth. The celestial cryptograms of Mariner II have given physical scientists an amazing amount of knowledge about the formidable surface and inhospitable atmosphere of Venus. This visit to Venus was a once-only event. The findings resulting from an analysis, interpretation, and explanation of Mariner II's coded messages are scientific, even though this visit occurred but once. Likewise, historical analyses, interpretations, and explanations of kaleidoscopic human events can be scientific as well.

Without attempting to offer the final word in the controversy, we shall classify history as being one of the social sciences upon which the discipline of education rests.

Education, like other social activities, has a history. The historical approach to education seeks answers to such questions as these. Are educational establishments old or new in America? When were the first elementary schools and secondary schools and colleges begun in America? Why were they begun? What was taught in these schools a hundred or two hundred years ago? Why? What were schools like in the past? Why? What teaching methods were employed? Why? Are there some methods of teaching that were used once but that have since been abandoned? What were they? Why were they abandoned? Has education fluctuated with the times like a weather vane, blowing this way and that with the changing winds, or has it been a leader of social change? Why? What trends in American education can be identified? Why have these trends existed?

When one can thoroughly answer questions of this sort, he has a far more sophisticated understanding of education in American life than he could have otherwise. He is not like Oscar Wilde's character who knew the price of everything and the value of nothing. It is difficult to appreciate the present, to know how to act wisely in the present, to know how to improve the present without a solid knowledge of what has gone before and of why past events occurred. Many colleges in the United States offer courses in the history of education.

Political Science and Education

The ancient Greek philosopher and naturalist, Aristotle, is credited with making the oft-quoted statement that man is a social animal. Human social life is never in a state of complete anarchy for long. In order to both perpetuate the group and encourage individual members to remain in the group and not become hermits, group life must be satisfying to its members. Human beings, as social animals, seek security in group life. Security is not easily achieved unless group life is stable, ordered, cohesive. In order to feel secure in a group, an individual needs to know his proper place in that group. He needs also to know how the other people in the group might reasonably be expected to behave toward him. Security, therefore, is based on mutual expectations, which imply some sort of social regulatory system as well as some means of social compulsion by which the members will be encouraged to abide by the precepts of that regulatory system.

Except for the most primitive of human societies, social regulatory systems may be classified under one of two broad categories. The first is that of political controls which are enforced through the power of some type of formal governmental arrangement. The policeman who arrests the speeder on the boulevard, the judge who convicts the criminal and has him locked in a prison cell, and the Federal Bureau of Investigation are examples in our society of those who implement political controls.

The second broad category of controls encompasses those nonpolitical ones that sometimes are buttressed by tradition and that rely on public opinion for their enforcement. The refractory adolescents who conform slavishly to styles set by their teenage peers, or the organization man of suburbia who finds it expedient to keep his yard and home neat and tidy, or the person who feels very uncomfortable when he wears the "wrong" clothes to some social gathering give evidence in our society of the enforcement and execution of nonpolitical controls.

Political science as a social science emphasizes the study of those regulatory practices and their enforcement which stem usually from formal governmental agencies. Political science mainly is a study of government or the state. It is a study of political regulatory practices—how these practices are formulated and made into policy, and how these practices are enforced through the coercive power of the state. It includes also a study of those individuals and groups that seek formally or informally to use the power of the state to initiate, to block, or to change the societal regulatory practices. Only incidentally are the nonpolitical controls of a society included in the discipline of political science. That trio of social sciences, cultural anthropology, sociology, and social psychology, gives serious attention to the nonpolitical regulatory systems of human societies.

Political science is one of the most specialized and, in this sense, narrow social sciences. Unlike the vast, all-encompassing discipline of anthropology, political science centers attention on governmental affairs and gives but passing recognition, and then only when germane to government, to the other aspects of human social life.

There is a very close relationship between education and political science, because the school *is* a government and because the school is much affected by other governmental activities. Political science presents educational questions such as the following. What is the power structure within a school system? Who administers our public schools? How does the federal government affect schools, public and private? How do state governments affect these schools? How do county, township, district, or municipal governments affect these schools? What must be taught? Who says so?

Such questions are the concern especially of school administrators. However, anyone employed in a school system needs to know something about how schools are administered and about the laws which govern one's actions at school. Several states require that any student planning to teach must study the school laws of his state before being certified. It is common for colleges to offer courses in school law to students in the teacher preparation program.

Economics and Education

Economics, like political science, is a specialized social science. Economics is that discipline which studies the necessary compromises that must occur between virtually boundless human wants on the one hand and limited goods and services to satisfy those wants on the other. It is a study of getting and spending scarce resources, and of those processes whereby resources are allocated for the purpose of satisfying human wants. Human beings want goods and services in order to survive and in order to enjoy those amenities which their society encourages them to desire. Some economic goods and services, such as food, protection from the elements, and health, are essential if a person wants to stay alive. Other goods and services are desired by the individual so that he might live comfortably at a pleasant level of existence. He wants nice clothes, a soft bed, a shiny car, entertainment, books and magazines, the latest electrical gadgetry—even an education. The economist studies the production, distribution, and use of limited resources to satisfy human wants.

Economics began as a highly theoretical social science, despite the fact that its weighty, technical language and its use of mathematics have given rise to the myth that it is the most "scientific" and factual of the social sciences. Economic theory was constructed out of a set of ideals based on what was considered a perfect society. With this "perfect" society, economic theoreticians could rule out or ignore extraneous forces which might affect economic functions in the real world. Since the society was perfect, the members of this society could be treated as perfect also. From this simple, theoretically ideal standpoint, laws and principles of economics were developed—for example, the laws of supply and demand. The laws of supply and demand were said to determine—certainly in the long run and to some degree in the short run—which goods and services would be allocated to which human wants and under what circumstances. In this perfect theoretical society no extraneous forces such as war, crises, acts of government, or "acts of God" had to be taken into consideration. Also, since this society was peopled by perfect men, it could be assumed that all humans as consumers or producers would behave rationally and that none would attempt to block or tamper with the impersonal functionings of economic laws.

This now remote beginning laid a theoretical basis for the contemporary study of economic phenomena. Economists today are much more sophisticated than those pioneers of the past. They recognize increasingly the vast chasm that exists between the "ideal" and the "real" in economics. In fact, there are economists who doubt that the ideal ever existed or ever will exist in actuality. Economic phenomena do not take place in a vacuum, either social or natural. Some contemporary economists are persuaded that economic conditions considered at one time as abnormal are actually normal, and conditions once described as normal are actually abnormal. Contemporary economists have a growing realization that so-called extraneous factors cannot be ignored or dismissed, since economic causation, like other social causation, is multiple, not unitary. And man himself, as an economic being, cannot actually be expected to behave rationally at all times, especially when his fellow men, with such techniques as high-pressure advertising and propagandizing, may try to make him behave irrationally.

While economic laws are much less inviolable today than they were thought to be a half-century ago, economics as a social science is much stronger now than in the past. The theoretical principles of the past have made possible an extensive and intensive study of the complexities of economic affairs as they actually exist. New theories are supplanting some of the old, and economics as a social science has matured greatly.

There is a direct relationship between the social science of economics and the field of education. Exposing a person to an education is the performance of an economic service that people value. Adults want their children to be educated. It is very costly to offer educational opportunities to all of America's children, and the financing of it is complex and intricate. Money must be procured somewhere to keep the schools in operation. Financial wizardry is needed in order to provide as many educational services as are desired from the limited resources available. It is here that economics comes into the educational picture.

Economics helps to answer questions such as these. Who finances our schools? Since most of our schools are public, what is rightly the federal government's role in providing money for education? What financial role do state governments play? What financial roles do county, township, district, or municipal governments play? What strings are attached to the local schools by the governments that finance them?

School administrators cannot perform their functions adequately without having answers to questions of this sort. Other people in educational work have interests in school finance, too, not the least of which is their salaries. Frequently, colleges include the topic of educational finance in a course on school law since the two are connected, particularly in public education. (They cannot be separated completely in any area.) Those agencies that pay the piper expect to have a right to call the tune.

Sociology and Education

Half a century ago it was a simple task to define the science of sociology. The study of society, or the analysis of societal phenomena, or a study of the social order, or a study of the structure and functionings of society would have been sufficient. But an adequate definition of sociology is becoming increasingly difficult to formulate. The primary difficulty lies in the merging of cultural anthropology with sociology. A secondary difficulty lies in the slightly less obvious merging of psychology with sociology.

At one time a person could say glibly that sociology is to civilized societies as cultural anthropology is to primitive or prehistoric societies: whereas cultural anthropology was a study of simple savages and long-dead societies, sociology was a study of contemporary civilized societies. This simple dichotomy is becoming increasingly less tenable. At one time, also, a person could say glibly that sociology is to groups as psychology is to the individual: whereas psychology was a study of individual behavior, sociology was a study of group behavior. This dichotomy also is becoming less and less true because of the increased awareness that people, since they are group animals, are deeply affected as individuals by the groups in which they live. At the same time, groups are what they are because of the behavior of the individuals who comprise them. This lack of a clear, distinct line to separate either cultural anthropology or psychology from sociology means that any person who tries to develop an exact definition for sociology is in trouble from the start. Yet, at the same time, there is a legitimate social science known as sociology which is taught and studied as a separate discipline from both anthropology and psychology.

One approach for identifying sociology is the historical. In the mid-nineteenth century a French social philosopher, Auguste Comte, created the word "sociology" by combining a Latin prefix with a Greek suffix. Comte believed that a society goes through three stages in the development of its store of knowledge. The first stage is one in which the society attributes all phenomena (social or otherwise) ultimately to gods or to godlike forces. The second stage is one in which all phenomena are attributed ultimately to inexorable metaphysical forces. The third stage is one in which scientific techniques are used as the basis of knowledge. Comte applied the term "sociology" to a scientific study of the mainsprings of human societies, the purpose of sociology being to amass usable scientific knowledge about social life. Contemporary sociology, even though it is far from Comtian in its outlook, reflects still the Comtian dream of approaching social phenomena scientifically and of acquiring a body of knowledge about society through empirical and rational means rather than through supernaturalistic means.

Another approach for identifying sociology is to cite tendencies found in sociology itself. First, sociology tends to be narrower in its investigations than cultural anthropology. Anthropologists give just as serious attention to the social ways of icebound Netsilingmiut Eskimos, or capitalistic Manus people of the South Pacific, or head-hunting Jívaro Indians as they do to the way of life of civilized Americans. Sociologists, on the other hand, tend to use knowledge about noncivilized societies in a somewhat incidental fashion. They emphasize, instead, the ways of civilized people, especially the ways of their fellow citizens in their own civilized societies. Most books on the subject of sociology published in the United States, for example, focus primarily on an analysis of various functionings of the social order in the United States.

Second, sociology tends to stress those patterns of behavior that accompany interpersonal relationships and group life. People themselves receive less attention in sociology than the groupings and networks of relationships that can be found among people. Thus, in a sense, the backdrop and the play's setting is more important to sociology than the individual actors are. In psychology the emphasis is on the actor—although these two emphases cannot be kept entirely separate.

Third, sociology tends to emphasize interrelationships among all social phenomena. In fact, an acceptable definition might well be that sociology attempts to demonstrate how an entire society is of one fabric. Economic, political, religious, educative, recreational, familial, governmental, and all other social activities form a single tapestry in a given society. Sociology tends to stress this point. Sociology has been called a generalizing social science because of this very tendency to show how social parts are joined together into a single, whole social structure.

The sociological technique of showing interrelatedness leads to numerous questions which bear on education. What effect does the social life of a community have on the educational system of that community? How do community attitudes affect the attitudes of pupils? How does home environment affect the progress of children in school? How do population shifts in the community, or in the state, or in the region, or in the nation affect the school? These are a few of the sociologically oriented questions that have significance for education.

School administrators, curricular planners, and classroom teachers are vitally affected by sociological matters such as those implied in the above questions. These people must have answers to many questions of a sociological nature if they are to perform their educative tasks effectively. Many colleges offer courses in educational sociology to students who are preparing for teaching.

Psychology and Education

The previous sketches have indicated the overlapping of psychology, anthropology, and sociology. The same difficulty of exact definition regarding the latter two is also encountered with respect to psychology. This is one reason for the current move to combine these three disciplines into one all-encompassing human behavioral science.

Psychology, in a very narrow sense, began as a scientific study of the mind or soul. The princess of classical mythology, Psyche, for whom psychology is indirectly named, symbolized the love and anguish, the joy and torment, and the supposed immortality of the human soul. People in many societies and many ages have looked upon the mind-stuff of man as being separate from his body—a sort of person inside the person, who directs the activities of the body.

Psychology as a field of study developed in the nineteenth century as a scientific attempt to investigate a subject that has intrigued mankind for ages. As psychology has developed, the inadequacy of defining it as a scientific study of the mind or soul has become increasingly apparent. The word "soul" belongs to the vocabulary of metaphysics, not science. No one, in dissecting the human body, has ever found man's soul. The study of the soul is beyond the present capability of a scientifically oriented researcher. The word "mind," while sounding somewhat less metaphysical than soul, is equally elusive. However, because it is handy to have a short term to designate thought processes, some psychologists continue to use the word "mind." But mind is not identified usually as either a substance or an entity in itself. These facts have led to a redefinition of psychology. Psychology nowadays is defined briefly as a scientific study of behavior, conscious and unconscious.

In their study of behavior, psychologists have not limited themselves to an investigation of human behavior only. They have studied rats, cats, dogs, frogs, worms, pachyderms, and many other species. Realizing that behavior is traceable in great measure to the nervous system, the functioning of glands, the chemistry of the body, the physiological structure of organs such as eyes, ears, and the brain, and the processes of maturation, some psychologists have become specialists in branches of physiology and neurology. Those psychologists who center their attention on animal psychology and physiological psychology are not at all certain that they should be classified as social scientists. They tend to think of themselves as life scientists. We shall not attempt to argue with them; instead, we shall grant them their wish and not include them among the social scientists.

Other psychologists, sometimes called social psychologists, while recognizing the biological basis for all human behavior, stress the importance of societal factors. Human behavior is traceable not only to physiological functions but also, and in great measure, to environmental determinants which start to work certainly at birth—maybe before—and continue throughout one's lifetime.

Identical twins, more alike than two peas in the proverbial pod—by definition they possess identical heredity equipment—will behave differently when reared in different environments. In fact, they are likely to behave rather differently even though they grow up in what is apparently the same environment. Environmental factors are not simple; on the contrary, they are knotted and tangled and snarled. They are far more complex than the network of nerves that affects behavior. Psychologists who emphasize the study of environmental factors in human behavior are classified correctly as social scientists.

When psychologists probe deeply into the cultural and social factors which interplay with the functions of man's biological equipment, they find themselves in the domain of anthropology and sociology. This again points to the interrelatedness of these three human behavioral disciplines and the impossibility of separating them completely.

Education is defined sometimes as the modification of behavior. This definition stresses the strong link between education and psychology. Schoolteachers ask questions of a psychological nature. What are children like at each grade level? How do people learn? How can learning be accomplished with most efficiency? How can materials be presented in such a way that people will apply what they have learned? How does one measure effectively what pupils learn?

College and state departments of education are deeply convinced that education and psychology are related. They are convinced that a trained teacher *must* be familiar with the psychological side of teaching. Virtually all students planning to teach in the public schools are required to study educational psychology under some label or other.

Philosophy and Education

A "philosophy" is a frame of reference, a starting point. It is also a basic orientation pointing to goals deemed desirable. When a person philosophizes, he attempts to define his aims, to analyze what he is doing, to understand why he is doing it, and to decide what he ought to do in a new situation in the light of his inquiry.

Strictly speaking, philosophy is not a social science. It is rather the great matrix of all scholarly inquiry. Philosophy is the mother—or at least the grandmother—of scientific inquiry. If one were to make a study of the history of biology, chemistry, or political science, for example, he would find that each science began with philosophical speculation. The fact is that numerous materials taught as science (either natural or social) in school and college are tinged still with philosophical colorings.

Education, as an applied social science, demands application now. The teacher cannot wait until earth's last picture is painted or until every datum of social life is twisted and tabulated before he begins to teach. If all facts were known and understood, there is the possibility that there would be only one proper way to teach in a specific situation. (Such a situation is hard to envisage, however.) From a practical standpoint, we still have very limited knowledge as to how to teach in a given situation. The conscientious teacher is forced to philosophize and ask, "Which of the facts related to education are the most important? Why? What do I believe to be the goal (or is it more appropriate to say "goals") of education? Why? What, basically, do I want my pupils to learn, not just for today but for tomorrow and the years to come? Why? Then how shall I weigh, organize, and supplement the scattered and often incomplete social-scientific facts which I have at hand so that I may do my best in teaching these children today?"

It is easy to get a variety of answers to these questions. The last hundred years in America have been a particularly fecund period in the production of philosophical notions about education. Most college departments of education are sensitive to the contributions that philosophy has made to education, and, either in separate courses or as part of other courses, will offer instruction in the philosophy of education.

Review and Preview

Anthropology, history, political science, economics, sociology, psychology, and philosophy have something worthwhile to contribute to that consequential aspect of mankind's way of life called education. It is out of these social sciences and philosophy that the study of education developed. Materials growing out of these disciplines are the stones that together form the substructure of education. The remainder of this book is devoted to a survey of social-scientific bases of education.

Chapter 2 shows why people need to be educated and how various societies deal with this matter. (An Anthropological Approach to Education.)

Chapter 3 offers an interpretation of what has been happening in America with regard to education. (An Historical Approach to Education.)

Chapters 4 and 5 delineate governmental and financial issues that affect education in America. (A Political and Economic Approach to Education.)

Chapter 6 suggests the relatedness of education to the larger, encompassing society and the schools. (A Sociological Approach to Education.)

Chapter 7 deals with the learners themselves in the educational setting. (A Psychological Approach to Education.)

Chapter 8 describes some of the current issues in education that involve aims, goals, and varying viewpoints. (A Philosophical Approach to Education.)

Education as a Vocation

Although education is a vocational field, many people are but vaguely aware that there is a *legitimate* body of material upon which the vocation is based. To complicate matters, some people who earn their livelihood by teaching have received specialized vocational training in education and others have not. Furthermore, there are teachers who are untrained in the vocation of education but who do a remarkably fine job of teaching. These facts serve to confuse students of education, teachers, and the general public.

The situation is not entirely unlike the one found in the vocational field of music. There are people who, with little or no formal training in music, become star performers. By inserting a dime in a jukebox or turning on your radio, you can hear these people sing or play. If you were to interview one of them, you might find that he cannot read music, that he has never taken voice or instrumental lessons, that he is self-tutored. Yet this same person may be touring a night-club circuit, may be making recordings by the dozen, may be the featured guest on some spectacular television program, and may be in one of the top income brackets.

There are other people in the field of music, too: Leontyne Price,

Yehudi Menuhin, "Van" Cliburn. These people have studied long and hard to learn both the fundamentals and the techniques of music. They are musically *trained*.

To the outsider this may be confusing. He may put all of these performers, trained and untrained, into one category and classify them by the same label—musician. He may become cynical about the vocation of music. He may contend that musical talent is all one needs to be a successful musician—thus brushing aside a venerable field of knowledge.

The vocation of medicine has emerged from somewhat similar conditions. One can still find the trained and the untrained practicing medicine side by side. There are churchmen who do not know a tibia from an ulna, but who nevertheless cure the sick by using occult techniques suggestive of the jungle. The deaf hear. The blind see. The lame walk. The cancerous are cured. There are also salesmen who offer remedies for everything in bottle, jar, or tube. The patent medicine market offers a variety of cure-alls. One can even find back-fence gossips who know how to nip colds with asafoetida, or cure a rash with catnip tea, or restore vigor with a special diet of eggs. Then there are physicians who have studied for years and years to learn the fundamentals and the techniques of their vocation. To the outsider this also may be confusing. If a churchman, or a salesman, or a gossip can cure the infirm, is not a study of medicine a waste of time? Again the outsider may brush aside a venerable field of knowledge.

One need not spend years at a conservatory of music in order to sing a song, or graduate from a medical college in order to diagnose the mumps. By the same token, one need not study education in order to teach. However, the person who has the talent for singing will sing more beautifully with the understanding that comes from training. The person who is interested in medicine will be far more accurate and helpful with the understanding that comes from training. The person who wants to teach will do much better with the understanding that comes from training.

There is a significant difference between the self-styled songstress who carries a tune lustily and the vocalist who has graduated from a conservatory of music. There is a significant difference between the twentieth-century medicine man who claims to cure anything from fallen arches to falling hair and the doctor of medicine who has passed successfully the lengthy and gruelling requirements of the medical college. There is a significant difference between the person who can speak Spanish and, therefore, is hired to teach a college course in Spanish and the trained educational specialist whose further education has prepared him to teach Spanish. What is this significant difference? In each case the latter is *trained* in his vocation, whereas the former practices without formal training. The latter in each case is familiar with the fundamentals and techniques of his specialty, whereas the former may be utterly insensitive to the vocational body of knowledge which exists. The latter in each case acts according to the training he has received, whereas the former is likely to rely on such nebulous props as clairvoyance, intuition, or trial and error. Finally, if the latter in each case is successful in his calling, it is because he understands what he is doing; if the former is successful, it is in spite of his ignorance.

The body of knowledge concerning music is highly useful to the person who wishes to earn his living in the field of music. Familiarity with the body of knowledge on which medicine is based is imperative to the person who wishes to practice medicine. The body of knowledge surrounding education is highly useful to the person who wishes to be a teacher. The final chapter of this book will discuss further the vocation of education, surveying its changing status.

The Educationist

The matter of nomenclature poses problems, too. Medicine has the matter rather well under control with its many labels ranging from faith healers, medicine men, and herb doctors to gynecologists, pediatricians, and ophthalmologists. But the terminology is still hazy in music. The term "musician" does not distinguish between the untrained tune carrier and the highly trained lyric soprano.

In the field of education there are terms that still remain vague. The term "teacher" does not distinguish between the amateur and the professional, the untrained and the trained. A fourteen-year-old girl can be a "teacher" of a Sunday-school class with no prerequisite qualifications whatsoever. One's neighbor or roommate can be a "teacher" of the latest dance steps or of the latest modifications of Canasta. At the same time, a trained specialist in primary education may be a *teacher* of a first-grade class. Notice that the word "teacher," as such, gives no indication of the vocational preparation of the person so identified. He may or may not understand the techniques involved in presenting new materials vividly, meaningfully, and lastingly to learners.

The term "educator" is sometimes used. It is a more discriminative term than "teacher." It suggests a person who earns his living by teaching or by other educative work, such as school administration. But, at the same time, it does not distinguish between the person who is trained only in the subject matter that he is teaching and the person who is trained in both the subject matter and the techniques of teaching. A chemist who teaches college courses in chemistry, even though he has never been trained to teach, can be called an educator. At the same time, a licensed teacher whose academic preparation has qualified him to teach chemistry may be called an educator also. The term "educator" lacks sufficient precision, although it is more specific than the term "teacher."

Another word used occasionally is "instructor." It has two main connotations. In the first, "instructor" and "teacher" are synonymous. Thus, "instructor" has the same vagueness as "teacher." One cannot be certain that an instructor has been trained in the fundamentals and techniques of instruction. The second connotation is more specific. Colleges and universities often rank the members of their teaching staff according to degrees earned, the number of years spent teaching, books published, and the like. The lowest rank is instructor. But even in this second use of the term one cannot be sure that an instructor is trained in teaching as well as in the subject matter.

There is also the term "professor." Once in a while, anyone who teaches under any circumstances is called a professor. It is more common, however, for the term "professor" to be reserved for college or university teachers. In higher educational circles the word "professor" is used in any of three ways: first, to denote any teacher of college-level courses; second, to identify a high-ranking member of a college faculty (whereas the rank of instructor is low, that of professor is high); third, as a title of address for a member of a college or university faculty. Instead of Mr. Doe or Dr. Doe, a college teacher may be addressed as Professor Doe. The term "professor" usually is reserved for a person who earns his living by teaching. It usually implies also that such a person teaches at the level of higher education. The term does not, however, indicate whether he is trained in the fundamentals and techniques of teaching as well as in the subject matter, or whether he is untrained in the vocational aspects of teaching.

There is another word, which is more exact than any of the preceding terms and is coming into use more and more. That word is "educationist." An educationist is a trained teacher. He is a person who has received instruction in the fundamentals and the techniques of teaching. He is familiar with the body of knowledge that has been developed in the realm of education. He has taken course work in education. Often, though not invariably, such a person has earned one or more college degrees in education. The term "educationist" is far more precise than other labels in identifying trained teachers. It automatically rules out, by definition, the amateurs, the untrained, the unequipped. Throughout this book the term "educationist" will refer to the person who is trained in the vocational field of education.

The Chapter in Capsule Form

1. Education, as a field of study, is classified as an applied social science. This means that it rests on a body of material that has grown out of the social sciences.

2. The study of education involves work in two types of courses.

2.1 *Foundational courses.* These are the "why to teach" courses. They draw directly from the social sciences.

2.2 *Methods courses.* These are the courses in educational techniques. They grow directly out of the foundational courses in education and indirectly out of the social sciences.

3. The following social-scientific fields offer materials out of which foundational courses in education are constructed.

3.1 *Anthropology,* the study of mankind, identifies the role of education among human beings and demonstrates how different societies have dealt with the matter of education. Foundational work in education based on anthropology is often called comparative education.

3.2 *History* is the critical review of mankind's past records. It offers perspectives on educational activities through the use of the dimension of time. Foundational work in education based on history is called the history of education.

3.3 *Political science and economics.* Political science is concerned particularly with governmental power. Economics deals with the production, distribution, and use of those resources on which a society places value. These two social sciences are closely tied together with regard to their relationship to education. Our various levels of government underwrite the American school system. At the same time, these various levels of government finance educational endeavors. Foundational work in education based on political science and economics is called school law.

3.4 *Sociology,* a generalizing social science, attempts to show the interrelatedness of the numerous activities that make up the fabric of a human society. Among these are educative activities that affect and are affected by other parts of the society. Foundational work in education based on sociology is called educational sociology.

3.5 *Psychology* is a study of behavior. Since education deals with the modification of human behavior, psychology has many insights to offer. Foundational work in education based on psychology is called educational psychology.

3.6 *Philosophy* is not, strictly speaking, a social science. Nevertheless, it is included as one of the bases of the applied social science of education because of its close relationship to the social sciences and to the field of education. Philosophy seeks to clarify aims, objectives, and viewpoints, including those of educational significance. Foundational work in education based on philosophy is called the philosophy of education.

4. The next seven chapters of this book are devoted to a survey of the foundations of education, which are based on anthropology, history, political science, economics, sociology, psychology, and philosophy.

5. Not everyone who teaches is a trained teacher. This generalization is true of some other fields, too, such as music and medicine. Education is still a developing vocational field. The final chapter of this book discusses more fully the professionalization of education.

6. The term "educationist" is being used more and more widely to identify the person who has received vocational preparation in education, and who, therefore, is a trained teacher. This term will be used from time to time in the remainder of the book.

For Supplementary Reading

BIERSTEDT, ROBERT, *The Social Order,* 2nd ed. New York: McGraw-Hill Book Co., Inc., 1963, Part I.
   Sociologists seem especially prone to define the relationship of the social sciences to one another as they introduce beginners to the field of sociology. Bierstedt's outstanding introductory volume is no exception to the rule, and suggests what one might find in the first chapter of other elementary books in sociology.
CHASE, STUART, *The Proper Study of Mankind . . . ,* rev. ed. New York: Harper & Brothers, 1956.
   A lucid, popular presentation of the work of social scientists in studying human behavior.
Encyclopædia of the Social Sciences. New York: The Macmillan Co., 1930–35.
   See the introductory article in Vol. I as well as the articles on each of the social sciences and education. This encyclopedia has been an indispensable reference work for social scientists.
HARRIS, C. W., ed., *Encyclopedia of Educational Research,* 3rd ed. New York: The Macmillan Co., 1960.
   See the articles on the various subfields of education. This volume is an important reference work for people in the field of education.

HUNT, ELGIN F., *Social Science: An Introduction to the Study of Society,* 2nd ed. New York: The Macmillan Co., 1961, Ch. II.

Several surveys of the social sciences have introductory chapters which identify and define major social sciences and their place among the scholarly disciplines. Hunt's book offers a well-written chapter of this nature.

Social Science Research Council, Committee on Historiography, *The Social Sciences in Historical Study.* New York: Social Science Research Council, 1954.

Chapters III and IV are especially pertinent. This is a sophisticated description of the social sciences. It may be difficult for the beginner to understand.

2

An Anthropological Approach
to Education

The ultimate foundation of a free society is the binding tie of cohesive sentiment. Such a sentiment is fostered by all those agencies of the mind and spirit which may serve to gather up the traditions of a people, transmit them from generation to generation, and thereby create that continuity of a treasured common life which constitutes a civilization.

from *Minersville School District* v. *Gobitis*, 310 U.S. 586 (1940).

Thinking It Over Beforehand

What would a person be like if he never learned anything from any other human being?

How much of what you know was learned outside of school?

Why do we have schools?

What did Bismarck mean when he said, "The nation that has the schools has the future"?

In what ways are schools alike throughout the world?

Learning and Mr. Jones

Here is a sketch of the social development of one John Jones as he grows from birth to maturity in the United States.[1]

[1] Reprinted from R. L. Sutherland and J. L. Woodward, *Introductory Sociology* (Chicago: J. B. Lippincott Co., 1937), pp. 180–182, from a compilation of materials gathered from the following sources: Arnold Gesell, *The Mental Growth of the Pre-*

[27]

At birth:

>   cries when pinched or when hungry
>   salivates, digests, defecates
>   sneezes, yawns, vomits
>   sucks and swallows

At three months:

>   holds head erect
>   smiles responsively to approval of parent
>   shows anticipatory excitement at feeding
>   shakes rattle
>   cries when mother leaves the room
>   follows moving pencil with eyes
>   cries if feeding is delayed

At one year:

>   walks with help
>   says two words (such as "ma-ma" and "da-da")
>   holds cup to drink from
>   inhibits simple acts on command (stops banging with spoon)
>   scribbles with pencil on paper
>   imitates adult beating two spoons together
>   plays peek-a-boo

At two years:

>   runs
>   tells name
>   "shows it to mama"
>   blows nose, tries to brush teeth
>   tells experiences
>   identifies picture of mother or nurse
>   has bladder control, except at night
>   goes on simple errands
>   about 250 words in vocabulary

At five years:

>   draws a man
>   crosses street alone
>   tells age
>   defines "chair," "horse," "fork," "doll"
>   wants to be a locomotive engineer when he grows up
>   plays follow the leader

School Child (New York: The Macmillan Company, 1925); Rachel Stutsman, *Mental Measurement of Preschool Children* (New York: Harcourt, Brace & World, Inc., 1931); Charlotte Buhler, *The First Year of Life* (New York: The John Day Company, 1930); Ada H. Arlitt, *Psychology of Infancy and Early Childhood* (New York: McGraw-Hill Book Company, 1930).

asks "Why don't we see two things with our two eyes?" and "Why does
water go out of the way when anything goes in?"
dresses himself, except for tying shoe laces
uses about 2,000 words

At sixteen years:
plays complicated team games like baseball and basketball
is active in school clubs and social life
has had his first ("puppy") love affair
objects to parental control over his social life and friendships
wants to be an automobile manufacturer
writes "poetry"
has an allowance from parents and lives within it
smokes occasionally when away from home

At twenty-one years:
has a job as a filling station attendant
is in love with a girl named Jessamine and wants to get married
belongs to the Eagles, a local lodge
wants to be a garage superintendent
plays billiards, poker, baseball
knows the names of the governor of the state and the local mayor but
not those of his congressman or his two senators
thinks it is all right to drive past a red traffic light if no "cop" is
watching
about 12,000 words in his vocabulary

This account is out of date in parts. Today's five-year-old may want
to be an astronaut or a replica of the latest idol of the moppets from the
magic screens of television or the drive-in theatre, whether a frontiersman,
an Indian scout, or some other creation of the delight-makers of the entertainment industry. Today's twenty-one-year-old may be married already
and have a John Jones of his own. He may also be rendering military
service rather than service in a filling station.

Whether brought up to date or left as it is, this fictitious account
illustrates a basic anthropological and educational point. Human beings are
born little more than animated alimentary canals that receive nourishment
at one end and expel waste from the other. Through the course of a decade
or two, they learn how to conduct themselves as human beings. Notice how
John Jones *learns* words, *learns* to respond to the activities of other people,
learns to identify and manipulate artifacts of our culture such as spoons,
chairs, and clothing, *learns* to participate in groups, and *learns* the ideology
of our culture, including the value of marriage, the value of becoming important occupationally, and the value of joining social organizations. Learning is critical, vital, basic to all of these human activities.

Insufficient Learning and Mr. Smith

It would be useful here to further illustrate the point by conjuring up another individual, perhaps one Sam Smith, who has had no opportunity to become acquainted with human cultural ways for twenty-one years. He could be contrasted with the above John Jones. This contrast is difficult to make with exactitude because such Sam Smiths are lacking in quantity, as is reliable scientific data. Rarely indeed does one have occasion to discover a child who has been so utterly abandoned that he has had no opportunity whatsoever to learn the cultural ways of human beings.

For many centuries there have been rumors about young children who, apparently, have grown up without contact with other human beings. Some of these accounts are supposedly authentic, but unfortunately, they lack sufficient scientific accuracy to be above suspicion. In passing, it should be noted that those accounts that seem to carry a kernel of authenticity despite their suspect nature are in agreement on one point. These wild children behaved strangely. They seemed more like beasts of the forest than like their contemporaries who had grown up in human surroundings.

The famous eighteenth-century life scientist, Carolus Linnaeus, had heard accounts of wild children. He considered these children to be so different from average children that he classified them as an entirely different species. The human being has the biological label, *Homo sapiens;* Linnaeus classified the wild children as *Homo ferus.* He was mistaken, of course; they are not a separate species. But despite the Linnaeus error, a shortened form of his Latin term is used today. These children are referred to as feral children. Caution forces the scientifically inclined person to disregard for the most part the accounts of feral children, absorbing though such tales may be.

There have been a few scientifically reputable reports of children who, while not entirely abandoned in infancy, have had *inadequate* contacts with other human beings. These children cannot be called feral, because they did not grow up alone in the wilderness. They do represent, however, cases of extreme isolation. These cases give the most reliable hint that we have of what Sam Smith would be like if he were to grow from birth to maturity away from other human beings and without the opportunity to learn human cultural ways.

The most authentic records of an extreme isolate are those of an Ohio girl.[2] In the scientific literature she is given a pseudonym, Isabelle, to hide

[2] The full account may be read in Kingsley Davis, "A Final Note on a Case of Extreme Isolation," *American Journal of Sociology,* LII (March, 1947), pp. 432–437.

her real identity. Isabelle was discovered in 1938. Her age at that time was estimated to be about six and a half years. She was the illegitimate offspring of a deaf-mute woman, a recluse who had been deaf almost all of her life. Isabelle was kept by her mother in a room separated from the rest of the household of her mother's kinsmen in order to spare them from having to gaze upon the product of the mother's indiscretion. Isabelle and her mother spent hours together in this remote room, which was usually kept darkened. Lack of sunshine and a poor diet had their harsh effects on the girl: when she was found, she was in very poor health. So bowed were her legs that the soles of her feet almost touched each other. She could walk, but her gait was strange to behold because of her deformity.

The extent of her deformity was not only physical; she was deformed mentally as well. The child had not learned to talk because her mother could not, and there was no one else who would talk to her. Occasionally the girl uttered random croak-like noises. These sounds were not speech because they did not carry any meaning. Isabelle scarcely responded to noises. The people who worked with her after she was found said that she acted much as a deaf child might act, although she was not deaf. She was extremely afraid of strangers, especially men. This characteristic she may have learned from her mother, who responded in similar fashion.

When Isabelle was discovered, a crew of specialists, including educationists, social scientists, and medical experts, converged upon the girl to study her every move and reclaim her as a human being. So different was this six-and-one-half-year-old from the average child of the same age that the experts at first shook their heads and classified her as feeble-minded, a practically hopeless case. It would be impossible to teach her to speak or to do much of anything, they thought.

But in two years, working continuously, the experts were able to teach the child what the average John Jones, American, would have learned during his first several years. Medical care improved her physical condition. By the time Isabelle was eight and a half, she had become normal in spite of her wretched earlier childhood.

People Learn to Be Human

Cases such as Isabelle's and the feral children's emphasize the significant educational fact that human children must learn how to be human. A typical John Jones behaves in an average way because he has learned to behave that way. A child such as Isabelle, deprived of adequate human associations, fails to act in a normal fashion. If children do not have the chance to interact sufficiently with other people, they will not behave in a normal human way.

Apparently this is less true of cocker spaniels, or chickens, or cats, or crickets. A dog can be taken away from all associations with other dogs and will still grow into a dog that will snap at intruders, bark at strangers, eat meat, shun dandelion leaves, and run after moving objects. Isolated from adequate associations with other human beings at an early age, the human child, it seems, will not talk and certainly will not behave as one would expect him to behave. Dogs are born to be dogs. Human beings are *not* born to be human beings. Somehow, in the very genes and chromosomes that go into the making of a dog, much dog behavior is transmitted biologically. Human beings do not inherit humanity through genes and chromosomes. They *learn* it.

Biologically inherited behavior is called instinctive behavior. Life scientists often speak of the "instincts" of lower forms of animals. They tell of the instinctive manner in which bees gather the nectar of flowers, feed and care for the queen and her young, and build honeycombs so exactly that some scientists have suggested that the dimensions of the honeycomb be used as the universal unit of measure. So precisely do bees follow the same pattern of living that one is able to predict, without ever visiting their hives, how bees will behave in Cairo, Illinois, or in Cairo, Egypt; in Moscow, Idaho, or in Moscow, Russia; in Toledo, Ohio, or in Toledo, Spain. Life scientists report the instinctive ways of birds: how robins always build nests of straw and twigs; how swallows always build nests of mud. Here, too, the methods are so exact that one can predict how birds will build their nests in Rome, Georgia, or in Rome, Italy; in Paris, Kentucky, or in Paris, France; in Waterloo, Iowa, or in Waterloo, Belgium. Herein lies an important distinction between human beings and lower forms of animal life. Through instincts, nature provides for the perpetuation of much of the lower forms' ways of life. Nature provides no such instinctive guarantee of the perpetuation of human cultural ways.

No one knows how the first human beings who came into the world cared for themselves, nor how they managed to survive. Nature had for some reason failed to give them an automatic way of knowing how to obtain nectar from a flower or how to get meat by pouncing on some luckless prey. Nature had failed to give them an unreasoned way of sipping the dew from leaves or crushing the contents of a barrel cactus and quaffing the liquor. Nature had neglected to give them an uncritical urge to burrow into the ground or curl up in a hollow log. The lives of these first human beings are still draped with many unpenetrated mysteries.

We do know, however, that human beings the world over have *invented* means of finding wholesome food, have *invented* means of finding non-poisonous liquids to drink, have *invented* means of protecting their bodies from the elements. We can surmise that these techniques were learned at the dawn of human existence and that the resultant knowledge was pooled, preserved, and passed on from generation to generation; otherwise, we would hardly be present to ponder such a question now.

We know also that different people in the many areas of our planet have learned different ways to provide themselves with the necessities for sustaining life. This suggests that different groups, with their different historical backgrounds, have pooled, preserved, and passed on their own unique methods of survival from generation to generation. Anthropologists who have delved into this topic are impressed by the variability of human behavior in different parts of the world. Various groups of people, representing various historical backgrounds, have cultures which vary from one another.

One can predict very accurately how birds, bees, and other lower forms of animal life will behave, wherever they are found, because they are controlled largely by instincts. Mankind, however, is not so predictable. Even though one is told that *Homo sapiens* inhabits the island of Dobu, one cannot predict what foods he will eat there, what clothes (if any) he will wear, or what his housing will look like. There is no universal, exactly duplicated, regular, detailed way of life that characterizes all of mankind in any way comparable to that of the lower forms. Human cultural ways, instead of being kept alive through heredity, are acquired after birth through the learning process. He who is denied the chance to learn how to act in a manner appropriate to some human group falls short of achieving humanity. If a representative of the species *Homo sapiens* survives in the wilderness or in some attic, segregated at a tender age from adequate human contacts, he fails to act "human" and is branded as half-witted. Lacking sufficient instinctive mechanisms, man must learn from other human beings how to become human.

The Rationale for Education

Theoretically one might conjure up a feral person, devoid of human associations in early childhood, who might find out by trial and error how to provide the necessities for his existence. However, if all children had to be subjected to such an ordeal, it would be an excessive waste of effort, especially when all groups of human beings now inhabiting the globe have already found out how to meet their basic wants by some means or other. Besides, the children might die by experimenting with harmful materials. The simpler, shortcut method would be, rather, to *teach* the children how to

Bob Noble of the New York Herald Tribune

CULTURE IS A MAN-MADE ENVIRONMENT WHICH MUST BE LEARNED.

satisfy their bodily needs successfully through the ready-made techniques developed by their elders.

This suggests, on a very rudimentary level, the motive behind education: namely, to teach the young the noninstinctive means of survival which the group has found practical in order (1) to make unnecessary the trial-and-error experimentation which must have taken place when the ancestors of the group found out how to keep alive, and (2) to insure the survival of the neophytes. *At its most basic level,* education is the shortcut means of insuring the perpetuation of human life. This is a universal principle of education among human beings.

Such a picture of the role of education is too simple. Living (even on a rudimentary level) is not just a matter of satisfying elemental drives. Quickly people develop sentiments, values, ideologies, folkways, mores,

[34]

and taboos that go far beyond the problem of merely staying alive. There are *right* ways, *right* modes of conduct, *right* attitudes, *right* frames of mind that are looked upon as being fully as important for survival as getting food. These intangibles take the form of rules, of customs, of laws. It is not unusual for religious sentiments to get so intertwined with them that an individual is looked upon as offending the spirit world if he violates accepted behavior. Among the civilized as well as the primitive, some acts are considered so dangerous that if they are committed (so it is thought), the very foundations of that society are irreparably weakened. Anyone daring to commit such acts probably would be called a corrupter of morality, an atheist, a Communist, or whatever epithet contained the most venom at that time in that society. Such a person probably would be dealt with physically, too, by being incarcerated, exiled, executed, or tortured.

In order to perpetuate the sentiments, values, and ideologies that are precious to the group, it must inculcate rules, customs, and laws in its youth so that they will believe them, revere them, and follow them. This is the second universal principle of education among human beings, and is largely what we in the United States really mean when we say that we must have an educated citizenry if democracy is to endure. An education not only teaches the neophyte how to survive; it also teaches him to value the way of life prized by his elders so that this way of life may be continued for another generation. These are the two universal principles of education.

Typically, the values, sentiments, ideologies, folkways, mores, and taboos are so excellently instilled and so deeply implanted and internalized that by the time a person reaches maturity he is convinced that the way of life he has learned and now practices is the *only* appropriate way of life for *any* human being.[3] He is shocked, amazed, or filled with disbelief when he hears about people in other societies who have ways of life far different from his own. Apropos of this, the teacher of anthropology often encounters such an ethnocentric attitude in his beginning students. The students are alternately horrified, amused, and stunned by the "ridiculous" practices of "heathen" people in "strange" lands.

A child, far from being born into a vacuum, finds himself in a social and cultural maze, a human environment. The people in this environment begin at once to mold him so that he will respectfully follow the ways of these people. This process happens in all societies throughout the world, including the United States. In this manner the two universal principles of education are put into effect. The information considered essential for both individual and group survival is taught to the child.

[3] The technical term for this way of thinking is "ethnocentrism."

The Two Universal Principles of Education in Cross-Cultural Perspective

Stimulated by the iconoclastic writings and pronouncements of the European physician, Sigmund Freud, behavioral scientists have developed a growing interest in the impact of culture on children. Freud had pointed out that adult behavior cannot be divorced from events, even though forgotten, that have transpired earlier in an individual's life. Social scientists and applied social scientists have made many intensive studies of children in a variety of cultural settings—savage, barbarian, and civilized. They have watched children being exposed to many different kinds of cultures and many different kinds of social environments. They have noticed the ways in which children have reacted to a wide range of materials presented to them. They have attempted to determine the effects of learning on the behavior of the learners.

From these cross-cultural investigations, several anthropological conclusions significant to students of the educative processes have been formulated. Reasoned judgment suggests that the transfer of culture from the group to the child is not at all simple. At the risk of making this transfer seem too complicated, we shall present very briefly in the next few paragraphs some of the major anthropological conclusions concerning the teaching and learning of those materials that are vital to individual and group survival. These conclusions give deeper insight into the functionings of the two universal principles of education.

Every culture has within it a network—often a complex network—of interpersonal relationships. These interpersonal relationships are not random or unstructured; on the contrary, they are patterned and prescribed. For this reason they are predictable. In fact, their predictability makes possible the social life of human beings. In order for human beings to live together in a social group, it is absolutely necessary for each member of the group to know how he should act with regard to other people. It is equally important for each member of the group to be able to predict accurately how other people in his society will behave. It is exceedingly discomforting for an individual to find himself in a social situation in which he does not know what he should do or how other people will behave toward him or toward one another. To illustrate, pretend for a moment that you are a backwoodsman who has never traveled before. You find yourself for the first time in a huge metropolis, such as New York, Chicago, or Los Angeles. How do you behave in a hotel, or on the street, or in a department store, or in a theatre, or in a restaurant, or in a crowded elevator, or on a bus, or in the offices of some commercial organization? Imagine the confusion, the ludicrous behavior, and even the insecurity that you would experience. "Like a fish out of water" describes the feeling that comes from not knowing the prescribed modes of behavior. Now, if you will multiply this illustration by all of the interpersonal relationships that occur in a society, you can begin to realize how important it is for individuals to know what behavior is expected of them and to be able to anticipate the behavior of other people. If nobody knew what to do, the result would be chaos. When people spend their lives with other people (and, of course, they do), patterns of prescribed behavior are absolutely essential. The people involved must learn the folkways, mores, customs, and habits which regulate the reciprocal relationships of human social life. The only alternative is social chaos, which, of course, is no alternative at all.

The newborn child arrives in the world with no knowledge of human cultural and social ways. He is as naked culturally as he is physically. He cannot inherit his culture, and this is a singularity. It is man, not the lion, who is king of the beasts, yet the humblest of woodland creatures and the wee things that crawl from under a log can do what man, with all his power, cannot do. These lowly animals are capable of transmitting genetically their means of meeting elemental needs, through the medium of instincts. Man's mass of knowledge, called culture, cannot be transmitted genetically, but must be learned. The child of the genius and the child of the person of average intelligence are equally lacking in culture when they are born. A learned man and his learned wife are unable to transmit genetically to their offspring the superior cultural knowledge they have acquired. If the elaborate social networks and complex cultural ways of humans are to survive, they must be taught to the young by use of the intellect.

The average child could be taught from birth to conform to the cultural ways of any human society. In the course of two decades or less he would so absorb one culture that he could learn the culture of some other society only with great difficulty. Historically, this has been demonstrated in the United States on a grander scale than in any other nation. People representing all races and many of the cultures of mankind have come to America to live. It is only with exceeding difficulty that the mature, first-generation immigrant abandons entirely the habits and ways of his childhood and takes on the mantle of American cultural ways. His pronunciation of an American version of English will itself attest to his inability to adapt himself completely to a second culture after a first culture has been fully acquired. And yet, the children, the grandchildren, or the great grandchildren of this same immigrant will have no difficulty in learning the cultural and social ways of the United States if they are given an adequate opportunity to do so. If he is at all normal, a child born cultureless could acquire any human culture, but, having once learned a culture, he can abandon that culture only with great difficulty. These facts formed the basis for an extremist point of view which was popular approximately a generation ago and which is expressed succinctly by one of its major exponents, John B. Watson:

> Give me a dozen healthy infants, well-formed, and my own specified world to bring them up in and I'll guarantee to take any one at random and train him to become any type of specialist I might select—doctor, lawyer, artist, merchant-chief and, yes, even beggar-man and thief, regardless of his talents, penchants, tendencies, abilities, vocations, and race of his ancestors.[4]

Most behavioral scientists today agree that Watson was too enthusiastic in his claims. It remains true, however, that children are plastic and pliable when they are born.

Even though culture is acquired, human beings are still biological organisms. The lack of human instincts and the plasticity of human infants should not be allowed to hide from view the fact that human beings are a form of life. As a form of life, human beings possess elemental needs that cannot be ignored totally if human life is to continue for generation after generation. In order for a society and its culture to survive, the basic needs of the people who constitute that society must be met. This includes the basic needs of children, of course, for without them there would be no people to perpetuate that culture.

Sometimes human cultural ways are at cross purposes with human biological needs. In such a situation, if the need is elemental, it cannot be ignored totally, even though its satisfaction may be withheld temporarily. These facts also have been the basis for elaborate theories—including the psychiatric theory of child development of Sigmund Freud himself. Out of the semiconflict between human customs and biological desires comes enough learning of folkways, mores, taboos, and other aspects of culture to effect, in part at least, compromises between these two conflicting forces. The compromises make it possible for an individual both to live with other people and to stay alive himself. Notice, for example, the warfare between culture and biology with regard to personal bodily habits. Human biology demands that the body rid itself of waste materials from time to time if that body is to remain alive and healthy. Culture—for example, of the United States—is just as insistent that prescribed procedures be followed rigorously, such as concealing oneself from heterosexual public view and using specially designed equipment in prescribed fashion, when one attends to the biological urge to excrete. The infant, all biology and no culture, is

---

[4] J. B. Watson, *Behaviorism,* rev. ed. (New York: W. W. Norton & Co., Inc., 1930), p. 104.

completely oblivious to the prescribed folkways, mores, and taboos. As a growing child, however, he will learn to undergo discomfort and will permit his biological needs to be thwarted sufficiently to conform to the prescribed customs of the group, even though, if he were granted his wishes completely, he might prefer being more biological and less cultural in his behavior. Stated differently, learning a culture is not all sweetness and light. The ways of man make demands on individuals. The end result may be a deep modification of biological man in order to create cultural man in a social setting. Culture usually wins even at the expense of temporary thwarting of some biological drives and elemental wishes.

Culture usually wins because the child has really no choice but to conform to the ways of the society into which he is born. Since the child begins life without culture, he has no basis for deciding which cultural items he shall select or reject. The child born in the United States, for example, has no opportunity to say, "Please do not teach me English; I would rather learn French, because it is more musical (or German because it sounds very weighty and important, or Arabic because it uses interesting throaty consonants)." Unless the child learns the language of his society, he cannot be a full participant in that society. Humanity is achieved, not inherited, and unless one interacts effectively with other people, he will never fully achieve humanity. Isabelle and the ferals are cases in point. The child, furthermore, is dependent totally on other people for his very survival. In a sense, he cannot afford to refuse to learn cultural ways even if the choice were his to make. He depends on other people to meet his needs for him, and he must interact successfully with these other people in order that his needs may be known and cared for. Since these other people have useful patterns of behavior that the child lacks, the child himself soon learns to use these pre-existent cultural patterns when he interacts with the people in his environment. Moreover, societies reward those who accept their cultural ways and punish those who defy them. Early in life the child begins to feel social pressures that encourage him to conform. He finds these pressures, both positive and negative, hard to resist. For these reasons the child typically follows the cultural ways of the society into which he is born. One writer states these ideas in the following words:

> You will, if you are intellectually honest, realize very quickly that nine-tenths of all you do or say or think or feel from the time you get up in the morning until the time you go to bed at night is done and said and thought and felt, not in independent self-expression, but in uncritical, unconscious conformity with rules, regulations, group habits, standards, codes, styles, and sanctions that were in existence long before you were born.[5]

[5] Russell Gordon Smith, *Fugitive Papers* (New York: Columbia University Press, 1930), pp. 100–101.

People who grow up in the same society behave similarly. Children who are exposed to similar, if not practically identical, social manners and cultural procedures display this common background in their behavior. This anthropological conclusion forms the basis for still another type of theorizing about the behavioral development of the child. Each society is said to have a unique national character that can be identified through patterns of behavior. The child, as he matures, takes unto himself the patterns of the society in which he lives, thus becoming similar in behavior to the other children in that society and, of course, different from the children of other societies of the world. When seen in terms of adult behavior, this makes the people of one nation behave differently from the people of other nations. Here is the basis for generalizations such as the "muddling-through" Englishmen, the neoclassical Frenchmen, the schematic Germans, the pragmatic Americans, and the metaphysical Russians.

But people who grow up in the same society are different from one another, also. Differences as well as similarities can be found among children in the same society, the same village, the same family. Watson failed to adequately take this into account, as do some educational programs. It is true that children in the same society begin life equally devoid of culture; however, they do not begin life with precisely identical biological backgrounds (unless they are identical twins, triplets, etc.), because they are different genetically. The functioning of their bodies will not be absolutely identical either, as any physician can demonstrate, nor will the human cultural environment. Growing up in the household of a bank president is not identical to growing up in the household of a tavern keeper. (We shall return to this point in later chapters.)

These seven anthropological conclusions are suggestive of the fact that the transfer of culture from generation to generation is an involved, many-sided phenomenon rather than a simple one. At the same time, despite the complexities, the two universal principles of education remain: Education is necessary in order for a human being to stay alive, and education is necessary in order for a society to remain in existence.

Informal Education and Formal Education

Much of the teaching and learning that takes place in a society is unplanned, coincidental, or spontaneous. Instruction is a concomitant of other activities. When education is unplanned, coincidental, spontaneous, or a mere concomitant of other activities, it is called *informal*. A person receives an informal education merely by living in a human environment and by interacting with other human beings.

An informal education goes on much of the time with neither the teachers nor the learners being especially aware that education is taking place. On some occasions the teaching is quite consciously done, but it is treated as secondary to some other activity. The harassed mother who complains, "How many times must I tell you that the knife and spoon

Courtesy of Metropolitan Life Insurance Company

MUCH LEARNING IS INFORMAL.

always go to the right of the plate?" is aware that she is instructing her offspring. But the education is informal since it is a concomitant of the family's dietary activities, which are designed primarily for alimentary and not educational purposes.

Not all education is informal. Education is called *formal* if it is carried on through a special instructional program organized and instituted by the society. In less elaborate language, all the various sorts of schools offer formal education. A school is created for the purpose of offering instruction. It is a formalized means of educating people.[6]

Informal Education Is All-Pervasive

Usually, when a person talks about getting an education, he has in mind a formal education. Never underestimate, though, the significance of informal education. Informal education starts at one's birth and continues until the instant of one's death. So obvious and so omnipresent is informal education that anthropologists for years were unaware of its very existence. Only recently have anthropologists begun to pay informal education the attention it deserves.

Every time you have a conversation with someone, every time you read a book, every time you listen to a radio or television program, every time you play a game with someone, every time you eat a new delicacy prepared by someone, informal educative processes are functioning. From informal sources such as these you *learn* the details of your neighbor's operation, you *learn* more about the subtleties of the perennial battle between the sexes, you *learn* the words to the latest popular song, you *learn* to play bridge more expertly, you *learn* that zucchini tastes better when it is cleverly seasoned or disguised. Informal education continues as long as a person is alive. It affects young and old alike.

Consider, for example, what a child in our nation learns informally before he ever enters kindergarten. He can speak and understand the English language with remarkable facility. He knows that mothers cook food, clean house, wash and iron clothes, and sew. He knows that fathers work away from home much of the time, do most of the driving when the family rides in the car, handle hammers, screwdrivers, and other tools with dexterity, shave, and wear somewhat different clothes from mothers. He knows that children are smaller than adults, that a person has two parents and four grandparents, that people live in houses and eat three meals a day with knives, forks, and spoons on an array of dishes. He knows that spinach is supposed to be good to eat, but does not taste as good as chocolate bars. He knows that water quenches thirst, that snow falls in the winter,

[6] For the sake of accuracy, it should be noted that some authorities use either the term "enculturation" or "socialization" in place of the expression "informal education." They use "education" without any qualifying adjectives to mean what I have described as formal education. It is my opinion that the great importance of the informal educative process is beclouded when the use of the word "education" excludes it.

that trees have leaves on them. He knows that birds can fly, but cows cannot. The list of all that a child of five knows in our modern civilization is stupendous. A child is considerably educated before he goes to school. The child of five has absorbed virtually all of this information through social osmosis, by living among human beings in human situations. He is unaware of how he learned much of it. His informal teachers also are unaware, for the most part, of their role in the learning process.

So significant is informal education that it may be said without reservation that an individual during an average lifetime does more learning informally than formally, even though he may earn several college degrees. Stated somewhat in reverse, it is not absolutely necessary to go to school to get an education, because there is a lifetime of learning that occurs to the person who is exposed sufficiently to human social and cultural ways.

An Informal Education Is Sometimes an Adequate One

The literature of anthropology is replete with illustrations which indicate that some societies depend entirely on informal educative processes as the means of instructing children in the way of life of the group. Formal education is by no means universal. When a society's way of life is simple, informal educative devices are adequate to insure both the perpetuation of the individual and the perpetuation of the group. Thus, for some societies, schooling is unnecessary.

It is not difficult to identify some of the things that any normal child might learn by informal means in a primitive setting. Speech, a distinctive characteristic of human beings, is their most important means of communication. The normal child, whether he is a Carib, a Crow, or a Chinook, will learn to speak. All societies place restrictions on their members with regard to relieving the body of waste materials. The normal child, whether he is a Nuer, a Navajo, or a Nootkan, will learn the prescribed folkways or mores with regard to intimate personal hygiene. Every society has prescribed dietary customs. The normal child, whether he is an Andaman Islander, an Arapaho, or an Arunta, will learn what foods are acceptable, how they shall be eaten, and under what circumstances. In every society males and females are expected to behave somewhat differently from each other. The normal child, whether he is a Tuareg, a Toda, or a Tasmanian, will learn to identify with the role appropriate to his gender. And so the list grows.

Sometimes there are items both difficult and intricate to learn. But even these can be taught or learned without formal schools. Yurok women weave baskets capable of holding liquids. There is much skill involved, but girls can learn the technique in the same informal, tutorial way that a girl in our culture learns to knit well. Ituri Forest Pygmies kill elephants daringly by standing next to them and stabbing them with spears—an extremely dangerous technique. Boys can learn this in the same informal, tutorial fashion that a farm boy in America learns to steal up beside a coiled rattlesnake and kill it with a stick. Witoto women take the deadly poisonous root of the manioc and process it to make it edible. Girls can learn this in the same informal, tutorial way that a girl in America can learn from her mother how to preserve string beans so that there will be little danger of botulism. Jívaro men skillfully shrink human heads for trophies. Boys can learn this in the same informal, tutorial fashion that a boy in America can learn from his hunter father how to skin and butcher a deer.

An Informal Education Has Its Limitations

Through informal means a great deal of lore can be imparted from one person to another and passed on from generation to generation. There comes a point, however, at which formal instruction is superior for some subjects. The distinction is most apparent regarding skills. We have just noticed that some difficult and intricate techniques can be taught under haphazard conditions. From the standpoint of both adequacy and efficiency, highly complicated skills are taught *better* under formal conditions. In fact, some complicated skills can be learned only after hours and hours of deliberate and careful instruction. A person can learn to talk with informal instruction, but he will never learn to write without painstaking instruction. A person can learn to hum a tune with informal instruction, but he will never learn to play a Chopin selection correctly on the piano by reading the music without painstaking instruction. It is preferable for a society to have special educational establishments for the teaching of many skills.

Skills are only part of the picture. Remember, according to the two universal principles, education not only insures the perpetuation of the life of the individual; it also insures social immortality—guarantees that the group's cherished way of life will be relayed from one generation to the next. Knowledge gained by informal education may be garbled, may have gaps, may even be incorrect, because informal education is likely to be unsystematic, unorganized. In order to make certain that children are exposed to the correct version of the correct ideas, it is desirable to have specialized educational establishments where the children may learn. So it is that schools come into existence.

Even though schools are not universal, both primitive people and civilized people have them. Whether among simple savages or among civilized sophisticates, formal education serves a common purpose. Essential knowledge (as defined, of course, by the society) will be taught deliberately by specialists and will not be left to the chance techniques of informal education.

Some specific examples will clarify the above generalizations. The next portion of this chapter will be devoted to a discussion of the formal educational systems of three societies. The first is a primitive one, the Mano society. The second is an ancient civilized society, the city-state of Athens. The third is one of the most ancient non-Western civilized societies still in existence: China. In each instance, we shall see that the knowledge deemed crucial by a particular society becomes the basis of the curriculum and thus is not left to the random fortuitous processes of informal education.

The Bettmann Archive

FORMAL EDUCATION EXISTS BECAUSE <u>SOME</u> KNOWLEDGE IS TOO PRECIOUS TO LOSE.

Some Generalizations about Primitive Schools

As we turn now to a description of a primitive school system, a few introductory statements may assist the reader in understanding it more fully. Schools among nonliterate people are most prevalent in the islands of the Pacific and in Africa south of the Sahara Desert. Strands of similarities are usually found in these schools. Following are four such strands.

Primitive schooling is interwoven usually with the ceremony (or *rite of passage*) that marks the acceptance of the youth as an adult into the society. It carries something of the flavor of the debutante party which announces to the world that the child has become an adult.

Primitive schooling includes usually an initiation into the cult. Here the comparison might be made to the initiation of a new member into a fraternity, with all of the hazing that usually accompanies it. The instructional part of primitive schooling may appear to be pushed into the background because of the emphasis placed on ceremonial or initiatory practices.

The primitive school curriculum typically includes essential vocational and moral training.

Primitive schooling is usually of short duration: a few days, a few weeks, a few months at most. In order to offset the brevity of the school term, the educational scene is frequently made so intense emotionally that it burns itself into the minds of the students. The pupils could not possibly forget even if they would like to.

With this introduction, the reader may be somewhat better prepared to witness a scene that may be distasteful to him: the bush (or jungle) school of the Manos. Remember, primitive education is not just schooling. It includes a rite of passage and the gaining of membership in the cult. Remember also that of these purposes, the latter are likely to overshadow the former.

Education in a Primitive Setting: The Manos

The Mano tribe lives in the African nation of Liberia. The following description is based on studies that date back to the period between the two world wars.[7]

[7] An excellent description of the Mano bush school may be found in G. W. Harley, "Notes on the Poro in Liberia," *Peabody Museum Papers,* Vol. XIX, No. 2 (Cambridge, Massachusetts: 1941). I have borrowed heavily from this source.

The Mano bush school was presided over by a group of religious specialists who were educators secondarily. What schooling there was rested in the hands of this clergy. These religious specialists were both respected and feared, since they were thought to possess powerful magic which could be used effectively against the irreverent. Even chiefs stood in fear of their power. These specialists conducted bush schools for girls and for boys, but the latter is more important for our purposes.

There was no stated time at which the school would be conducted. The usual procedure was to wait until there were enough boys coming of age to make a school session worth the trouble and expense. Also, it was considered desirable to have a son of the chief in each class to become its alumni leader later. Several years could elapse between sessions.

Certain key religious figures were empowered to decide, amid pageantry, when the next bush school would be held. The time being agreed upon, a special campsite in the jungle was cleared to serve as the campus. Huts were constructed for the officials and the initiates (students). Roads leading into the area were blocked, and unauthorized persons were prohibited from entering the camp. Across the main entrance was constructed a huge, waterfall-like curtain of raffia streamers, so thick that no one could see through it.

When all was ready, the adolescent boys who were to be initiated assembled in front of the raffia curtain. Here they bade farewell to any family members or friends who had come to say good-bye. The boys would be at school for approximately two years. During this time they could neither leave nor communicate with any unauthorized outsiders.

The initiation began at the raffia curtain. Passage through (or sometimes over) the raffia curtain symbolized death. The boy was dead. A new man would emerge from the camp at the end of the school session. Once inside, the boys were sworn to secrecy and pledged not to run away. The penalty for breaking the oath was death. As a grim reminder, the boys were shown a tray containing fingers or toes of former initiates who were said to have broken the promise.

The program was divided into two major categories: initiatory practices and subject-matter instruction. The initiatory practices consisted principally of a series of operations on the body. Each boy was circumcised shortly after he entered the school. As soon as the wound healed, his body—particularly the back and the chest—was scarified. The scarification was a tedious and far from simple operation performed with pinchers and a razor. It was very painful. A rather intricate, even delicate pattern suggestive of the tooth marks left by a crocodile was cut into the initiate's flesh. There were dangers of infection and blood poisoning from these wounds, of course. If a boy did get blood poisoning, he was burned alive until his body was so charred that it could be reduced to a powder to be used as a medicine to keep the other boys from meeting the same fate. Any boy dying a natural death during the school session was treated somewhat differently. He, too, was put on the fire—but only until tender. Members of the school feasted on him. Boys who deserted the camp underwent a similar fate.

Subject-matter instruction consisted of teaching the boys the secrets of the cult, the lore of the culture, the moral and legal precepts, and basic native arts and crafts. The boys learned by doing those things they would do as adults. They learned how to build a house, how to clear a farm, how to grow crops. They learned how to hunt and capture wild animals. They learned the use of wild plants. They were taught trades of their choice if they showed special aptitudes. For example, the camp witch doctor taught able lads the art of mixing and administering herbal remedies.

At the end of approximately two years, each boy who had survived went through a final set of ceremonies—a graduation exercise of sorts. He was given a new name, by which he would be known for the rest of his life. A celebration was held as the graduates, pretending to be newly born, returned to their village and to their families. Those youths who did not survive the schooling were neither mourned nor ever spoken of again, because, after all, they had died two years earlier at the raffia curtain.

From Primitive to Civilized Schooling

Similar anthropological examples can be found among other primitives in other parts of the world. If one were to make further explorations among the primitives, one would find in each case that the school program (as distinct from the ceremonial and initiatory program) is designed to augment informal education. The school program is designed to give the younger generation those cardinal facts that young people are thought to need in order to survive in the society. The school program is designed also to insure the continuation of the cherished way of life of the society, thus guaranteeing group immortality. Here again are the two universal principles of education at work.

Primitive schooling lasts but a few weeks of the student's lifetime. When the way of life of a society becomes more and more complex, more and more time must be devoted to the formal teaching-learning processes if the pupil is going to learn what the society deems essential. Among civilized people (including ourselves) formal education may take years to complete. For example, in the United States a student must complete at least nineteen years of formal education before he is eligible to receive the highest degree of our universities, the Ph.D. degree.

The remaining two examples of formal education in this chapter deal with civilized societies. In each one, the formal educational system is somewhat elaborate and occupies the student for several years. In each one, also, the formal educational system, like that of the primitives, is designed to impart information deemed essential for individual and group survival.

Now to ancient Greece . . .

Education in Hellenic Athens

One of the outstanding civilizations of pre-Christian Europe was that of the city-state of Athens. The Athenians' way of life then was far more complex than the Manos' is today. Formal education there was much more time-consuming than it is in the society of the Manos.

Athens has a lengthy history. The following survey will be confined to roughly the four centuries between the two convenient dates of 700 and 300 B.C. This span of years is sometimes called the Hellenic period. It was during this time that Athens experimented with a brand of democracy and set in motion some of the political ideas which, indirectly and subtly, would have profound effects on the political structure of the Western world two millenia later.

Citizens of Athens had an opportunity to participate in the government of the Athenian democracy and in governmentally related activities. The formal educational system that developed was designed to reinforce the state by producing suave potential citizens. The goal of education was political: the creation of highly select gentlemen of political promise who could ably handle themselves and their city-state. Education had a practical basis in Hellenic Athens, as it has in the primitive Mano society.

Among the Manos the educative rites were for all boys and girls. None could escape unless he or she preferred to be put to death. But in Hellenic Athens formal education was limited in the sense that it was offered to male citizens only. Citizenship was also limited. Apparently only about one-eighth of the people under Athenian rule could consider themselves citizens. Education was limited to the crème de la crème of the society; not even all of the male citizenry went to school. Schools were for the most part private, and students had to pay their own way. So a trio of artificial barriers to education presented themselves: the barrier of sex (boys only), the barrier of citizenship (boys of citizens only), and the barrier of wealth (boys of prosperous citizens only).

Two distinct levels of formal education are discernible in the Hellenic period: an elementary level and an advanced level. In contemporary America we are familiar with three traditionally defined levels of education: elementary, secondary, and higher (or collegiate). It was not until the close of the Hellenic period that an obvious distinction between secondary education and higher education began to take shape in Athens. Thus, for the sake of accuracy, it is preferable to combine these latter two levels of education when describing the Hellenic period, and to call them the advanced level.

The Bettmann Archive

AN ATHENIAN MUSIC SCHOOL.

On the elementary level there were three distinct curriculums. Often the three were taught in separate schools; occasionally some combination was arrived at. In any event, the young male citizen-to-be, whose family could afford the expense, studied letters, music, and gymnastics. The teacher of letters gave him the rudiments of the three R's: reading, 'riting, and 'rithmetic. The teacher of music taught him singing, chanting, dancing, and instrumental music. The teacher of gymnastics taught him such body-strengthening pursuits as jumping, swimming, wrestling, and how to walk handsomely.

The citizen-statesman would have to be literate. He would have to be adroit in the use of words, since he would speak publicly on political issues. The citizen would be expected to participate in politico-religious or civic celebrations involving music and the dance. The citizen might be called upon to defend his city-state. A strong, healthy, well-developed body would be important in warfare. The education offered in the elementary schools was designed to produce a well-rounded individual—a literate, aesthetic, physically sound person.

Advanced education in Athens was not as organized as elementary education, even as late as the fourth century B.C. The Athenian government erected three "gymnasiums," strategically located in different parts of the city. These gymnasiums were not "gyms" in the American sense of the word. Rather, they were primarily athletic fields. To these athletic areas came older boys and men of leisure to engage in muscular exercises or to spend their free hours. This relatively unorganized arrangement sounds as much like an advanced educational establishment as an American city park would. In a sense, it was not; yet, such a conclusion is hasty. Athletic activities were important to the citizens. The gymnasiums gave the men an opportunity to retain what they had learned earlier from their teachers of gymnastics. The gymnasiums were practice grounds. The learning that occurred in them was somewhat similar to that which takes place when an amateur pianist practices to retain his skill.

From time to time, shrewd men of letters—astute professionals—visited the gymnasiums and sought pupils for themselves. These men were known as Sophists. Sophists offered to teach any and all comers how to manipulate words cleverly, how to overpower a person in a debate, how to defend oneself with words. In fact, the Sophists would teach anything of a verbalistic nature. Of course, the teaching was done for a fee, and the fee usually was as high as the traffic would bear. Some of these men were excellent teachers and had accurate and correct information to offer. Others were opportunists. It was they, selling claptrap, who tended to give all Sophists the bad name which the label still carries today. The Sophists did not have school buildings. They were itinerant teachers, selling their verbal wares wherever they could find temporary quarters and enrollees.

At the end of the Hellenic period, some advanced educators became permanently located and founded advanced educational establishments in Athens. The two most famous were Plato, who founded a college known as the Academy, and Aristotle, who founded a college known as the Lyceum. And there were others.

One more sphere of advanced education in Athens deserves mention. Older adolescents were expected, at first through custom and later through official pressure, to spend some time in military training before achieving full status as adult citizens. (Need I point out the educative aspects—both formal and informal—of military life? They differ little today from what they were then.) During the fourth century, the final years of the Hellenic period, a military college called the Ephebic College was instituted. Unlike the other Athenian educational arrangements, except the gymnasiums, it was government operated. The terminal years of the Hellenic period were troubled times for the Athenian city-state. In a move of desperation, military training for male citizens was made obligatory, and the Ephebic College, a sort of West Point of the Athenian world, was established to insure adequate training. However, the history of Athens shows that the horse had bolted before the barn door had been. Athens fell to the armies of Alexander.

Education in Athens was limited to the privileged few. Only sons of the elite studied music, letters, and gymnastics. Only the select young men practiced at gymnasiums, or attended lectures of Sophists, or trained at the Ephebic College. On the shoulders of these youths was placed the responsibility of guarding and preserving the Athenian way of life. Once more the two universal principles of education can be seen at work. Formal education is designed to transmit to students that knowledge which is essential for them to function well in their society. Formal education is designed also to protect and to preserve the society—to give it social immortality. Basic knowledge is not left to chance.

Education in China [8]

The most populous nation in the world is China. Depending on which set of statistics one employs (and each is less than satisfactory), China's current population may be estimated at somewhere between one-fifth and one-fourth of the total population of the Earth. For this reason alone China would be an important nation, and there are other reasons. China is considered by some to be the world's leading "backward" nation, which now is coming out of a lengthy period of dormancy. It is now striving to match or surpass in economic and political influence the most advanced of the Western nations. The less powerful underdeveloped countries watch with interest as this ancient nation of the East rouses from its long sleep. China may indeed set the pattern for other underdeveloped nations. When one bears in mind that the majority of the world's population now and in the foreseeable future is in the so-called backward areas of the world, what

[8] Two up-to-date sources of information that have influenced the following discussion are:

Chang-Tu Hu, ed., *Chinese Education under Communism,* No. 7 of *Classics in Education,* ed. by L. A. Cremin. New York: Bureau of Publications, Teachers College, Columbia University, 1962.

L. A. Orleans, *Professional Manpower and Education in Communist China.* Washington: National Science Foundation, 1961.

China does may have a decisive effect on the future history of all mankind.

Even though the history of China covers several millenia, its educational system changed very little during much of that time. However, during the past hundred years, swift changes touching the entire culture have occurred. In describing briefly the Chinese educational scene, we shall divide the materials into three periods. The first extends from the time of Confucius to the middle of the nineteenth century. The second runs from the middle of the nineteenth century to 1949. The third is the current one, dating from the establishment of the Communist regime in 1949.

Period I: Traditional Education in China

In order for a society to remain unified over a period of years, there must be some cohesive force that holds its people together. Without such a force (or forces) a society rapidly disintegrates. In the Western world one of the powerful cohesives has been religion. China has lacked a state religion; one might even say, with qualifications, that the Chinese have never been a religious people, although several religions have been able to survive and even flourish side by side in China for centuries. Another powerful societal cohesive force has been imperialism, or a similar political force. China has had its dynasties; several have come and gone. But politics has not been the glue that has held the age-old Chinese society together. Instead, China has used a third binding societal force—a humanistic philosophy of life known as Confucianism.

Although Confucianism is often classified as a religion, it is more accurate to call it an axiologically oriented philosophy which stresses ethical and sociopolitical values. In this philosophy man is thought to achieve peace with himself, peace with his fellow man, peace with nature, and peace with the world through the understanding that comes from education. The truly learned person is an ideal citizen. He is loyal, faithful, just, kind, righteous, and proper because he has learned to be moral. An individual does not fully achieve humanity without learning. Thus, education is seen as the highroad to personal and social ethics and to becoming fully human. This point is illustrated in a somewhat humorous fashion in the following excerpt from a letter written in the sixteenth century by a Chinese scholar to his son. The letter concerns some European Jesuit priests whom the scholar had seen in China.

These "Ocean Men," as they are called, are tall beasts with deep sunken eyes and beak-like noses. . . . But the strangest thing about them is that, although undoubtedly men, they seem to possess none of the mental faculties of men. The most bestial of peasants is far more human, although these Ocean

Men go from place to place with the self-reliance of a man of scholarship and
are in some respects exceedingly clever. It is quite possible that they are sus-
ceptible to training and could with patience be taught the modes of conduct
proper to a human being.[9]

According to Confucian thought, one is not born moral. Nor is one
born to a position of leadership. The person who has studied carefully,
who becomes learned, achieves that sort of ethical character that equips
him to be a leader. This point of view had a direct bearing on the government of China. Leadership, said Confucius, is too precious a social function
to be left to the chance operations of heredity. Therefore, the man who
has become wise through education should rule and be the leader in all
other social undertakings as well. At least in theory, this point of view
worked against the establishment of hereditary social classes in China. It
also led to an overlapping in meaning of such terms as "scholar," "leader,"
"official," and "gentry." A man who is truly educated is moral and trust-
worthy and need not be feared as a leader, because he will do nothing to
harm the society. He also deserves respect. Such a person was deemed
worthy to be the custodian of Chinese culture and society.

But a question arises. Among the learned people, which ones are best
suited to positions of leadership in governmental affairs? In time an answer
was developed: there should be examinations. These examinations could
be used to cull out the least promising people and identify the most able.
Different levels of civil service positions in the government could be filled
by different levels of scholars. The least able scholars could be assigned the
least crucial governmental offices, while the most notable could be recruited
for vital governmental positions. Eventually there was instituted an elaborate series of examinations extending from the community level up to the
imperial level. As this occurred, the examinations began to crystallize and
become ends in themselves. Anyone who wanted the prestige of being
identified as a scholar and who desired social advancement and high office
needed to study not to become wise and moral, but to pass examinations.
Schooling became oriented toward preparing students to pass examinations.
Schools tended to become what we call colloquially in the United States
"cramming schools." The crystallization of examinations was accompanied
by a formalization of teaching, which in turn was accompanied by a formalization of materials for study, which was accompanied eventually by
a formalization of the culture itself. The Chinese culture became virtually
static and self-contained, and in this state of torpor China entered the nineteenth century.

[9] Quoted in R. T. LaPiere and P. R. Farnsworth, *Social Psychology,* 2nd ed.
(New York: McGraw-Hill Book Co., Inc., 1942), p. 154.

Period II: The Westernization of Chinese Education

The nineteenth and early twentieth centuries were a neocolonial period for several European nations, transplanted European nations, and other nations that had been imbued with the expansionistic spirit of Western manifest destiny. Africa and numerous Pacific islands felt the effects of neocolonialism. So did China. By the dawn of the twentieth century, China had become in part a colony of Western and Westernized nations.

China's first reaction to contact with the West was to borrow enough Western ideas and methods to combat ideologically, socially, and militarily further inroads of the West on her traditional, orthodox, Confucian way of life. Thus, during the last third of the nineteenth century, foreign-language schools for training diplomats, schools of technology for training scientists, and military schools for creating a fighting force in a traditionally peace-loving nation were instituted. The purpose of these new schools was not to supplant the traditional schools. It was, rather, to equip China sufficiently to resist any further erosion of her self-contained culture and her territories through Westernization.

The disastrous outcome, from the Chinese standpoint, of the Sino-Japanese War at the end of the nineteenth century was enough to indicate to the leaders of China that their efforts to retain the old by veneering it with the new were unsuccessful. Thus, as China entered the twentieth century, she was ready to abandon the ancient orthodoxy of Confucianism and become thoroughly Westernized in order to survive as a nation. By 1905 the venerable system of examinations was abandoned—a symbol that Confucian learning had become outdated. Following the lead of various Western nations, and that of the United States especially, China established a new educational system much like our own. This system had three levels of education: elementary, secondary, and higher. The shift in education was hastened by missionary organizations and other Westernized groups that established their own schools in China. Many young Chinese scholars went abroad for their advanced education and brought back Westernized notions about education.

The younger generation of scholars, educated abroad or in Westernized Chinese schools, felt no allegiance to the traditional orthodoxy of Confucianism. Their ideal was to be as Western as possible in activity, outlook, and ideology. Thus, the past-oriented, traditionalistic, self-contained culture of previous centuries was abandoned in favor of the West. The time-honored Confucian scholar was replaced by a Westernized intellectual. The new intelligentsia were fervent in their desire to convert China overnight into a leading Westernized nation.

The zeal of the intelligentsia was thwarted, however, for various reasons.

During its period of Westernization the government of China was unstable. It changed and changed again—a factor upsetting to the entire society. The masses of people were ignorant, and China was poor. These characteristics made Westernization itself difficult and an effective competition with advanced Westernized nations almost impossible. In addition to all this, a second war between Japan and China broke out within half a century of the first. This second war lasted more than a decade, merging in its latter phases with World War II. The war greatly impeded China's development, not only economically, but socially, poltically, ideologically, and educationally. China was a shattered, dislocated nation after World War II, and its intellectuals were demoralized. They had abandoned the traditions of their ancestors in the hope of creating a new, modernized China that would take its place among the leading Westernized nations of the world. But Westernization seemed a failure, because China was in worse condition after its contact with the West than before. She was a nation without roots; she had severed her connections with the orthodoxy of tradition, but the new ties with the West had failed to develop to the satisfaction of the intelligentsia. Like Luigi Pirandello's *Six Characters in Search of an Author,* the intelligentsia of China were searching for a new orthodoxy to take the place of the ancient Confucianism, since it appeared that Westernization had not been the answer.

Period III: Education in Communist China

It was in this setting of unrest and disillusionment that the Communists came into power in China by offering a new orthodoxy for the seemingly unsatisfactory ones of the past. Zeal, enthusiasm, and an aggressive sense of mission characterize present-day China, as the new orthodoxy permeates the thinking of the Chinese. China hopes now to accomplish through totalitarian tactics what it failed to accomplish through Westernization— that is, to become a leading nation, perhaps *the* leading nation, of the world. China is a nation in a hurry; she feels an urgent need to fulfill her destiny.

Education assumes a vital place in the new China. She must become a leader in science and technology if she is to come close to realizing her goal. Leadership in technology is possible only in a country in which literacy is widespread and advanced training is readily available.

Communist China faces numerous educational problems. A key one is the problem of making the population literate. When the Communists came into power, an estimated 80 to 90 per cent of the population was illiterate. A second basic educational problem is that of highly educating many people along scientific lines while at the same time keeping these educated people from questioning the dogma that Communist ideology is

Gillhausen, from Black Star

AN EDUCATION FOR THE PERPETUATION OF THE IDEALS OF ITS SOCIETY STARTS EARLY IN COMMUNIST CHINA.

infallible. The main trait of the true scientist is an inquiring mind, since science, by its very nature, must challenge everything and accept nothing at face value. Communist jabberwocky might be in danger if the Communistic educational system produced enough people with the spirit of scientific inquiry. This presents a very real dilemma: without skilled scientists the future of Communist China is in peril, and with highly educated scientists trained to challenge and question, the future of Communist China is also in peril. A third key educational problem is that of finding sufficient resources in an underdeveloped country to support a universal system of education for the most populous nation in the world. If the United States, a wealthy nation having less than 7 per cent of the world's population, has financial problems in maintaining its schools, imagine the problem confronting China, a poor nation with perhaps as many as one-fourth of all of the people of the world. How is Communist China meeting these educational problems?

[57]

In order to overcome illiteracy, China has established a dual educational system. Diagram II identifies the major elements of this dual system. One of the two major branches is composed of what may be termed full-time schools. The other major branch is composed of part-time and spare-time schools. The full-time schools follow the traditional Western hierarchy of lower schools, then middle schools, and then advanced schools, institutes, and colleges.

The curriculum of the elementary school centers around linguistic studies. Chinese is a difficult language in which to become literate; its characters usually stand for words rather than sounds. This means, in effect, that one must learn a separate character or combination of characters for almost every word in the language. The characters are somewhat similar in function to the arbitrary symbols that we use, such as % (per cent), # (number), £ (pound), $ (dollar), & (and), * (see footnote at bottom of page), and so forth. By the time a child completes the sixth grade, he is expected to have mastered some four thousand characters—no mean undertaking. It is easy to understand why the language arts take up a great deal of time on the elementary level.

Secondary education in the full-time schools is divided into three overlapping, but separate, curriculums: college preparatory, teacher preparatory, and technical. The last is an obvious imitation of the Soviet *technicum,* with its applied scientific curriculum designed to produce skilled laborers and lower-level technicians. Higher education is specialized also, the prime emphasis being on scientific and technical subjects for the preparation of professional and semiprofessional people.

Paralleling the full-time schools somewhat are half-time and spare-time schools. They have two major purposes: to bring literacy to the masses of older people who are not enrolled in full-time schools, and to improve the general public's understanding of the sciences in their applied forms. These schools correspond roughly to the various extension services of a semi-educational nature that we have had or do have in America, from Chautauquas and women's-club "study groups" to educational television programs and night schools. They are much less organized than the full-time schools.

In order to overcome the perplexing dilemma of cultivating scientific minds without kindling the spirit of scientific inquiry at the same time, Chinese education uses various approaches. One is to include sturdy courses in indoctrination on all levels of education, in both full-time and part-time schools. These courses, no matter what title they may carry, have the single purpose of inculcating propaganda. Students are saturated with Communist ideology. A second approach is to undermine the status of the scholar. Children are taught that it is important to study diligently, but

STRUCTURE OF EDUCATIONAL SYSTEM (CIRCA 1960)

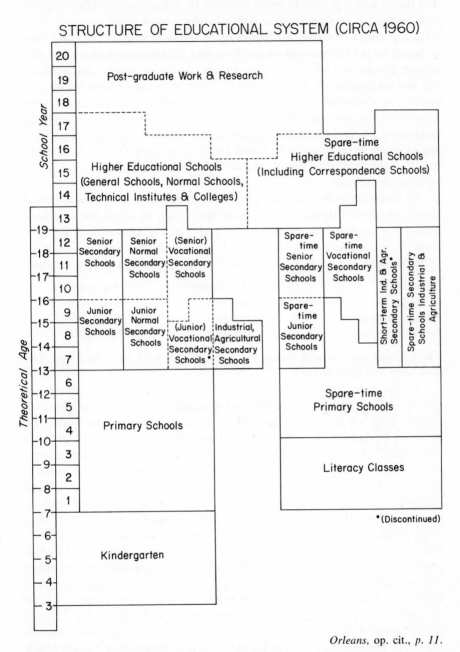

Orleans, op. cit., p. 11.

DIAGRAM II.   STRUCTURE OF THE EDUCATIONAL SYSTEM IN COMMUNIST CHINA
(*circa* 1960).

that the practical person is more valuable than the scholar. The "impractical" scholar is suspect and not worth listening to. A third approach is to judge a person's academic excellence on the basis of what he says and does in behalf of the Communist cause. Informal questioning sessions and discussion groups are held from time to time to make certain that students can and do express the new orthodoxy. Students are also expected to participate in Communist political activities in order to demonstrate their devotion to the new order. Still another approach is to insist that *all* students from every level of education engage in productive economic work. Some schools even have factories or farms attached to them. This arrangement, it is thought, will unite the practical and the theoretical, and will proletarianize the scholar.

In order to overcome the problem of financing a vast educational enterprise, several shortcuts have been taken, each of which has sacrificed quality for quantity in education. Official Chinese Communist statistics suggest remarkable strides in universalizing education. Here are some for 1958,[10] a year the Communists called the year of the great leap forward.

Grade Level	1957 Enrollment	1958 Enrollment
Kindergarten	1,000,000	30,000,000
Primary Schools	64,000,000	86,000,000
Secondary Schools	7,000,000	10,000,000

The Chinese government claimed that 85 per cent of its school-age children were in school in 1958.

A closer look reveals woeful inadequacies from the standpoint of quality—reflecting China's inability to adequately finance her educational system. Here are three examples. Many Chinese kindergartens would not be called kindergartens in the United States. At best, we might term them baby-sitting agencies. The "teachers" often are illiterate or semiliterate old women or young girls who merely watch the children while the mothers are away at work. The children receive scant instruction, if any. A second example of inadequate financing is the fact that all students must work at least part time. Having students on all levels of education work part time helps reduce the cost of education, but it means that the students have fewer hours to devote to their studies, a penny-wise but pound-foolish practice. A third example is the caliber of literacy expected of those adults who are enrolled in spare-time literacy classes. Four thousand characters is the criterion of minimum literacy in the full-time lower schools; but in the spare-time schools a person is considered literate if he has learned fifteen hundred characters. Such an individual could read only the simplest materials. His reading ability in his own language would be not greater than

[10] Adapted from Orleans, *op. cit.*, p. 18.

the average American high-school student's ability to read a foreign language after one year of the traditional language course. Thus, the universal literacy now striven for is truly minimal. These three aspects reflect some of the financial shortcuts that have been taken to make universal education a reality in this most populous of nations.

Summary Comment

Details in the formal educational systems of the Manos, the Athenians, and the Chinese vary greatly. The basic reasons for formal education remain the same, however. The motives behind formal education in China parallel the motives seen in the other school systems under survey. Some subject matter is so essential to the welfare of the individual and the group that its inculcation cannot be left to the haphazard techniques of informal educative processes. Therefore, it becomes subject matter for formal education.

Traditional Chinese society recognized education as indispensable to the survival of the Chinese way of life. The scholar was thought to be the protector of the values of the culture, because it was he who became fully human through study. During the transitional period also, formal education was used to preserve the integrity of the Chinese society. At first, education was used as a weapon to resist Westernization. Later, it was used as an implement to encourage Westernization. The educated person was essential in both cases in effecting these social goals. Under Communism the values of formal education are also recognized. The Communists turn to education as a means of reaching national goals as well as of creating a citizenry capable of functioning effectively under China's new regime.

Social Institutions and Education

All human societies are structured around one or more major units of social organization known among anthropologists and sociologists as social institutions. A social institution is an enduring, self-perpetuating, sometimes elaborate blueprint for group activity which satisfies one or more needs considered basic to the maintenance of the society's way of life. The family, education, religion, government, and economic affairs are examples of such institutions. The lives of the human beings who compose a society are built around the specifications designated in the institutional blueprints of that society. Most of the time of the average person, whoever he is, wherever he is, is spent performing some of those activities and satisfying some of those needs identified in the institutional blueprints of his society. The institutionalized activities are pervasive. In fact, one method of understanding the ways of a particular society is to study carefully that society's institutions.

All of the institutions of a society serve an educative function. This is one of the reasons why institutions are self-perpetuating. The child in America, for example, is taught those social expectations that reflect the institutional blueprint of economics through such means as working occasionally at odd jobs, having an allowance, or making purchases at stores. He is taught those social expectations that reflect the institutional blueprint of government through such means as seeing policemen enforce laws, noticing people's behavior when the national flag is unfurled, or watching news broadcasts on television. He is taught those social expectations that reflect the institutional blueprints of religion through such means as attending Sunday school, accompanying his parents to services of worship, or participating in religious holidays.

Even though every institution in a society has an educative function, there are two social institutions in particular that are of foremost importance educationally. One is the family, and the other is the school. The family, from a world standpoint, is the main agency of informal education. The school, from a world standpoint, is the main agency of formal education.

The Family and Education

The family's role as the prime agency of informal education may be somewhat difficult for the American to appreciate fully, because in America the family serves fewer functions than it does in most societies. Americans spend less time in familial activities than do people in most other societies. The nuclear American family is usually small in size and typically separated both geographically and psychologically from the larger kinship unit (the extended family) of which it is, both legally and sociologically, a constituent part. These factors may lead the American to the conclusion that the family is not much more important as an informal educative agency than the neighborhood, the peer group, or the television set. This conclusion, while understandable, is not supportable from either the geographical or the historical standpoint. In most societies the nuclear family takes part in a larger cluster of activities than its American counterpart, is composed of a larger group of people than the American family, and has closer affiliations with the kinship group than in our society. The Pueblo Indians of New Mexico and Arizona, for example, have a familial institution that is closer to the human average than the prevailing family pattern in the United States. The Pueblo child grows up in a household that is not only the primary family unit, but also the primary economic unit and the primary educational unit. He lives in an abode that adjoins or is close to the residences of his mother's kinsfolk. All of the relatives who surround the Pueblo child interact with him and participate in his informal education. The pervasiveness of the Pueblo family is rather typical of the human family, especially among nonliterate and peasant people.

Child-rearing is primarily the duty of the mother in America. Cross-cultural evidence suggests that in the majority of human societies the child-rearing functions of the family are diffused among several people. In most societies there are surrogate mothers and surrogate fathers, as well as the natural parents themselves, who educate the child. The relatives living nearby act as parent substitutes. When a society is homogeneous (a characteristic more often found among primitives than among civilized people), those who practice the culture are in basic agreement as to what behavior is acceptable or unacceptable. In such a homogeneous society, with surrogate parents as well as natural parents to educate the child informally, his learning to behave in the accepted way is well reinforced. Anthropologist Margaret Mead, writing of the Samoans, contrasts the child in America with the child in Samoa.

> The close relationship between parent and child, which has such a decisive influence upon so many in our civilisation, that submission to the parent or defiance of the parent may become the dominating pattern of a lifetime, is not found in Samoa. Children reared in households where there are a half dozen adult women to care for them and dry their tears, and a half dozen adult males, all of whom represent constituted authority, do not distinguish their parents as sharply as our children do. The image of the fostering, loving mother, or the admirable father, which may serve to determine affectional choices later in life, is a composite affair, composed of several aunts, cousins, older sisters and grandmothers; of chief, father, uncles, brothers and cousins. Instead of learning as its first lesson that here is a kind mother whose special and principal care is for its welfare, and a father whose authority is to be deferred to, the Samoan baby learns that its world is composed of a hierarchy of male and female adults, all of whom can be depended upon and must be deferred to.[11]

Whether the family is stripped of kinsfolk, as in the United States, or is rich in nearby kin, as in most human societies, the family remains the key agency for transmitting informally the patterns of behavior, the value system, the ideologies, and the way of life which comprise a culture. Through this process the child becomes a functioning member of both the family and the larger society. The range of materials taught by the family is usually vast. In a nonliterate society that has no formal educational

[11] Margaret Mead, *Coming of Age in Samoa* (New York: The New American Library of World Literature, Inc., 1928, 1949), pp. 138–139.

Courtesy of The Travelers Insurance Companies

THE FAMILY IS THE MAIN AGENCY OF INFORMAL EDUCATION.

system, the full gamut of ideals and techniques necessary to adulthood are customarily taught by the extended family. The methods employed to emphasize this learning include such negative ones as ridicule, deprivation, or chastisement and such positive ones as praise, promises, and rewards.

Schools and Education

As we have remarked earlier, formal education is not universal. Many nonliterate societies have no formal schools. Even though the average American may not be very well informed about schools or other educational media throughout the world, he is quite aware of the fact that an educational institution has one paramount function: to educate. The educating that is done in the educational institutions of human societies may be summarized in the five following generalizations:

Unlike informal education, formal education is a very conscious process. Sometimes people are unaware that informal education is taking place. This may well be a basic reason why pioneer anthropologists neglected the topic of informal education. But formal education is far too obvious to be overlooked. The school buildings, the special personnel, the delegation of resources for the support of education are all too imposing to be missed.

Formal education is much more limited in scope than informal education. This generalization holds true if for no other reason than the fact that formal education is of short duration when compared with informal education. Among the Manos, for instance, the bush school lasts for only two years. This does not give them enough time to include everything in the curriculum.

This leads to a third generalization—that the educational institution is a reflection of the society's value system. Since the educated person spends only a fraction of his lifetime at school, only those materials that are far too important to be left to chance can be included in the curriculum. Notice how, as the cultural values of the Chinese changed, their curriculums changed also. For years and years China's outlook was Confucian, and education in China mirrored it. Then, after its contact with the West, China's outlook became Westernized, a change that its educational system duly reflected. At present, China's value orientation is in terms of industrialization and Communism, and its educational structure is an extension of this new set of values.

The effects of value systems on educational procedures can also be seen when one seeks answers to the question "Which people in the society shall receive an education?" Schooling is expensive in time, manpower, and monetary resources. The value system of a society will determine who will receive a formal education and under what circumstances. Each of the three societies whose formal educational organizations we described had different value systems. The Mano answer was that everyone expecting to survive at least until adulthood was obliged to receive an education unless he preferred being raked over the coals. In Hellenic Athens education was reserved for the sons of prosperous citizens. In contemporary China all children (in theory) attend school. Competent students continue their education at the secondary and higher educational levels. All older people whose education previously was neglected attend, supposedly, part-time or spare-time schools in Communist China.

The school's curricular offerings and the composition of the student body reflect the point of view, the outlook, and basic aims of a society. This generalization applies to other school policies as well.

Formal education exists because some knowledge is too precious to lose. This generalization takes us back to the second universal principle of education: a fundamental reason for education is to insure that the most precious components of a society will be preserved. In order to preserve them, human beings purposely implant these most precious items in the minds of the young, which education in China clearly illustrates. For centuries Confucian morality was thought to be indispensable, so formal education was designed to perpetuate Confucianism. Early in the twentieth century, Westernization was thought to be a social necessity, so the schools sought to develop in China a thorough understanding of the Western way of life. Nowadays an industrialized, Communized culture is thought to be essential, so China's dual school system attempts to preserve this new heritage. In each case a primary endeavor of the changing Chinese educational system has been to perpetuate that which the society does not wish to lose.

Formal education exists to insure competency among those members of the society who receive schooling. This generalization takes us back to the first universal principle of education: a fundamental reason for education is to insure the survival of the individual. Mano youths went to the bush school to learn what their society considered necessary for their welfare. Likewise, the Hellenic Athenians offered formal education to the sons of citizens in order to transform these boys into refined men capable of surviving in Athens. And the Chinese educational systems, whether Confucian, transitional, or Communistic, have had as one of their aims the well-being of the people who would receive an education.

Institutions other than the family and the school also have educational functions. In the next chapter we shall see, for example, that both church and state have had deep educational influences on American life. The family and the school, nevertheless, are the primary institutions of education among human beings. The remainder of this book will be concerned principally with formal education rather than informal education, and, therefore, with the institution of education rather than the family.

In Conclusion

Human beings are bundles of potentials when they are born. These potentials can become realized through educative processes. Informally, a child learns much, mainly about the way of life of the group into which he is born. If the group is very simple, he may receive no other sort of education at all. Many societies, civilized and primitive alike, do not like to leave education to the random, chance processes of informal education. Thus, they institute special, formal educative organizations, or schools, to insure that the young will be exposed systematically to those subjects that are basic both to their own welfare and to that of the society. So it has been with the Manos, with the Athenians, and with the Chinese. And so it is, we shall find, with the Americans.

The Chapter in Capsule Form

1. Human beings, born little more than animated alimentary canals, learn how to behave in a human fashion.

2. From evidence which is not altogether scientific, it appears that a potentially normal child will not behave in a human way if he is deprived of adequate opportunities to interact with other human beings.

3. Whereas the way of life of lower animals is largely instinctive, human culture is learned after birth and is highly variable from society to society.

4. It is through education that a society teaches the child those noninstinctive means of survival that have been transmitted socially from generation to generation.

5. Education is also the means whereby the cherished values of the society are perpetuated by being transmitted from generation to generation.

6. The transference of culture from generation to generation is complex and involved.

7. Much education is informal. That is, much of what one learns is learned casually or in an unplanned, coincidental fashion.

8. Formal education is education received in an organized, systematized, instructional program that is purposely devised by the society.

9. Informal education continues throughout one's entire lifetime. In fact, one does more learning informally than formally during a lifetime.

10. In very simple societies an informal education may be sufficient to teach the individual the way of life of the society.

11. Many societies, including primitive ones, are unwilling to leave an individual's education to the rather haphazard processes of informal learning. Thus, schools are instituted. The school system offers in its curriculum those materials the knowledge of which is considered indispensable both for the welfare of the individual and for the perpetuation of the society itself.

11.1 For example, the Manos have a bush school designed to prepare boys (or girls) for the responsibilities of adulthood.

11.2 For example, the Hellenic Athenians had a formal educational system designed to prepare boys for the responsibilities of citizenship.

11.3 For example, China, during the three periods of its formal educational system, has endeavored to perpetuate cherished ideals and insure competency in its citizens.

12. In each of these cases, the materials which the society deems crucial are the materials taught. In each of these cases the individual is exposed to those subjects that it is thought he will need in order to be a valuable member of the society. In each of these cases, the educational system helps insure the continuation of the values prized by the society.

13. All social institutions serve an educational function. The family, however, is the prime agency of informal education, and the school is the prime agency of formal education.

For Supplementary Reading

ARIÈS, PHILIPPE, *Centuries of Childhood,* translated by Robert Baldick. New York: Alfred A. Knopf, 1962.
A unique and revealing social history of children and their education in Western Europe.

BEALS, RALPH L., and HOIJER, HARRY, *An Introduction to Anthropology,* 2nd ed. New York: The Macmillan Co., 1959, Chapter XX.
Several current introductory textbooks in anthropology contain a chapter on education. This is a representative chapter from a standard college textbook.

KLUCKHOHN, CLYDE, *Mirror for Man.* New York: McGraw-Hill Book Co., 1949, Chapter VIII.
A very readable, nontechnical analysis of the interplay between culture and personality.
GOLDSCHMIDT, WALTER, *Exploring the Ways of Mankind.* New York: Holt, Rinehart and Winston, 1960, Part IV.
A well-selected anthology of anthropological readings about education, prefaced by a succinct introduction.
PETTITT, GEORGE A., "Primitive Education in North America," *University of California Publications in American Archaeology and Ethnology,* XLIII (1936), 1–182.
This is the only systematic analysis of educational practices of North American Indians ever published.
RADIN, PAUL, *The World of Primitive Man.* New York: Grove Press, 1953, 1960, Chapter VII.
An inquiry into primitive rites of passage related to puberty.
SPINDLER, GEORGE D., *Education and Culture.* New York: Holt, Rinehart and Winston, 1963.
This is one of the very few books about the anthropology of education. It is a book of readings, and thus presents a heterogeneous treatment of the subject.
STEPHENS, WILLIAM N., *The Family in Cross-cultural Perspective.* New York: Holt, Rinehart and Winston, 1963, Chapter VIII.
While this book is not concerned principally with education, it contains one interesting chapter on child-rearing customs.

The following books are included for pleasure reading rather than for serious study. These books not only complement each other, but also amplify some of the materials discussed in the present chapter.

HAYES, CATHY, *The Ape in Our House.* New York: Harper & Brothers, 1951.
A husband and wife "adopt" a chimpanzee and raise it as though it were a human child.
JACKSON, SHIRLEY, *Life Among the Savages.* New York: Farrar, Straus and Young, 1948.
A humorous description of the ordeals of childhood and parenthood in American life.

3

An Historical Approach to Education

It being one chiefe &iect of y^t ould deluder, Satan, to keepe men from the knowledge of ye Scriptures, . . . — It is therefore ord^{r}ed, y^t ev^{r}y towneship in this iurisdiction . . . shall . . . forthwth appoint one wthin their towne to teach all such children as shall resort to him to write & reade, . . .

from a law passed by the Massachusetts General Court in 1647.

Thinking It Over Beforehand

Why does social change affect social institutions?

What subjects ought the school to teach?

Would it be better to have private schools or public schools predominate in America?

Should all of America's children be required to go to school?

How different are today's elementary and secondary schools and colleges from their counterparts in the American colonies?

An Age of Change

When colleges were founded on the eastern seaboard in Colonial America, all of the enrollees studied for a three-year period the same scant series of courses: classical and Biblical foreign languages, mathematics, philosophy, rhetoric, natural science, history, and religion.

Pick up the catalog of a contemporary land-grant college, and you will find enough courses listed in it to keep a student occupied for a century. And what courses! Many bear little resemblance to their Colonial counterparts. The following are from the current catalog of a western land-grant college:

Aerial Photointerpretation
Agricultural Cooperation
Alcohol Studies in School Curriculum
Cement and Concrete Laboratory
Credits and Collections
Currents and Water Masses
Data Processing
Drosophila Genetics
Educational Personal Relations
Field-Plot Technique
Flower Shop Operation
Fluid Flow
Fungus Deterioration of Wood Products
Gas Dynamics
Glass Blowing (a course in chemistry, not art)
Greenhouse Construction and Management
Human Factors in Engineering
Marriage
Mineral Dressing
Naval Weapons
Pattern Making
Photogrammetry
Photo-Journalism
Potato Growing
Poultry Judging
Program Report Analysis
Public School Camping
Pulp and Paper Chemistry
Recreational Use of Music
Rodent Control Methods
Salesmanship
Speech for Foreign Students
Sports Officiating
Sterile Products
The Chick Embryo
The College Student
Utilization of Dairy Products
Wholesale and Retail Meat
Wood Properties

Many changes have taken place on all levels of education during the three and a half centuries of American history. This cataclysm in education cannot be explained other than by a similar unheaval in the entire society. When the way of life of a people is severely altered, its social institutions must change, too, or else they will cease to be of any more than sentimental value to the society. The social institution of education is no exception.

Tremendous and spectacular changes have occurred in American life since 1607. Indeed, a series of cultural revolutions has shaken the entire culture. As colonists settled North America, the series was being born; as the American nation wrested its independence from Great Britain, the series

Courtesy of "Steelways" Magazine, published by American Iron and Steel Institute

A VAST, TECHNOLOGICALLY ORIENTED WAY OF LIFE HAS DEMANDED CHANGES IN AMERICAN EDUCATION.

was being cradled; and today, as the American nation matures, that revolutionary way of life is stretching toward adulthood.

There have been attempts to attach a name to this series. It has been called the Industrial Revolution, the Scientific Revolution, the Technological Revolution, but no single name quite captures the vibrant qualities of the new way of life. The revolutions have been revolutions in power. Certainly industrial power has been unchained as little mills have become gigantic factories. Certainly scientific power has been unleashed as scientific discoveries have been applied to virtually all phases of life. Certainly technological power has been released as muscle power has given way to steam, electrical, or atomic power and as sweat-shop labor has given way to automation. But much more has been involved in these power revolutions.

Commercial power has brought an unprecedented standard of living to the average person. Communication power has made events "no sooner done than said" around the world. Transportation power has shrunk a huge earth to the size of a golf ball by means of beat-the-clock vehicles. Military power has grown so great that no longer is there any place to hide from the sabre-rattling. Political power has dethroned monarchs and set up a vairety of people's governments. Social power has transformed the serf into an indulgent suburbanite and the bourgeois entrepreneur into a magnate. Secular power has encouraged a taste for the comforts of the present life. Recreational power has converted the sports of kings into sports of commoners. Feminine power has brought women from behind lace and fans into almost social equality with the masculine sex, and from behind spindles and butterchurns into the world of business affairs.

The revolutions have brought bigness into strategic areas of life. Commercial motives loom large in accounting for the discovery of the New World. *Big commerce,* involving tons and tons of materials and worldwide markets, has come to overshadow the embryonic commerce of Columbus' day. Industry, finance, and agriculture played significant roles in the founding of settlements in America. *Big industry,* as symbolized by "the generals"—General Tire, General Telephone, General Motors, General Mills, General Foods, General Electric, General Dynamics—*big finance,* which, Titanlike, holds the economic purse strings of the land, and *big agriculture* of a factory-in-the-fields variety have dwarfed the exploits of the London Company of Virginia. At a time when colonies were being planted in America, Galileo was toying with simple scientific ideas in Europe. *Big science,* mother of an age of synthetics and interplanetary rocketry, has augmented Galileo's rudimentary concepts. The Colonial Americans were rural in setting and small in numbers. *Big cities,* sprawling outward into suburbia and even into exurbia, blotting out the bucolic landscape, and *big population,* now increasing yearly in America by an amount almost equal to the total number of people living in the United States at the time of the first census in 1790, make the miniature settlements of the past seem Lilliputian. With all this bigness, it would have been impossible to hold the nation together, to meet civic needs, and to cope effectively with international stresses without *big government.*

The late anthropologist, Ralph Linton, suggested that George Washington would have had more in common, culturally speaking, with the Sumerian monarch Hammurabi, who lived some four thousand years ago, than he would with the current occupant of the White House in the city that bears his name. More basic cultural changes have occurred in the last century and a half than in the four millenia that preceded Washington.

Change and American Education

How are these cultural revolutions related to education in America? Remember the two universal principles of education. First, through education the newcomer acquires that ready-made knowledge and those tailored techniques considered indispensable for survival in his society. Second, through education the way of life cherished by the group is perpetuated.

When America was a fragile, rather impotent cluster of poorly integrated colonies, formal education could be uncomplicated and unstable and yet fulfill its basic functions. But industrial power, communication power, transportation power, military power, political power, social power, secular power, recreational power, and feminine power in our day all demand educational power sufficient to offer students an immeasurably more involved body of learning. When America was little, little formal education was needed. But big commerce, big industry, big finance, big agriculture, big science, big cities, big population, and big government demand in our day big education if our youths are to be prepared to wrestle competently with their intricate environment and to hold in esteem the cultural legacy bequeathed to them. The simple educational structure of the past has been overwhelmed. The cultural revolutions have forced the educational system to change accordingly.

From a Religious to a Secular Orientation

The motives of the American colonists to develop educational systems were many. No single motive, however, was stronger or more significant than the religious. The colonies were founded primarily by Protestants at a time when Protestantism was still close, historically and emotionally, to that rupture in Christianity which had brought Protestantism into being, the Reformation. This religious motivation was particularly obvious in the

Courtesy of the Publications and Information Bureau, Oregon College of Education

THE CULTURAL REVOLUTION HAS BROUGHT NEW EDUCATIONAL MEDIA INTO BEING.

Puritan colony of Massachusetts, where Calvinist leaders attempted to establish a theocracy. As early as 1642, the legislature (known as the General Court) of the colony passed the first compulsory education law. It required children to learn to "read and understand" the principles of religion and the basic laws of the colony.[1] Within the same century the Puritan legislatures of Connecticut and New Hampshire passed similar statutes.

---

[1] This was a compulsory *education* law, not a compulsory attendance law. The children involved did not have to go to school, but they did have to learn to read.

The middle colonies, settled and inhabited by diverse groups—diverse in both their Old World origins and their religious leanings—had a diverse array of church-dominated parochial schools. The Southern-plantation way of life, both geographically and socially, discouraged the development of schools. By the eighteenth century, however, the Society for the Propagation of the Gospel in Foreign Parts, sponsored by the Anglicans, was performing philanthropic work in the South by providing an oblation-financed education for children of poor white parents.

Higher education also rested in church hands in Colonial America. Before the American Revolution, eight colleges founded by church groups were in operation. In fact, six years before the General Court of Massachusetts passed its compulsory education law, the first church-instituted college, Harvard, was established by the Puritans at Cambridge.

Rather typically, church groups had a voice in the hiring of school-teachers, to insure that they were orthodox in their views. Collegiate-level instructors were also clergymen. Often they were more eager to save souls than educate minds. College students were watched, guarded, and prayed over by their clergymen-professors.

In elementary schools little children learned to read by poring over religiously oriented materials. One of the earliest readers, *The New England Primer,* was filled with religious selections, such as the alphabet in rhyme beginning with:

> A. In *Adam's* Fall
> We sinned all

and ending with:

> Z. *Zacheus* he
> Did climb the Tree
> His Lord to see.

Today the scene is decidedly different. Most pupils are public-school pupils. Most college students today attend either public or independent colleges. Parochial schools remain, but they are greatly outnumbered by public schools. Two Christian groups in particular continue to maintain parochial schools—the Roman Catholics and the Lutherans—yet many of their communicants' children attend public schools. Numerous colleges and universities in America were founded under religious auspices. The general trend, however, has been for these colleges to become independent of religious sponsorship. From an advertising standpoint it is not unusual for some of them to emphasize their religious heritage, but from both administrative and financial standpoints their current denominational ties ordinarily are either very weak or nonexistent. Thus, for example, the venerable

College of William and Mary, begun by the Anglicans, is now state-supported, and the relative newcomer, the University of Chicago, organized under Baptist leadership, is independent today.

The curriculums on all levels of education usually are scientifically oriented or naturalistic rather than being supernaturalistic. Children learn to read not by perusing incidents in the lives of Biblical personages, but by studying the adventures of such characters as Dick and Jane or Tom and Betty. Teachers and professors are selected not according to religious views but according to academic background. The clergyman-professor has disappeared, except for those found in a department of religion or a college that has remained under the guardianship of some church group.

The shift from religious to secular domination of education goes back certainly as far as the latter half of the eighteenth century. The American Revolution was far more than a political upheaval; it was also an ideological revolt. Advanced thinkers of the mid-eighteenth century in America, such as Franklin and Jefferson, unsatisfied with the traditional way of life, dreamed of a more perfect society. In such a society an improved method of education was needed. The leaders in the revolution of ideas envisaged the removal of education for ecclesiastical (or, in fact, any private) hands. Education should be protected from becoming either hidebound or stunted by backward-looking special-interest groups. To these thinkers, the traditional church organizations represented narrow-mindedness, stagnation, a failure to keep pace with the kaleidoscopic times. This attitude toward organized religion has been tempered by more recent generations. The attitude did help, however, to stimulate the growth of public elementary schools and public colleges. Later, the attitude helped to stimulate the growth of public secondary schools.

The American population has been a heterogeneous one. From many lands, from many cultures, from many societies the people came. The heterogeneous immigrants brought with them a sizable number of varying religious beliefs, and adding to these, America itself has been fertile ground for the spawning of new religious sects. America has more different sects and denominations than any other comparable nation in the modern world. There are well over two hundred and fifty different religious bodies in the United States. Add one more ingredient: no established (government-sponsored) church exists in America. Purposely, those men commonly referred to as the "founding fathers" sought to keep church and state separate. The multiplicity of faiths and the lack of an established church in America pose a real problem with regard to education. Shall each religious group in each community have its own school system? If so, this could mean that a little town of five thousand inhabitants might easily have twenty-five or thirty schools. Such an arrangement would make education extremely expensive and meager, particularly for the smaller church groups. Or, if a religious group were too small or impecunious to support a school, could it run the risk of having its children educated in the schools of rival sects? The delicate and pliable minds of the children might be exposed to what their parents would consider the "wrong" theological dogmas. The solution to this many-sided problem has been to divorce religion from education, to the extent that the two can be divorced, and create in each state a civil educational system that offers secular studies only, leaving the theological training of the youths to home or church. A few groups (as noted earlier) are unsatisfied with this arrangement and continue their own parochial education.

It was Jefferson who suggested that there be a wall of separation between church and state. Attempts to build such a wall in the domain of public education have been far from easy. Public schools in early America reflected the Protestant orientation of American life. It was customary not only for textbooks to have a religious bent, but also for religious exercises such as the singing of hymns, the recitation of prayers, and the reading of the Bible to be included in the school curriculums. In a very real sense, public schools used to be Protestant schools, although nondenominational in nature. The prime reason was that the highest law of the land, the Constitution of the United States, made no reference to religious practices in schools. To be sure, the First Amendment, passed early in Washington's administration, forbade the federal government from establishing a religion or from prohibiting "the free exercise thereof." But the amendment applied neither to the states nor to civil agencies within the states. It was not until the passage of the Fourteenth Amendment, a product of the Civil War, that the same prohibitions applied to the states and lesser civil units. The Fourteenth Amendment specifies, in part, that a state may not "abridge the privileges or immunities of citizens of the United States." It makes the First Amendment (as well as the rest of the Bill of Rights) applicable to the states and their agencies.

Before the Civil War, states were quite free to inject as much religion as they saw fit into their state-sponsored activities. Usually this meant that Calvinistic ethics, ideas, and dogmas were a part of both the reading matter and the curriculums of the public schools. This was one of the reasons why some religious groups chose to establish their own parochial schools. They wished to protect their communicants from the creedal emphases of the public schools. With the passage of the Fourteenth Amendment, states have been restrained, albeit slowly, from using public schools for the establishment or aggrandizement of religion. Federal restraint of the states has been effected only with much labor and gnashing of teeth. A few examples of the conflict may be cited from the twentieth century.

eyes	seiz-ed	fight-ing	gath-er-ed
perch	pick-ed	feath-ers	re-veng-ed
vex-ed	show-ed	naught-y	con-quer-ed
crow-ed	larg-est	chick-ens	quar-rel-some

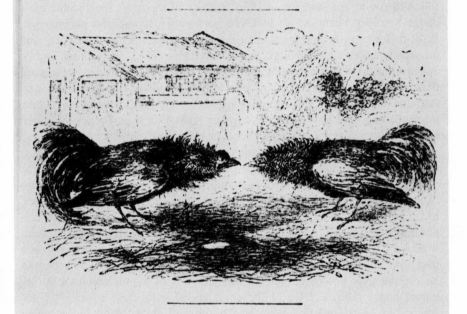

THE QUAR-REL-SOME COCKS.

1. HERE is a sto-ry a-bout two fool-ish cocks that were al-ways quar-rel-ing, which is ver-y naugh-ty. You do not quar-rel? No? I am glad of it. But if you see any lit-tle boys who quar-rel, you may tell them the sto-ry of the cocks.

A DIDACTIC STORY FROM *McGuffey's New Third Eclectic Reader: for Young Learners,* PUBLISHED IN 1857.

[79]

During the 1920's, several states passed laws designed to control instruction in public schools and colleges by making it illegal to teach materials that might injure the religious beliefs of the students. The most publicized law of this variety was one passed in Tennessee, where the legislature made it unlawful for any instructor in any educational establishment receiving money from the state "to teach any theory that denies the story of the Divine creation of man as taught in the Bible. . . ." A high-school teacher, John T. Scopes, purposely violated the law. The trial that followed during the summer of 1925 was one of the most spectacular trials of the "roaring twenties." It involved personages of national prominence. William Jennings Bryan, for years a key figure in the Democratic Party and an archdefender of orthodoxy, made what proved to be his final public appearance as the prosecuting attorney. Representing Scopes were such illustrious legal minds as Clarence Darrow, Dudley Field Malone, and Arthur Garfield Hays.[2] The case, if it proved anything, demonstrated how unenforceable and how futile this type of legislation was. Scopes, although found guilty, was freed on a technicality by a higher court.

In the 1940's and 1950's a different approach was used to insure that religion would be represented in the public schools. This time the technique was not to pass thought-control laws, but rather to broaden the curriculum of the public schools to include courses in sectarian religion. For instance, in Champaign, Illinois, religious instructors went into the schools at specified times and taught classes of those children whose parents wished them to receive religious training. In a much less notorious case than the Scopes trial, the federal Supreme Court ruled in the late 1940's that sectarian instruction may not be offered on the premises of a public school during school hours. The decision of the court ended with these words: "If nowhere else, in the relation between Church and State, 'good fences make good neighbors.' "[3]

Undaunted, religious groups sought still a different method of accomplishing the same purpose. Instead of religious instructors entering the public schools to offer their doctrinal courses, the children during the school day could, at the request of their parents, be dismissed temporarily to attend off-campus classes in religion. This practice was challenged unsuccessfully in the courts. A ruling in the early 1950's indicated that "released time" religious instruction away from the school grounds, during school hours, given only to those children whose parents indicated their willingness to have their children receive this sort of instruction, did not violate the intent of the First or Fourteenth Amendments. Many schools in numerous states follow this compromise practice today.

[2] See Arthur Garfield Hays, *Let Freedom Ring* (New York: Liveright, 1928), for an entertaining account of the trial.

[3] Illinois *ex rel.* McCollum v. Board of Education, 333 U. S. 203 (1948).

In the early 1960's another question involving the public schools and religion arose. Various groups, believing that religion should not be omitted entirely from the public-school program, sought to retain a vestige of the past by having a short devotional period for the pupils at the beginning of each school day. In New York State the Board of Regents recommended that local public schools begin the day with a brief, nondenominational prayer. In fact, to expedite matters, the State Board of Regents composed what it thought was an inoffensive twenty-two-word prayer and prescribed it for use in the schools. This was the prayer:

Almighty God, we acknowledge our dependence upon Thee, and we beg Thy blessings upon us, our parents, our teachers and our country.

The federal Supreme Court in 1962 ruled that this practice was unconstitutional. These were its words: ". . . government in this country should stay out of the business of writing or sanctioning official prayers. . . ." [4]

The Supreme Court a year later was faced with one more issue of a somewhat similar nature. For many years various states and school districts throughout the United States have required that a passage from the Bible be read or recited daily at school for devotional purposes. For example, the state of Pennsylvania and the city of Baltimore, Maryland, wishing to establish a religious atmosphere in their public schools, required that the school day begin with a devotional reading from the Bible. The city of Baltimore provided, further, that the recitation of the Lord's Prayer (which is a Biblical passage) might be substituted for the reading of another scriptural passage or might be used in addition to the reading. Suits were brought to court from Pennsylvania and from Baltimore to the effect that these practices violated the Constitution of the United States. With heterogeneity as a characteristic of religion in American life, several basic administrative questions are raised when either a devotional reading of the Bible or the recitation of the Lord's Prayer is instituted in a public-school program. Since different denominations sanction different translations of the Bible, which version of the Bible or of the prayer shall be used? Not all people of the Judeo-Christian tradition accept all portions of the Bible as sacred. And how shall the religious lives of children not of the Judeo-Christian tradition be nurtured? America's highest court ruled that the *devotional* use of the Bible or of the Lord's Prayer as part of the public-school curriculum violated the Constitution.

Not all religious issues are settled even yet. However, in a nation as heterogeneous as ours, the safest and soundest compromise seems to have been to leave instruction in creed and dogma to agencies other than our common public schools. This has been the direction in which public educa-

[4] Engel v. Vitale, 370 U. S. 421 (1962).

tion in America has been moving. Most Americans find this compromise reasonably satisfactory, and the compromise has encouraged our public schools and colleges to become highly temporal in their curricular offerings and to avoid sectarian materials. No wonder that Dick and Jane have replaced Adam and Zacchaeus in the primers. No wonder that the orientation of American education is scientific and naturalistic rather than supernaturalistic.

From Local Sponsorship of Education to Enlarged Public Responsibility

The maintenance of educational establishments was quite haphazard in Colonial America; nevertheless, the beginnings of public responsibility for education were there from the start. The colony of Massachusetts offers one example (by no means typical, because Massachusetts was in the forefront regarding educational matters). Mention was made earlier that Massachusetts was the first colony to pass an education law requiring youths to learn to read religious and civic materials. In order to implement this law, the General Court of Massachusetts passed a second law five years later, in 1647. The latter law is known as the Old Deluder, Satan, Law, deriving its name from the opening lines of the statute: "It being one chief object of that old deluder, Satan, to keep men from the knowledge of the Scriptures. . . ." The law continued by stating that every community having fifty families should appoint an elementary-school teacher for those children who might prefer learning to read from his tutelage rather than from some other source. If there were one hundred families in the community, a teacher should be provided for the secondary-school pupils, too. The salaries for these teachers were to come from tuition fees and/or the coffers of the local community. This was the first law in America providing for the hiring of school personnel. Consequently, it was the first law to organize schools, if one adheres to that maxim (applied especially to higher education) that a college consists of a log with a professor sitting at one end and a student at the other. It was also the first law in America which placed the responsibility for school support in the hands of the citizenry.

The attempt in the colony of Massachusetts to involve the public in the creation and maintenance of schools was not characteristic of Colonial America. In most of the colonies, education was private. Likewise, as noted above, education was church-sponsored, not government-sponsored. Since there was no permanent government *in America* that was higher than the colony's, no "federated" government could be involved in education. There was no move in the colonies to maintain public colleges. All of the Colonial colleges were private.

Present-day America has an elaborate network of schools and colleges that are supported by many public agencies—local, county, state, and federal. (Coincidentally, as I write these lines, the President of the United States is speaking on the radio and is pointing out the need for the federal government to take added steps to underwrite education in America.) The two following chapters will describe the roles of the various levels of government in education. Suffice it to say at this point that the public, through many of its governmental agencies, keeps our public schools and colleges in operation. The public even assists, to a considerable extent, in the maintenance of private schools and colleges. Education is no longer the business of only those people in the community whose children are directly involved; it is everybody's business in the United States. This is one reason why everybody is so willing to express himself regarding how our schools and colleges ought to be operated and what subjects ought to be taught.

Local and Colonial concerns for the establishment and maintenance of schools can be traced to seventeenth-century Massachusetts, as has been noted. Interest on the part of an interstate body in the support of education, while not so old, is still older than our federal government. Before the Constitution was written, the Continental Congress (that interstate body that tried unsuccessfully to hold together those thirteen newly independent and separate nations) had prepared a plan for the support of schools on the frontier. In 1785 the Continental Congress passed a law pertaining in part to public education in America's newly acquired Colonial possession, the trans-Appalachian west. The land ordinance of that year called for setting aside one thirty-sixth of the land in the Old Northwest for school purposes. The intent was that income from these acreages would be used for the support of public schools. Developing states were slow to make educational use of this source of funds, and much of the potential wealth assigned to education was squandered and virtually stolen. Yet the leaven was there, and eventually a public elementary school system did appear in the West. This law was the first instance of aid being given to education by a level of government higher than that of the state in the new American nation. Thus, "federal" aid to education is a venerable practice which, as the following chapters will document, has continued to the present.

Just as Massachusetts illustrated an early Colonial attempt to involve the citizenry in the support of education, so Pennsylvania illustrates an early state attempt (after the American Revolution) to institute public elementary schools that would be free to *all* enrollees. Numerous historians feel that the crisis, the point of decision, in the establishment of free, tax-supported, public elementary schools in America occurred in Pennsylvania.

The states that developed public elementary schools in our early national period tended to frown upon permitting children to receive this education free of charge. While some children were allowed to attend school without cost, usually there was an obstacle. Their parents were obliged to take the pauper's pledge before the children were admitted free. Any child whose parents were solvent economically, and any child whose parents were too proud to humiliate themselves by declaring themselves paupers, had to pay to go to school. Most people found it too distasteful to stigmatize themselves in order to have their children admitted to school free of charge. Public elementary schools developed the reputation of being schools for poor children, because parents who had to pay to have their children admitted often preferred to send them to private schools. This attitude toward public schools has not disappeared entirely, and remains in some areas to this day.

Pennsylvania had established a pauper school arrangement by 1802. A law enacted in that year called for the development of a system whereby outcast children might be instructed free of charge. Few people availed themselves of the provisions of this and subsequent pauper school laws— and understandably so. Poor people who wanted to retain their self-respect preferred to keep their children out of school rather than suffer the humiliation of advertising their threadbare circumstances. Completely impoverished people, for the most part, did not regard education highly enough to avail themselves of a free education for their children. Probably not over half the children of Pennsylvania of elementary-school age actually were in school a third of a century after the 1802 law was passed.

A group of people who were concerned about the educational welfare of the children of the state was instrumental in having a free-school law passed in 1834. This new law made it possible for communities to establish, through local option, public schools that would be free of charge for any student. Even though each district could decide whether or not it wanted to participate, the 1834 law aroused bitter feelings. The upper house of the Pennsylvania legislature, quick to sense the animosity of the public toward this optional free-school law, passed a bill that would have returned the state to the older practice of having free schools for paupers only. The majority of the members in the lower house favored the action taken by the upper house. This was the turning point. Would Pennsylvania break with tradition and institute free public schools for all children, or would it return to the pauper school system?

At this crucial point a very enigmatic political figure of the nineteenth century arose in the lower house of the legislature of Pennsylvania to cham-

Pennsylvania Historical and Museum Commission

THADDEUS STEVENS, PIONEER SPOKES-
MAN FOR FREE, TAX-SUPPORTED ELE-
MENTARY SCHOOLS.

pion the cause of free schools for all children. He was Thaddeus Stevens, the same Thaddeus Stevens who, a third of a century later, would cast himself in a villainous role in national politics. The speech that he gave in behalf of free, tax-supported elementary schools so electrified its hearers that not only the lower house but also the upper house passed a new school law in 1835 that guaranteed the eventual development of such schools open to all children of Pennsylvania. Stevens' speech has become one of the outstanding orations in behalf of public education in America. Stevens himself considered it his greatest speech.

Pennsylvania's battle for free public schools made it easier for other states to substitute free public elementary schools for pauper schools. Every state today has free public elementary schools available on equal terms to all children. These schools are supported through taxation of the citizens.

Half a century passed before the public was ready to tax itself for the

[85]

support of secondary schools for all youths. This time it was Michigan that took the lead. In 1874 the Supreme Court of Michigan ruled that the state had the right to tax any and all citizens within its borders for the support of public secondary schools. When public high schools developed, there was some doubt as to whether the tax money collected for the support of free elementary schools might also be used to extend the program beyond the eighth grade, and whether this post-elementary education could be offered to students on the same basis as elementary schooling. These questions led some citizens of Kalamazoo, Michigan, who were friendly to tax-supported public high schools, to obtain definite answers. The famous Kalamazoo Case resulted. It is considered by some educationists to be as significant in the development of public secondary education in America as the Pennsylvania law of 1835 is in the development of public elementary education.

In 1872, plans were laid for creating a public high school in Kalamazoo. One of the leading citizens of the community, former Senator Charles E. Stuart, agreed to find out through a court decision whether or not the public-school curriculum supported by tax money could be extended beyond the eighth grade. In other words, he wanted to know if a public school teaching high-school-level subjects might receive tax support. The case known technically as *Stuart et al.* v. *School District No. 1 of the Village of Kalamazoo,* 30 Mich. 69 (1874), ensued. Michigan's State Supreme Court ruled that

. . . neither in our state policy, in our constitution, or in our laws, do we find the primary school districts restricted in the branches of knowledge which their officers may cause to be taught, or the grade of instruction that may be given, if their voters consent in regular form to bear the expense and raise the taxes for the purpose.

Slowly other states came to agree with Michigan. By the end of the nineteenth century the place of the high school as a tax-supported public school was fairly secure. Today all states have tax-supported public secondary schools.

Collegiate education, originally in church hands, has gained increasing public support financially. In 1795, shortly after the Revolution, the first state university was established in North Carolina. All states have public universities today. Early in America's national history there was talk about founding a national university. Indeed, George Washington offered to help finance one. This dream, however, was never given substance, although the federal government is greatly involved in higher education at the present time.

No act of Congress has had more significance in its effect on higher education in America than the Morrill Act, or Land Grant College Act, of 1862. The act will be described in more detail later. Its intent was to encourage the founding of state colleges by offering federally owned land to any state that would develop a public college that conformed to the specifications of the act.

The foregoing sketch suggests the growing extent to which the citizenry underwrites education on all levels, and the growing extent to which governmental agencies are charged with the responsibility of maintaining schools and colleges. Again the reader is reminded that Chapters 4 and 5 deal with this subject at greater length.

From Selective Curriculums to Inclusive Curriculums

During the Colonial period and for a while thereafter, each type of curriculum was offered in a separate educational establishment. The situation was similar to that in Hellenic Greece. For example, on the elementary level, there was a school, known as the dame school, in which the rudiments of reading were taught. The name is derived from the fact that the teacher was a married woman (called formerly a dame) who would have children come to her house to learn to read. (It is rather amazing to note, in passing, that even though women were considered too uneducable to be sent to secondary school or college, the incongruity of using women as teachers was not apparent to the colonists.)

Elementary schools, as distinct from dame schools, frequently offered a wider curriculum—not just the skill subjects of reading and writing. Arithmetic and some geography and history might be taught in addition. In some cases a child would not be admitted to the elementary school until he knew how to read, although this selective admissions policy was not practiced in all of the Colonial communities. Typically, the elementary-school teacher was a man, as were the teachers at the higher levels of education. Women taught only in dame schools.

The original secondary school in Colonial America was the Latin grammar school. This establishment offered college-preparatory schooling. A boy who did not intend to go to college would have had no interest, nor reason for enrolling, in a Latin grammar school. In order to be accepted by a college, a lad had to have a command of Latin. Usually he was expected to have an elementary knowledge of Greek, also. Proficiency in Latin was a *sine qua non* for college students, because many college books were written in Latin, and sometimes college professors spoke in Latin, expecting their students to reply in Latin. Under these circumstances, a boy not highly conversant in the language would have been overwhelmed at college. The Latin grammar school curriculum was aimed at making boys fluent in the use of Latin. Some Greek and occasionally the elements of Hebrew were offered as well. The program of the best-administered Latin grammar schools lasted seven years.

Colonial colleges were not vocational institutes, despite a prevalent but spurious belief that the pre-Revolutionary ivy-league colleges were nothing more than vocational schools for the clergy. While religion was very apparent at these colleges, to assume that the curriculum was for prospective preachers only or that the graduates automatically entered the ministry is an oversimplification of the facts. Bear in mind that with the exception of George Washington, all of the Presidents of the United States who were of college age before the Revolutionary War had attended college. Not one of these men was a clergyman. The Colonial colleges were liberal-arts colleges. The curriculum, borrowed from Europe, was designed to fashion frontier lads into Christian scholars and gentlemen of a north-western European variety (the courses in the curriculum were identified in the opening paragraph of this chapter). Any college graduate who wanted to follow a learned profession such as law or medicine would, typically, become apprenticed to a practitioner and "read" law or "read" medicine under the practitioner's tutelage. An individual did not have to go to college, however, before reading law or medicine.

Today there is but one general type of elementary school. The dame school has disappeared, and the courses offered on the elementary level are varied and broad. The curriculum covers introductions to the humanistic studies, the nature studies, the social studies, the fine arts, and physical education. Sometimes there are applied-arts courses, too, such as manual training.

Today's secondary schools no longer are limited to the study of ancient languages. Our high schools are vocational schools, college-preparatory schools, cultivational schools, and serviceable-arts schools all assembled into a single package. Current terminology uses the adjective "comprehensive" to describe the modern high school. A well-directed comprehensive high school is very likely to have terminal vocational curriculums in agriculture and commerce as well as in various trades and industries. Vocational homemaking courses are taught also. The high school has a curriculum that can prepare a student for entrance into a liberal-arts college. It has courses designed to enhance the general knowledge of those students who do not intend to go to college but who at the same time are in need of an intelligent understanding of the complex American culture in which they will participate as adults. Finally, the high school has courses on subjects that are useful or serviceable in our technologically oriented society, such as the courses in auto mechanics and driver training.

Higher education has become a five-ring circus. One can major in viticulture or veterinary medicine, horticulture or hotel management, forestry or finance, physical education or pharmacy, dental hygiene or drama. One can even major in mathematics or philosophy or Latin. Universities have become universalities of knowledge.[5]

The movement toward a cafeteria-like secondary-school curriculum dates back to the final years of the Colonial period. Men such as Benjamin Franklin felt the need for a new type of secondary school. The old Latin grammar school did not adequately prepare youth for the new society that was coming into being. A more practical sort of intermediate education was called for—one that would emphasize the findings of the newly founded natural sciences, social philosophies, and humanities, one that would offer training for vocations calling for advanced study but not collegiate training, one that would recognize the educational needs of young women as well as young men. Such a school was the academy (at least in theory). By the middle of the eighteenth century, the academy movement had begun. Academies were to overshadow and eclipse the Latin grammar schools by the beginning of the next century.

Early leaders in the academy movement had envisioned making the academies public schools, thus keeping them out of ecclesiastical or other private hands. Their dreams were not to be realized yet. Academies, while often being secularly rather than ecclesiastically controlled, were private in management. As academies developed, they took over the curriculum of the Latin grammar schools and added to this curriculum both terminal vocational training (such as commercial studies) and broader cultivational subjects.

In time, academies, as private schools catering to families that could afford them, began to emphasize the college-preparatory subjects more and more and to neglect terminal subjects more and more. As this happened, there was a growing sentiment that still another sort of secondary school was needed, a school that would be truly a public school with a truly practical curriculum for youths who did not intend to go to college. This sentiment fostered what we now call high schools. Academies were private; high schools would be public. Academies catered to people of wealth; high schools would be open to all people on equal terms, although the support of these schools by taxation was fought over. The curriculum of the academies began to narrow because of the narrowed demands of the clientele. The high schools were to attempt, as the academies had tried earlier, to offer a set of courses that anticipated and met the needs of the students. The academies were located usually in centers of population and often

---

[5] To be accurate, I should point out that historically the term "university" did not mean a school that offered world-encompassing courses. It meant, rather, a corporation or guild, which medieval universities such as Bologna were.

boarded students. The high schools were to be for commuters—thus more accessible to students. The academies, like the Latin grammar schools before them, were college-preparatory schools to a considerable degree. The high schools, as first visualized, were to be terminal schools—almost people's colleges.

The idea of the high school was slow to develop, but as high schools gained strength, academies began to wither. During most of the nineteenth century the average adult saw little need for a secondary-school education. Elementary education was far from universal, and this kept down the potential number of youths who might otherwise have attended high school.

As compulsory attendance laws were enacted, the number of high schools and high-school students increased. Today every American child has access to a nearby high school. The character of the high school has been modified: today high schools are both terminal and preparatory schools.

Two great occurrences on the collegiate level aided the growth of the multiple-curricular university. One was the Morrill Act, or the Land Grant College Act; the other was the importation from Europe of the Germanic concept of graduate education.

As part of a tremendous program of parceling out federal lands by the newly installed Republican Party during the Lincoln administration, a land-grant college act was passed in 1862. The act reads in part:

. . . each State which may take and claim the benefit of this act, to the endowment, support, and maintenance of at least one college where the leading object shall be, without excluding other scientific and classical studies, and including military tactics, to teach such branches of learning as are related to agricultural and the mechanical arts, in such manner as the legislatures of the States may respectively prescribe, in order to promote the liberal and practical education of the industrial classes in the several pursuits and professions in life.

This act succeeded in opening wide the doors of the American colleges to the new subjects born of the cultural revolution. The act stipulated that states could qualify for portions of the coveted federally owned land provided they set up a new type of college. The new college was to be, on the collegiate level, what the academies originally intended to be and what the high schools purported to be on the secondary level. The traditional college curriculum was to be broadened to include new areas of training in vocations that demanded more than a secondary-school level of preparation. Prior to this time, the esoteric but nonacademic vocational fields were trained for in separate, noncollegiate, and frequently profit-motivated schools somewhat similar to our contemporary beauty, barber, and business colleges.

This most significant of all federal acts affecting higher education has

Courtesy of the Vermont Historical
Society

PORTRAIT BY THOMAS WATERMAN
WOOD OF CONGRESSMAN JUSTIN SMITH
MORRILL, FATHER OF THE AMERICAN
LAND GRANT COLLEGE.

left an indelible mark. It has made possible the growth of one of the ger-
minal ideas of the educational revolutionists of the American revolutionary
period. Those dreamers of almost a century before had hoped for a college
that would have up-to-date course offerings to augment the traditional,
past-oriented collegiate curriculum. The Land Grant College Act brought
about the contemporary type of higher educational establishment, in which
a student may study anything from how to reupholster davenports to
Caesar's Gallic exploits. Narrow course offerings designed merely to
produce Christian scholars and gentlemen were doomed to obsolescence.
The act forced colleges other than land-grant colleges to broaden their
curriculums also, in order to remain in business and compete for students.
It had the effect of paving the way for colleges (as with elementary schools
and high schools) to become establishments for common men, leading in

our day not only to Gargantuan curricular offerings but also to elephantine enrollments.

The founding of Johns Hopkins University in 1876 marked the beginning in the United States of a widespread interest in both higher learning and post-baccalaureate education. Higher learning, as distinct from higher education, emphasizes the discovery and collection of materials from the frontiers of human knowledge. Patterned after Germanic university practices, research projects became an integral part of the activities at Johns Hopkins University. At the present time many American universities have on their staffs people whose sole work is research. The reader may recall that the controlled release of nuclear energy, for example, was pioneered by researchers at the University of Chicago.

Before the Civil War, Americans who wanted to earn graduate degrees usually went to Europe—especially to German universities—to study for the master's or doctor's degree. Postgraduate offerings in America were practically nil. Johns Hopkins University was the first American university to emphasize course work toward advanced degrees taught by leading researchers. From this beginning grew the trend for American universities to develop graduate schools and link their graduate facilities with higher learning. This trend has contributed also to Gargantuan curricular offerings and elephantine enrollments at higher-education establishments.

From Sporadic to Regularized Attendance

In Colonial America no child was obligated to go to school. Even the colony of Massachusetts, which had passed a compulsory education law, did not require attendance at school. A child could stay home and learn how to read. As a matter of fact, most of the children did stay home—and most of them did not learn how to read. It is estimated that no more than 10 per cent of all of the youths in the thirteen colonies attended school. One of the early administrators of the colony of Virginia, Governor Berkeley, went so far as to offer thanks to God that there were no free schools available for the children of Virginia.[6]

Of the children who did go to school in the colonies, most were boys. Girls were considered inferior to boys and therefore less educable. Girls were not permitted to go to secondary school, and it was unthinkable to send one to college. She would not have been admitted to college even if she had tried to go.

The schools themselves were not arranged by grade levels as we organ-

---

[6] Berkeley's thanksgiving was statistically incorrect, however. There were two such schools in 1671, the year he made the remark.

ize them today. All children, beginners and advanced alike, studied in the same classroom. The situation somewhat resembles the one-room country schoolhouse, but the comparison is not exact. Even one-room schools today recognize grade levels, which were still undreamed of in the colonies.

Boys planning to go to college customarily did *not* attend elementary school. Instead, they went to a Latin grammar school, or else they studied for the college-entrance examinations under a private tutor. One did not have to have a single day of schooling behind him to be admitted to a college; the only requirement was to pass the entrance exams.

The school year was short in the early days; months might pass between sessions. By no means was it unusual for an elementary school to be in session for a dozen weeks once every two or three years—and that was all.

How different the scene today. The school year is from nine to ten months in length on a yearly basis, and is often augmented with summer sessions. Every state requires, under penalty of law, that its children (except in extreme circumstances) attend school for a specified number of years or until a certain teen age is reached by the student. Grade levels are recognized. Secondary school cannot be attended until elementary school has been completed, and one does not go to college unless one has been exposed to the curriculum of the secondary school. Almost all of America's elementary-school-age children—both boys and girls—attend elementary school. Most of America's secondary-school-age children—both boys and girls—attend secondary school, at least for a while. Approximately a third of the nation's college-age youths—male and female—are enrolled in higher-educational establishments.

The nineteenth century was the century of social emancipation for women, a development in which education played a vital role. When the century began, girls were guarded and carefully protected at home. For a woman to have a career was not socially accepted. The only ones who worked for a living were impoverished or degraded women. Unless a woman married, she was doomed to a life of depending on male relatives for her support if she wished to retain her self-respect socially. In both cases she could look forward to a life as a household drudge. Although she might work at a slave's pace in the home, she could not become a wage earner outside the home without loss of status and reputation. But by 1900 the picture had changed noticeably. In 1900 approximately 18 per cent of all people in the labor force were women. And today the percentage is almost twice that. Women have entered practically every vocational field. By 1900 there were women in such male-dominated occupations as medicine, law, and theology, as well as in the manufacturing and distributive trades. The taboos against women's working outside the home were becoming obsolete. Today there is only token resistance to the idea of women being employed.

The desire of women to be more than servants of men in the home was greatly strengthened by education. Coeducation had existed to a very limited extent on the lowest educational level in some colonies, and in the early national period girls could enter secondary schools. Sometimes secondary schools for boys had *separate* classrooms for girls. Sometimes there were "finishing schools" or "seminaries" that catered exclusively to young ladies. By the latter half of the nineteenth century, the idea of coeducation on the secondary level was fairly well established.

It was not until the second quarter of the nineteenth century that women began to go to college. A few colleges were for women only, such as Mount Holyoke, which opened in 1837. The Midwest took the lead in coeducation at the collegiate level. Oberlin College in Ohio was the first private college to experiment with coeducation (1833). The University of Iowa, the first state university to do so, began to admit women in 1855. By the turn of the twentieth century, approximately one-fourth of the college students were women. By 1960, approximately one-third of the college graduates were women, and most higher-educational establishments are coeducational. Women fare even better on the secondary level than they do on the collegiate level. A higher proportion of girls than boys who start high school eventually graduate. The idea of the mental inferiority of women has become an anachronism.

Compulsory attendance at school is a relatively new phenomenon. It was 1852 before the state of Massachusetts passed America's first compulsory attendance law. In this respect Massachusetts was following a practice initiated in Prussia almost forty years earlier. (Prussia tended to be the leading European nation in the field of education during the nineteenth century, and Massachusetts has tended to be a leading state in America in the field of education from the Colonial period to the present.) As late as 1900, only twenty-nine states had passed compulsory education laws. The average state law, as of 1900, required that children between the ages of eight and fourteen attend school. Current compulsory education laws apply only to the elementary and secondary levels of education. Attendance at college still is not compulsory, and it probably will not become compulsory in the foreseeable future. As late as 1900 only 4 per cent of all college-age youths were in college.

Related to the compulsory-attendance trend was the trend toward increasing the length of the school year. As schools themselves became more numerous and their tax support was guaranteed, as better training facilities for teachers were developed and better-trained teachers were available, the lengthening of the school year followed as corollary follows axiom. Even

Ewing Galloway

HORACE MANN, NINETEENTH CENTURY
EDUCATIONAL TRAILBLAZER.

so, the compulsory attendance laws of the various states generally did not require a student to stay in school throughout the entire school year. In fact, in 1900 it was an exceptional state that required the student to attend school as many as twenty weeks per year. Half of the states that had attendance laws in 1900 required the student to attend school only twelve weeks per year, and not more than eight of the twelve weeks had to be consecutive. Thus, both compulsory education and the rule that pupils must attend school during most of the year are rather recent phenomena.

Graded schools developed slowly, too. During the early part of the nineteenth century, the idea of separating students by grades began to develop in some of the larger American elementary schools. This development was a child of necessity. Common schools in urban areas accepted pupils of all ages from mere infancy to young adulthood. They offered instruction at a variety of levels in the same classroom. Sometimes over a hundred city children would attend the same one-room elementary school. The practice of assembling all of these children in a single room under the

[95]

tutelage of a single teacher became increasingly impracticable. Several schools began to experiment with various techniques of dealing with the situation. One entirely negative technique was to limit enrollment and not admit the youngest children if the total enrollment exceeded a predetermined number. Another method was to subdivide students into somewhat homogeneous groups, based on accomplishment, and to treat these groups as units. Still another method was to divide the instructional materials roughly into segments. The latter two practices paved the way for the development of the graded school.

That educational-administrative giant of the nineteenth century, Horace Mann, also helped to bring about the graded school. He sought to import the finest European educational practices into the United States, including the graded school. As one might expect, the idea came from Prussia, and Massachusetts was in the American vanguard. Horace Mann was secretary of the Massachusetts board of education, the first state board of education to exist in the United States. The first fully graded elementary school in America was Boston's Quincy Grammar School, which opened in 1848.

From this beginning, the practice of dividing schools into grades eventually spread throughout the nation. It should be borne in mind, however, that the division of schools into grades was an urban practice until recently, and most of the American population has been rural. Until the twentieth century, even though urban schools began to be graded, most of the schools in America remained ungraded. Thus, the grading of schools might also be considered a recent development in American education.

From Education for the Select to Education for All

The educational scene in the American colonies bore a resemblance to that of Hellenic Athens. For the most part, schooling was for the male children of the more substantial citizens. A secondary and higher education were reserved in large measure for sons of genteel families. Some weak attempts were made to insure that impoverished children would be exposed to a rudimentary education as a means of keeping them from becoming public charges as adults. Children of slaves typically were given no formal education. Most children fitted into none of the above categories, and they, as a group, received little, if any, formal education. Most education was class education for boys from the upper social strata. The Colonial colleges even followed the practice of listing their students not in alphabetical order, but according to family wealth and prestige, from high to low.

Today anyone can receive an education, whether from the classes or the masses, whether wealthy or poor, whether proud or humble, whether mighty or meek. Cradle-to-grave education is offered. There are child-care agencies, nursery schools, kindergartens, elementary schools, junior high schools, senior high schools, junior colleges, colleges, universities, and graduate schools, not to mention trade schools, correspondence schools, night schools, and extension programs. The average American adult has attended high school. The 1960 federal census reports that less than 3 per cent of the American adults of age twenty-five or over have never gone to school.

A shift from education for the select to education for all can actually be traced to the beginnings of the Colonial period. The American colonies were settled at a time when the mother country, England, was in the throes of working out governmental methods for dealing with impoverished citizens. One of the English sentiments imported to the New World was that education could be used as an effective means of fighting poverty. It would be unlikely, it was thought, for the person educated in some vocational art as well as in the general arts to become a public charge as an adult. Feeble Colonial attempts were made to convert sentiment into practice; New England's early compulsory education laws are an example. In various colonies, dependent children were bound out to masters as indentured servants in the hope that these youngsters would learn, through the informal means of apprenticeship, how to support themselves.

In the early national period of America's history, utopians, with one eye focused on dreams and the other on limited finances, attempted to put into effect the principle of a minimum formal education for all children. Three examples illustrate their efforts.

The first example is the Sunday-school movement, an idea brought to America from the British Isles. Poor children (and any others whose education was being neglected) were to convene one day a week—Sunday— when the children did not have to work. On that day they would be taught the rudiments of reading and writing. But churchmen effectively destroyed the movement by conducting their own Sunday schools. The curriculum was remodeled into the one with which the present-day American child who has gone to Sunday school is familiar. The old three R's gave way to a fourth R—religious indoctrination.

The second example is the monitorial or Lancasterian school, another British idea. This type of school was predicated upon two assumptions: first, that an education meant the memorization of certain facts, and second, that if an education is inexpensive enough, it will be well received by those who pay the cost. The basic arrangement of the monitorial system was simple. An instructor who was familiar with the method would teach a segment of a lesson to his brightest pupils. These pupils, in turn, would parrot to small groups of their fellow pupils the same materials they had just been taught. In this manner a single teacher might handle a hundred or more pupils in one classroom. The per-pupil cost was low, and the plan was popular for a few years in the early nineteenth century, before its obvious educational defects forced its abandonment. Teachers, whether student-teachers or masters, must be more than animated dictaphones. There is a vast difference between an education and the repetition by rote of memorized information.

The third example is the infant school. It, too, originated in the British Isles. The British socialist, Robert Owen, was aroused by the public neglect of little children whose parents labored in factories. He sought to help the very young children of laborers by educating them *en masse* in what was termed an infant school. American humanitarians adopted and adapted the practice. In several American cities in the 1820's, poor children below approximately age eight received philanthropically sponsored mass instruction in rudimentary subjects. In time, infant schools merged with elementary schools to eventually become the primary level of public education.[7]

Toward the mid-nineteenth century, people of both high and modest status had a vision of universalizing education so that all children could receive some formal education. The high-status people are well represented by Henry Barnard, commissioner of education first in Connecticut, then in Rhode Island. It was his view that education could be used as an effective sedative or tranquilizer to keep the commoners from becoming a restless, destructive force in America, as they were becoming in Europe. The least expensive way to keep the masses content, to keep them working at their little tasks, to keep them supporting the government, was to educate them. If these people were taught to appreciate how well they were thriving, if they were taught to admire private enterprise and its myriad benefits, they would respect and defend at all costs the nation that granted them such marvels of civilization.

Modest-status people, represented by the members of fledgling labor unions, also wanted education for all—but for different reasons. They saw education as a stairway, a means of social mobility, a means whereby children could rise to a higher position than the one their parents had reached. And they began to see schooling as a means of occupying the children during the day so that they would not be available to work in factories— thus taking them out of the labor market until they were older and releasing them from having to compete with adults for employment.

Jacksonian democracy, with its emphasis on manhood suffrage, was still another force pressing for widespread education. A democratic way of life can scarcely survive if uninformed illiterates do the voting. The people

[7] The kindergarten, another European import, must not be confused with the infant school. The latter was more like the Colonial dame school.

of a democracy must have those tools and attitudes, gained through education, that will enable them to decide political issues wisely.

Compulsory attendance laws and the popularity of obtaining an education have helped to complete the process of universalizing education in the United States.

From Poorly Equipped to Excellently Outfitted Schools

"Stark" and "meager" are the words that describe Colonial schools and their educative materials. Typical features of school buildings were these: one or two rooms; dingy lighting; small windows, or no windows at all; poor heating—too cold in bad weather, too hot in good weather; poor ventilation; backless benches; tables, perhaps; no blackboards; sometimes a dirt floor. Educative materials were scant. The Bible and occasionally other religious writings were used. Flat, paddle-like boards known as hornbooks, on which a few reading materials had been printed and which were covered with a layer of horn to preserve the writing, served as readers. Textbooks began to make their appearance before 1776; one of the first was *The New England Primer,* cited earlier in this chapter.

In contrast, one can find school buildings today that are beautifully designed and just as beautifully landscaped. Rooms are spacious. They resemble light, airy, well-decorated living rooms. Furniture, equipment, and air conditioning are designed for maximum comfort. Often the schools are in better condition than the homes from which the pupils come. This generalization frequently holds true on all levels of education. Educative materials abound. Various publishers vie with one another for the school market by printing excellent, delightfully illustrated textbooks geared to the interests and the abilities of all sorts of students. Audio-visual materials ranging from the ubiquitous chalkboards and bulletin boards to films, recordings, radio and television performances, and handsomely equipped laboratories are available.

Many of these enrichments are traceable to the cultural changes, discussed earlier, that have revolutionized the American way of life. An apt illustration of this is the use of television for teaching purposes. Both commercial and noncommercial television stations broadcast courses of instruction for elementary-school children, high-school pupils, college students, and adults. Many schools throughout the land make use of televised materials. Several colleges and universities offer academic credit for courses taken via television. Some educational establishments have their own closed-circuit instructional television programs.

Siegmund collection, Oregon State Library

A FRONTIER SCHOOL IN THE LATE NINETEENTH CENTURY.

Courtesy of Glenn Arbogast & Associates, Architects, Los Angeles.
Photo by Julius Shulman

SCHOOL BUILDINGS TODAY OFTEN RESEMBLE ATTRACTIVE HOMES.

Modern technology has also entered the field of school construction. Most of these improvements belong to the twentieth century. An interest in improving the features of the classroom and in enriching teaching aids, however, was present during the nineteenth century in America and even earlier in Europe. Such Europeans as Pestalozzi were aware of the importance of audio-visual aids in the teaching process. And such Americans as Horace Mann sought to import the finest European educative techniques to the United States.

As teaching became more of a vocation in our country during the nineteenth century, educationists sought to improve both the appearance of the schools and the devices used in teaching. Accompanying the enlargement of the school curriculum, and roughly along with the germination of the idea that the elementary school should be graded, was a trend toward increased use of textbooks. Hundreds upon hundreds of authors have written books to be used as school texts. Of the quantities of American textbooks, few have been so important as the "blue-backed" speller of the noted lexicographer, Noah Webster, and the graded readers of William Holmes McGuffey. Probably no schoolbook was more common in the nineteenth century than Webster's *The American Spelling Book*. And without doubt the most influential readers ever to be compiled were McGuffey's. Beginning in the 1830's, generations of American school children were taught middle-class Protestant American virtues from the pages of these books. McGuffey's readers also established certain basic principles for constructing graded readers—principles still used in elementary-school textbooks today.

From Scarcely Trained Teachers Toward Professional Educators

Unfortunately, there has been too much truth to the remark, "If you can, do; if you can't, teach." One need not go back beyond the early years of the twentieth century to find schoolteachers who had only rudimentary educations themselves and no formal teacher training whatever.

It was the ancient Roman author, Lucian, who wrote, ". . . whom the Gods hate they make schoolmasters." During the Colonial period, the Ichabod Crane type of schoolmaster was not entirely a caricature. The assumption on all levels of education was that if a person had been exposed to the materials taught on a given level, he was qualified to teach on that level. To teach on the elementary level, one needed only to have attended elementary school. Secondary-school teachers needed only to have attended a Latin grammar school or, later, an academy. To teach on the collegiate level, one needed only to have gone to college. An additional qualification occasionally used at the elementary and secondary levels was the candidate's religious and moral orthodoxy. (On the collegiate level it was taken for granted that professors would also be clergymen.)

Today the one level of education that continues the Colonial practice of requiring of a teacher only a knowledge of subject matter is higher education. In contemporary colleges and universities it is still common to find professors who are self-taught as far as the techniques of teaching are concerned. In order to teach in a public school on either the elementary or the secondary level, an individual must be certified by the state in which he plans to teach. Certification is withheld (except in an emergency) unless the candidate has studied in college both technical courses in education and academic courses in those disciplines represented in the school curriculums. Most colleges and universities prepare people for certification as teachers, and many offer advanced degrees in education. Teachers keep abreast of their fields through such means as nationwide teachers' organizations and learned journals. Thus, at least on the elementary and secondary levels, there are attempts to rewrite that acrimonious quip to read, "If you can, *teach; if you can't, try something else.*"

The move toward the professionalization of teaching began on the elementary level from European influences. Early in the nineteenth century, "normal schools" for the training of elementary-school teachers appeared. By the end of the century there were close to four hundred normal schools in the United States. That curious word "normal" is derived from the French *normale* and refers to the "norm," the "model," the "standard" which the normal schools offered to future teachers.

When normal schools began, they were indeed schools, not teachers' colleges. Their admission requirements were very low. As late as 1900 it was rare for a normal school to require a complete high-school education for admission.

With some reluctance, colleges began, during the nineteenth century, to offer courses in education and to set up departments of pedagogy. By the end of the century, graduate courses in education were taught.

As the academic field of education began to congeal and the curriculum in education began to take shape, state legislators began to demand specific requirements of schoolteachers and to certify candidates.

Accompanying the rise of normal schools was another movement designed to improve the competency and status of teachers: teachers' institutes. These institutes were not intended as alternatives for the academic training of teachers, but, rather, they were a stopgap means of offsetting the wretched qualifications of the average schoolteacher. Institutes first appeared in New York State in 1837, and other states quickly borrowed the idea. Teachers' institutes usually consisted of short-term instructional sessions for teachers. They were conducted when elementary schools were not open, so that the teachers would be free to attend. Condensed instruction was offered in both subject matter and teaching procedures. By means of institutes, teachers who had not been exposed to normal-school training were made aware of materials applicable to schoolteaching. Institutes continue to the present time. In earlier years they served a genuine purpose, when so many untrained and poorly qualified people taught school, but today's teachers' institutes, where they do continue to exist, too often demonstrate that they have outlived their usefulness. The needs they once met are better met elsewhere, in most cases. Teachers who have occasion to refresh or improve their knowledge can turn nowadays to readily available collegiate-level summer sessions and extension courses that are usually superior to institute courses.

The development of a higher status for the teaching vocation was stimulated further by the rise of teachers' organizations. Several had appeared by the middle of the nineteenth century. The most influential of the contemporary teachers' organizations include the National Education Association and the American Federation of Teachers. These organizations publish journals and other materials devoted to the teaching processes. The last chapter of this book elaborates on the topic of the developing status of schoolteaching.

From an Imported Framework to an American Plan of Education

The final trend to be identified here is in some respects a summary of the contents of the entire chapter. The United States had its origin in Europe. Western Europeans of the post-Columbian era brought to the New World the practices, schemes, artifacts, and institutional blueprints that they had known in the Old World. The culture of Europe was transfused into the wilderness of North America, to the extent that such an undertaking was feasible in a new and untamed socio-geographic setting.

The educational structures, the educational designs, the educational procedures of the American colonists came largely from Europe. The American elementary school was an imperfect counterpart of the European "vernacular school" for peasants. The American Latin grammar school was a defective copy of the European classical school for sons of elite families. The American college was an inferior duplicate of a segment of the European university. Even after the political rupture that made the United States an independent nation, American education continued to borrow heavily from Europe. The normal school, the infant school, the monitorial school, and the Sunday school are all European in origin. Compulsory attendance at school, graded schools, graduate education, and higher learning show European influences. From the early seventeenth century until the latter years of the nineteenth century, Americans looked across the Atlantic Ocean both for instructional clues and for educational plans that they might borrow. In many respects, American education was little more than a young nation's imitation, adapted to a wilderness environment, of the cultural ways of its parents.

Education in contemporary America is now sufficiently unique that one cannot with accuracy call it a cultural import. While its European ancestry has left an imprint, American education is different from that found in other countries of the world. Consider for analysis three of the many characteristics of contemporary American education that give evidence of this uniqueness.

First, American education has an egalitarian curriculum. Instead of separating schools of the same level by curriculum, the tendency is to place all curriculums under the same educational roof. In Europe it is common to find on the secondary level a dual educational system composed of academic secondary schools and trade-oriented secondary schools, one separate from the other. And the European university is an academic university. Advanced trade subjects are not dignified by being housed in the same higher-educational quarters as the venerable learned disciplines. As indicated already, both the American high school and the American university are cafeteria-like in their course offerings. In America the preparation of philosopher kings and cabbage farmers, of gifted students and retarded students, of Brahmins and plebeians, of nuclear physicists and housekeepers is thought to demand curriculums that are of equal seriousness, equal status, and equal place in the educational structure. These curriculums are offered in the same school or college.

Second, American education is egalitarian in its having universalized post-elementary-school education. Historically, very few people attended secondary schools in Europe, and even fewer people attended universities. Even today, for example, only a small segment of the British population is college-educated. As pointed out earlier, almost all American adolescents attend high school for a while at least. And higher-educational enrollments in recent years have multiplied so greatly that they are causing acute growing pains across the nation. Some Europeans, in fact, look upon the heavy enrollments in American high schools and colleges as prima-facie evidence of the inferiority of American education. They cannot believe that quantity education can exist without a sacrifice of quality.

Third, the American educational institution has increased its functions to include social work as well as education. A sizable school district or university is likely to have medical, dental, psychotherapeutic, counseling, and recreational facilities for its students, as well as classroom studies. The American school and college resemble more and more that social-work agency fostered by such people as Jane Addams and known as a neighborhood center or settlement house. This stands in direct contrast to the usual European practice of limiting the functions of the educational institution to strictly academic ones.

Change, revolutionary change, in the American way of life has brought revolutionary change in American education. Schools are different now from what they were in the past because the whole tenor of life is different from what it was then. When America had scarcely more than a neolithic culture, a plan of minimal education was sufficient to equip a citizen to cope with his environment and to perpetuate the ideals of the society. The new technological age in a new nation has brought with it such complexities that a new design of education was recognized as essential for the realization in America of the two universal principles of education.

The idea of a common vernacular school for the masses had been brought from Europe and transplanted on American soil to grow someday into the tax-supported public elementary school of the United States. As the effects of the cultural revolution became more obvious, more and more Americans who held positions of leadership were won to the belief that a vernacular-school education was insufficient for the common man if he were to be prepared adequately for the exigencies of an increasingly intricate way of life. This thinking, as early as Franklin's day and very obvious by the middle of the nineteenth century, gave rise to a belief that there should be a vernacular college to supplement the educational work offered by the vernacular elementary school. This belief, in turn, resulted eventually in the development of the tax-supported public high school. The high school would be the common man's college. It would be as practical in its approach on the secondary level as the common vernacular school was on the elementary level, which meant that its course offerings would be those best designed to benefit the common man in his ordinary pursuits.

But accompanying the movement to develop a people's vernacular school and a people's college was the even stronger nineteenth-century American democratic movement toward greater egalitarianism. It was this movement, in an extreme form, which helped to put the semiliterate bear hunter, Davy Crockett, in the Congress of the United States and which later hastened the emancipation of a group of people who, only weeks earlier, were totally illiterate and ignorant slaves. The spirit of egalitarianism turned away from the European dual school system, with its classical secondary schools for college-directed youths and its trade schools for commoners. This spirit of egalitarianism, put into words by Thaddeus Stevens, had helped to keep the public elementary school from becoming identified as a school for common people only. The same spirit of egalitarianism helped to keep the public high school from receiving a similar label.

Egalitarianism demanded that the people's college be also the preparatory school for youths who would seek a higher education. Egalitarianism demanded, further, that odious comparisons between courses and curriculums in this people's-college-preparatory-school should be minimized. A course in stenography should be just as respectable as a course in college-preparatory English. A course in manual training or cooking should be just as respectable as a course in Latin or geometry. The trend toward egalitarianism in the curricular offerings of the high school was encouraged and upheld by a series of powerful committees which, through their deliberations, helped formulate and organize the thinking of both high-school and collegiate teachers and administrators. These committees, such as the Committee on College Entrance Requirements, gave expression to their views in the late nineteenth century and early twentieth. Another of these committees, the Committee of Nine on the Articulation of High School and College, which met in 1910, had as a member Professor Charles H. Judd of the University of Chicago. It was his view, though a minority one, that there be no required courses whatever in high school and that each student should take whatever pattern of courses that he considered coherent. Judd went so far as to suggest that colleges should accept all courses, without an imposed pattern, for admission to college. While Judd's views have never prevailed to any degree, a spirit of egalitarianism regarding curricular offerings had enveloped the secondary school by 1920.

As the twentieth century continues, the public feels increasingly that a secondary-level people's college does not offer a sufficient amount of education to prepare the common man to meet life adequately. Thus, there is a growing trend toward converting higher education into an advanced people's college. The junior-college movement, the popularity of the many and varied collegiate extension services, and the burgeoning enrollments in higher-educational establishments all bear out this view. Senator Morrill's Land Grant College Act of a century ago had laid the foundation for offering a multiplicity of curriculums and a myriad of courses in colleges and universities, as well as for helping those curriculums and courses to attain equal status.

Accompanying the push for an extension of education for the common man and the trend toward an egalitarian curriculum, of course, has been the rapid expansion of the population of the United States. This population growth was fostered in large measure in the past by immigration. In some years, more than a million people came to the United States from foreign lands. No nation in the history of humanity has ever gained so many people from so many different lands in so short a period as has the United States. Cities such as New York have become Babels. The Statute of Liberty in New York harbor carries the words of Emma Lazarus:

> Give me your tired, your poor,
> Your huddled masses yearning to breathe free,
> The wretched refuse of your teeming shore,
> Send these, the homeless, tempest-tossed, to me:
> I lift my lamp beside the golden door.

And America received what she asked for!

Compulsory attendance laws, a deepseated belief in both the necessity for and the desirability of an education, a nativistic fear of the possible erosive effects that admitting the "wretched refuse" of alien lands may have on American culture, and the realization that there is no other institution in American life capable of offering a common heritage to people who lack such a heritage have helped to encourage American educational establishments to be and become agencies for Americanization. New courses and even curriculums designed especially to equip newcomers to become model citizens have been added to the already gigantic offerings of the schools— courses and curriculums that would be the ideological equals of the other multifarious courses and curriculums. These same forces also helped to encourage American educational establishments to assume functions other than strictly educational ones. The health, psychological adjustment, social adjustment, political adjustment, and economic well-being of the children of new Americans have become concerns of the schools. Schools have been prompted to rival settlement houses as social-work agencies.

Had there not been the rush of immigrants to America, the very opening of the doors of the elementary schools, high schools, and now colleges to all interested students would have been reason enough for schools and colleges to develop an interest in the general well-being of the students. As Chapters 6 and 7 will demonstrate, pupils themselves are heterogeneous, regardless of parental origin, and their environments are as varied as they are. Common vernacular schools, common high schools, and increasingly common colleges emphasize differences and disparities in students. Egalitarian forces, faced with human inequalities, have demanded and continue to demand that the educational institution enlarge its responsibilities to include the minimizing of differences that tend to tear people apart and the broadening of mutual experiences that tend to bring people together. The result is that the educational institution in America has become a social-work institution as well as an educative institution, a neighborhood center as well as a place for instruction.

Thus has American education become unique. Through the catalytic action of a cultural revolution, American schools and colleges attempt to put into practice the prophetic words of Ezra Cornell, founder of the university that bears his name: "I would found an institution where any person can find instruction in any study." And as they have taken "any person" as a student, schools and colleges have found it more and more necessary to concern themselves not only with his instruction but also with numerous needs once thought to be a part of other institutional blueprints. Through educational changes such as these, American education has grown different from its European sources.

The Chapter in Capsule Form

1. America has undergone a power revolution during its three-and-a-half-century history. Drastic changes have occurred in industrial, scientific, technological, commercial, communication, transportation, military, political, social, secular, recreational, and feminine power.

2. American culture has become swollen with big commerce, big industry, big agriculture, big science, big cities, big population, and big government.

3. This dynamism in America's way of life has acted as a catalyst upon, and has speeded changes in, education.

4. There has been an educational trend away from a religious orientation toward a secular one. Colonial church-dominated education has been supplanted largely by state-dominated, temporal education.

5. There has been an educational trend away from local sponsorship toward enlarged public responsibility. The Colonial schools and colleges were primarily locally controlled. Today, both public and private education is aided by all levels of government.

6. There has been an educational trend away from selective and toward inclusive curriculums. Colonial schools and colleges specialized in one type of curriculum only, as a rule. Today, highly varied curriculums are offered in the same establishment.

7. There has been an educational trend away from sporadic attendance toward regular attendance. In the colonies, school attendance was haphazard, and many children were slighted. Today, compulsory attendance laws and social pressures insure that practically all children

attend elementary and secondary school. Increasing numbers of youths are receiving higher educations.

8. There has been an educational trend away from schooling for only the select toward schooling for all. In the colonies the upper classes were the ones most likely to be exposed to a formal education. Today, education is available for all people.

9. There has been an educational trend away from poorly equipped and toward excellently outfitted schools. Whereas Colonial schools were stark and meager, twentieth-century schools are often beautifully designed and elegantly furnished with a profusion of teaching devices.

10. There has been an educational trend away from poorly trained teachers toward professional educators. The training of teachers, beginning at practically the "zero level" in Colonial America, has grown into a widespread enterprise. Standards for teachers have risen. A genuine teaching profession is being developed.

11. There has been an educational trend away from borrowing European educational ideas and practices toward developing a unique American plan of education. Once America was little more than an extension of Europe. During its three-and-a-half-century history, America has developed a culture of its own, including a distinctive educational institution.

For Supplementary Reading

CUBBERLEY, ELLWOOD P., *Public Education in the United States.* Boston: Houghton Mifflin Co., 1934.

Cubberley's style of writing can hardly be called inspirational. Even so, this was the standard textbook about the history of American education for years.

————, *Readings in Public Education in the United States.* Boston: Houghton Mifflin Co., 1934.

The book's subtitle summarizes well its contents: *A Collection of Sources and Readings to Illustrate the History of Educational Practice and Progress in the United States.* Excerpts from the Stevens speech of 1835 are contained in it as well as several other materials alluded to in the chapter.

EDWARDS, NEWTON, and RICHEY, HERMAN G., *The School in the American Social Order,* 2nd ed. Boston: Houghton Mifflin Co., 1963.

This essentially is a cultural interpretation of the history of education in the United States, which demonstrates the interplay between the social order and the educational institution.

GOOD, H. G., *A History of Western Education,* 2nd ed. New York: The Macmillan Co., 1960.

There are many books that view the history of American education from the perspective of the development of education in the entire Western world. Good's book is one of the more readable and less voluminous treatises of this nature.

KNIGHT, EDGAR W., *Education in the United States,* 3rd rev. ed. Boston: Ginn and Co., 1951.

This book has rivaled Cubberley's *Public Education in the United States* as a leading textbook concerned with the history of American education.

MAYER, MARTIN, "Last Chance for Our Schools?" *Saturday Evening Post,* CCXXXVI, No. 31 (Sept. 14, 1963), 24–36.

This popularly written article by an important and outspoken interpreter of American education suggests that most schools have not changed enough to keep in step with the times.

MONROE, PAUL, ed., *A Cyclopedia of Education.* New York: The Macmillan Co., 1911–1913.

This old encyclopedia is still very useful to the student of education. It contains numerous entries that elaborate on materials mentioned in the chapter.

WIGGIN, GLADYS A., *Education and Nationalism.* New York: McGraw-Hill Book Co., Inc., 1962.

An up-to-date interpretative history of American education in which education is viewed as a vehicle for developing a sense of nationalism in the United States.

WILLIAMS, T. HARRY; CURRENT, RICHARD N.; and FREIDEL, FRANK, *A History of the United States,* 2 vols. New York: Alfred A. Knopf, 1959.

Several general textbooks in American history give serious attention to the history of American education as viewed by the historian. Here is one of the better ones. Consult the index of each volume for specific references to education.

4

A Political and an Economic Approach to Education

Part I: The Federal Government and Education

> *Religion, morality and knowledge being necessary to good government and the happiness of mankind, schools and the means of education shall forever be encouraged.*

from the Northwest Ordinance of 1787.

Thinking It Over Beforehand

What does the federal Constitution say about education?

How does the Department of Health, Education and Welfare affect education?

Should Indians or Negroes go to separate schools from whites?

Must federal involvement in education damage the status of American education?

What bearing does the federal Supreme Court have on education in America?

The Relatedness of Politics and Economics in American Education

Instead of treating the subjects of school government and school finance separately, they will be combined in this discussion. School government and school finance are closely interrelated in America. Most of our schools are public schools. As such, the public, through its governmental agencies, not only regulates how our schools shall be operated and managed, but also taxes itself for the support of public schools. In other words, it is through government that we, the people, conduct and finance our public schools. Laws prescribe how schools shall be administered; laws also prescribe how the costs of schools shall be defrayed. The same legislative body that passes an act requiring all children to attend school until they are sixteen may pass an act requiring that so many cents out of every tax dollar shall be used to support public schools.

The Constitution of the United States

At first it may seem odd, in a prefatory book about education, to devote an entire chapter to the role of the federal government in education. One might well ask, "What role?" The functionings of the federal government are based on an important political document, the Constitution of the United States. Not once in that document is either the word "education" or the word "school" mentioned. Furthermore, the Tenth Amendment states very plainly, "The powers not delegated to the United States by the Constitution, nor prohibited by it to the States, are reserved to the States respectively, or to the people." An easy conclusion is that there is no federal government of education.

This conclusion is far too simple. It overlooks two cardinal facts. First, the Constitution has been interpreted very liberally through the years. It has resembled a stretch stocking that fits the varying sizes and shapes of different users. Even though education is not alluded to specifically, federal officials have found flexible terminology in the Constitution which they have interpreted as meaning that education is, at least in part, a federal function. For example, the Constitution calls upon the federal government to provide for the common defense and to promote the general welfare of the nation. If people do not have the opportunity to receive an education, is our democratic nation adequately defended? The integrity of a democracy rests upon an enlightened citizenry. If people do not have the opportunity to receive an education, is the welfare of our nation promoted? Ignorant people overburden a democratic society.

Secondly, precedent is as important as the Constituition in determining what the role of the federal government should be. If the federal government has concerned itself with a given activity in the past, the federal government probably will continue to concern itself with similar activities in the future. During the nearly two hundred years that our federal government has been in existence, it has involved itself many times with educational issues. A tradition has been developed to the effect that the federal government has a rightful role to play in the matter of education in the United States. So important is that role that one of the cabinet posts in the executive branch carries the word "education" in its title. The federal government, in actuality, has been a powerful force in the field of education, as we shall see.

School children quickly learn that the federal government has three branches: the executive branch, headed by the President, the legislative branch, run by a two-chamber Congress, and a judicial branch, dominated by the Supreme Court. Each of these three branches concerns itself with education. The following discussion will examine the three branches one at a time, in the order given above, and will indicate the relationship of each branch to education in the United States.

The Department of Health, Education and Welfare

The most obvious starting point in a discussion of the executive branch as it relates to education is the cabinet post that has the word "education" in its title. The Department of Health, Education and Welfare is a new cabinet office, initiated in 1953. Several Presidents had wanted to establish a department concerned with human welfare, but pressure-group opposition

Courtesy of the Department of Health, Education and Welfare

THE MAIN BUILDING OF THE DEPARTMENT OF HEALTH, EDUCATION AND WELFARE, WASHINGTON, D. C.

was strong. The idea was first discussed during the presidency of Warren G. Harding. Special-interest groups, including the American Medical Association, scotched Harding's plan. Presidents Franklin Roosevelt and Harry Truman were eager to set up the new cabinet post, but they were no more successful than Harding. Finally, during the presidency of Dwight D. Eisenhower, the Department of Health, Education and Welfare became a reality after a truce was declared between the federal government and the opposing special-interest forces. Ironically, most people did not really care one way or another about the establishment of the department.

Diagram III identifies the major agencies of the Department of Health, Education and Welfare. Several of the subdivisions within the department are not concerned directly with education, but others are.

The Office of Education

Going from the obvious to the less obvious, the observer can hardly help noticing the educational significance of that agency of the Department of Health, Education and Welfare known as the Office of Education. There is little doubt that the Office of Education is one of the most important of the many federal agencies concerned with education.

The office is much older than the Department of Health, Education and Welfare. Educational pioneers of Horace Mann's generation had urged the establishment of a national agency that would act as a clearinghouse for educational affairs in the nation. It was not until after the Civil War, when the ravages of warfare on American social institutions became obvious, that such an agency was created. In 1867 Congress called for the formation of a "Department of Education," not of cabinet rank,

. . . . for the purpose of collecting such statistics and facts as shall show the condition and progress of education in the several States and Territories, and of diffusing such information respecting the organization and management of schools and school systems and methods of teaching as shall aid the people of the United States in the establishment and maintenance of efficient school systems, and otherwise promote the cause of education throughout the country.

Mann's contemporary, Henry Barnard, an outstanding educational figure of the nineteenth century, served as the agency's first commissioner.

Almost as soon as the Department of Education was created, its name was changed to the Office of Education, and, almost as quickly, its name was again changed to the Bureau of Education. It was assigned to the Department of the Interior. The agency's name was changed once more, in 1929, back to the Office of Education, its present name. In 1939 the office was moved from the Department of the Interior to the Federal Security Agency. When the Department of Health, Education and Welfare

DIAGRAM III.   STRUCTURE OF THE DEPARTMENT OF HEALTH, EDUCATION AND WELFARE.

Courtesy of the Department of Health, Education and Welfare.

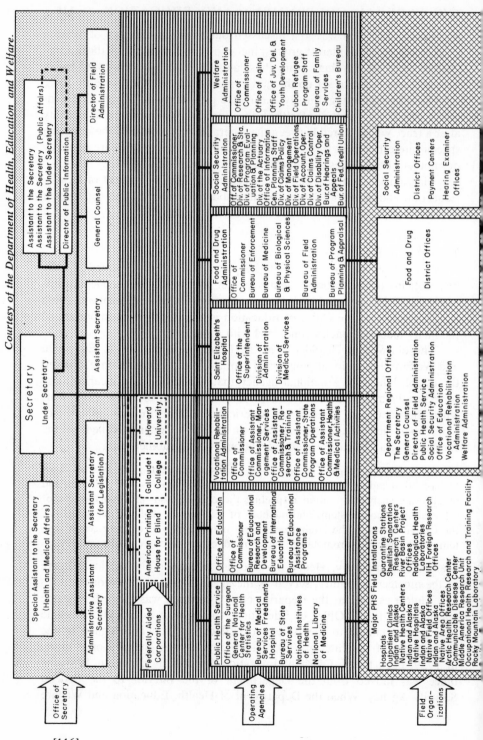

came into being, the Federal Security Agency became the nucleus of this newly formed department. This meant that the Office of Education was transferred once more to its present place in the federal government.

During its nearly one hundred years of operation, the work of the Office of Education has expanded as education in America has changed and grown. It now has four paramount functions.

First, the Office of Education advises and consults. When educationists want information or advice, they can turn to the Office of Education for much help. This office gathers statistics about what is happening to American education. Its surveys of education, published since 1918, are excellent sources of data about American education. The office also evaluates educational trends. It identifies and conducts research on special problems that have arisen and need study. It investigates foreign educational systems so that American educationists may become aware of new ideas from abroad. These activities are suggestive of the kind of investigative work that the Office of Education performs. When people who are interested in the field of education seek counsel, the Office of Education is prepared to offer answers based on sound knowledge.

Second, the Office of Education develops teaching aids and other educational materials. Several of these deal with techniques of teaching. The office publishes *School Life* and *Higher Education,* two important periodicals in the field. The office also issues captioned films for use with deaf pupils.

Third, the Office of Education helps to develop policy for some of the federally sponsored or federally aided educative programs. For example, the Office of Education develops the point of view that governs vocational training in federally aided high schools. The office cooperates with the Department of State in outlining policies for sending Americans abroad to study or for bringing foreign students to the United States. The office cooperates with the Veterans Administration in determining the minimum qualifications that schools must meet before federally sponsored veterans may enroll in them. The office works closely with land-grant colleges, also.

Fourth, the Office of Education administers certain federally aided programs, including grants-in-aid to higher education, grants for vocational education on the high-school level, monies for training people to teach handicapped students, school building assistance programs, and loans to college students.

The Children's Bureau

When the Department of Health, Education and Welfare was begun, the already existent Children's Bureau was moved to it from the Department of Labor. The Children's Bureau has various functions related directly or indirectly to education. It gathers statistical information about children. It issues many publications concerned with children, including a periodical called *Children*. The federally aided school health programs are administered by the Children's Bureau. The bureau is also very concerned about those children who have hurt themselves in the buzzsaw of crime. Technical assistance in combatting delinquency is available through the bureau.

The Office of Vocational Rehabilitation

The basic educative function of the Office of Vocational Rehabilitation is to administer federal funds designed to help handicapped persons redirect their energies into a new and useful vocational channel so that they may become self-supporting. The office is also the custodian of monies for the training of teachers who, in turn, will train the handicapped.

The Overseeing of Three Corporations

There are three federally assisted corporations each of which is dedicated to important educational purposes and each of which receives assistance from the Department of Health, Education and Welfare. While these corporations are not agencies of the department, they are under its guardian care.

The American Printing House for the Blind, Incorporated, is a private enterprise. At the same time, it receives federal help because the federal government is its chief client. The American Printing House for the Blind is located in Louisville, Kentucky, and was begun over a century ago. It prints books in Braille. It makes talking books (or educative phonograph records) for blind people. The federal government acquires these materials from the American Printing House for the Blind and distributes them, without cost, to state schools for the blind.

Gallaudet College in Washington, D. C., is unique. It is the only college in the world run especially for deaf people. It grew out of a school for the deaf, dumb, and blind that was started in the mid-nineteenth century, and it now specialized in work with the deaf. There is a lower school, Kendall School, connected with Gallaudet College which has two purposes. In the first place, it is an elementary and secondary school for the deaf. In the second place, it is a laboratory school for Gallaudet students who want to learn how to teach the deaf themselves. Gallaudet students specializing in education have an opportunity to perform student teaching at Kendall School.

Howard University, located in Washington, D. C., was started at the close of the Civil War. Although the university is open to any qualified student, it caters especially to Negroes. The federal government helps support the university, although money comes to it from other sources, too. Howard University offers a wide range of courses for both undergraduate and graduate students.

Courtesy of Gallaudet College

GALLAUDET COLLEGE IS THE WORLD'S ONLY COLLEGE FOR THE DEAF.

Schools and Colleges

George Washington and other founders of the American nation were eager to establish a national university system. While the system has never been literally established, we, the people, have come close to doing so. At the present time, the federal government sponsors a ponderous quantity of halls of learning. Mention has just been made of Kendall School, Gallaudet College, and Howard University, but these are only three from a lengthy list of federally linked educational establishments. The federal government also operates, directly or indirectly, the:

Air University
Armed Forces Staff College

Foreign Service Institute
Industrial College of the Armed Forces
National War College
United States Coast Guard Academy
United States Department of Agriculture Graduate School
United States Merchant Marine Academy
United States Military Academy
United States Naval Academy
schools for the children of personnel on military posts in the United
States or abroad
schools in federally held territories of the United States, including, in-
directly, those in Washington, D. C.

This list is incomplete, and it is impressive, yet there are those who believe that the federal government is *not* involved in the business of teaching. It is very much involved.

Department of Justice, Bureau of Prisons

The principal division of the Department of Justice that is connected directly with education is the Bureau of Prisons. This type of association between the Department of Justice and education is relatively new; it was the outgrowth of a change in viewpoint regarding the treatment of criminals. For ages the usual method of dealing with people who had committed crimes against the state was to kill, exile, or inflict physical punishment on them. Prisons in Europe, when they existed, were used not for punishment, but as a dumping place in which to rid the society of such nuisances as people who were insane, who were embarrassed financially, or who held heterodox views. The colonies attempted to repress crime in this same general manner.

The prison as a place of detention for those who commit crimes against the state can be traced in America to the efforts of Pennsylvania Quakers, who strove to substitute imprisonment for those earlier, more brutal methods of treating criminals. By the early national period, the practice of incarcerating criminals had begun. This move, while it was a vast improvement over the former techniques of dealing with criminals, still centered around the ancient view that criminals should pay for their transgressions— an eye for an eye and a tooth for a tooth. Society, by incarcerating its criminals, was avenging itself. By the end of the nineteenth century a new point of view was coming into being: prisons should not be dedicated to revenge; instead, they should be dedicated to rehabilitation, to the extent that the inmates could profit from it. While this new viewpoint was once thought to be visionary, it has come more and more to be the prevailing opinion of penologists today. The idea of reforming criminals has brought education into the picture as a means of redirecting human energy that has been misdirected.

During most of the history of the United States, there have been no special prisons for federal lawbreaking civilians. The federal government boarded and lodged its prisoners in state or local prisons until 1895, when Congress assigned the military prison at Fort Leavenworth to the Department of Justice. It became the first federal prison for civilian criminals who had violated federal law. Thus, the Department of Justice entered the field of prison management at a time when advanced ideas on the subject were being promulgated. In 1930 an act of Congress, signed by President Hoover, brought into being the Bureau of Prisons of the Department of Justice. The bureau is charged with the responsibility of the "safekeeping, care, protection, instruction and discipline" of federal prisoners.

The idea of educating prisoners predates both the Bureau of Prisons and the existence of federal prisons. In the early nineteenth century it was not entirely unusual for clergymen, on their own or as prison chaplains, to offer rudimentary instruction to some of the prisoners on an individual tutorial basis. Formal classes of instruction within the confines of a prison are primarily a twentieth-century phenomenon, and their popularity since 1930 is traceable, in part certainly, to the progressiveness of the Bureau of Prisons. Today it is no longer uncommon to find in federal prisons (and to some degree in state prisons) [1] a staff of teachers and a fairly wide range of courses. There is also a recognition usually that the interest of the inmates must be captured in the educational program if that program is to have a telling effect on the prisoners' lives. This last point is especially true for prisoners whose egregious past lives may have included a hatred of school.

A concomitant development emphasizing the importance of education in federal prisons is a change that has occurred in the make-up of the prison community. When our nation was founded, there were few federal laws to be violated, and thus few federal prisoners. As Congress after Congress has seen fit to pass law after law, there have been more and more laws to violate, and hence more prisoners. At the same time the number of acts defined as illegal have been enlarged to encompass a wider portion of the population. In the early days, such crimes as piracy and counterfeiting were principal crimes; today, the inclusion of such crimes as auto theft and traffic in drugs has changed the face of crime. Younger and younger people

[1] It is difficult to generalize about state prison administration, which, in the different states, runs the gamut from barbaric to highly informed.

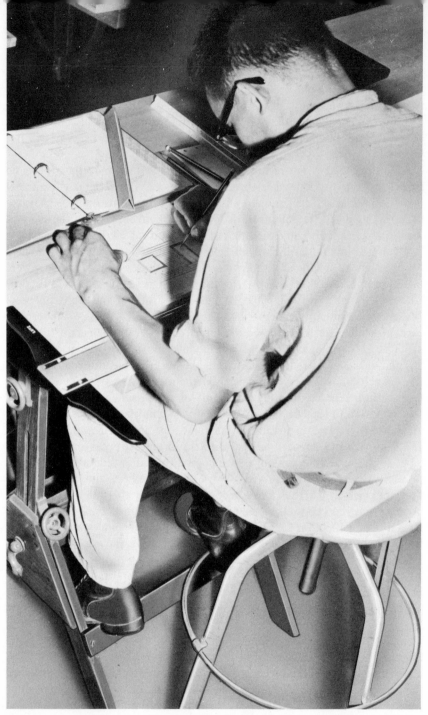

Courtesy of the Bureau of Prisons, Department of Justice

APPROXIMATELY 12,000 FEDERAL PRISONERS PER YEAR PARTICIPATE IN VOCA-
TIONAL COURSES. THIS YOUTH IS STUDYING CARPENTRY.

[122]

find themselves in trouble with federal statutes. Currently, a large segment of federal prisoners is composed of youths in late adolescence and early adulthood. This factor has contributed to a feeling that education is a *sine qua non* if these youths are to be truly rehabilitated and if they can spend the remaining days of their lives in useful activities.

Federal prisoners at the present time are required to achieve an education of at least fifth-grade level. They are encouraged, if educable, to advance their education as far as possible beyond this level. Not only are academic courses taught; vocational training is an equally important facet of education in federal prisons. On-the-job training is offered also in those fields that coincidentally must operate in order for the prison itself to function; cooking is an example.

Department of Interior, Bureau of Indian Affairs

The key agency of the Department of Interior that deals with education is the Bureau of Indian Affairs. Originally assigned to the War Department, the bureau was moved to the Department of Interior over a century ago— where it has remained.

The Bureau of Indian Affairs is responsible for overseeing the general welfare of American Indians and Eskimos, including the education of Indian youths. Presently the bureau functions with the understanding that American Indians eventually should need no special supervision from a federal agency. Eventually Indians should be able to direct their own social, economic, and political affairs in this complex world. But that was not always the attitude.

Since the inception of our federal government, there have been three official governmental points of view with regard to American Indians: Indians as foreigners, Indians as wards, and Indians as citizens. Before 1870 the Indian tribes were treated as foreign nations and were dealt with by means of treaties or wars. By 1871 the federal government had set up reservations for Indians on lands that were mainly submarginal. In order to offset inevitable poverty, the federal government began to provide for the Indians as a trustee does for his ward. Begun as early as 1887 and completed by 1924, citizenship was bestowed upon all Indians within the boundaries of the continental United States. The education offered to Indians has reflected these three historical points of view.

Long before the federal government came into being, Catholic and other church groups had established missionary schools for Indians. When the federal government began to concern itself with Indian affairs, it was quite logical for it to make use of the educational programs of church

Trover collection, Oregon State Library

A FEDERALLY OPERATED SCHOOL FOR INDIANS AT THE BEGINNING OF THIS CENTURY.

groups. Treaties between the United States and various Indian tribes occasionally promised that the government would provide educational facilities for the Indians. In 1819 Congress passed a law setting aside $10,000 per year for the education of Indians. This money was assigned to missionary groups as federal aid for the support of church schools for Indians.[2] This law remained in effect until 1873. It was not until 1860 that the federal government began to operate its own schools for Indians.

Borrowing upon the experiences of the missionaries, the federal government built boarding schools away from the reservations for the most part. The government wanted to civilize the Indians. It was believed that if Indian children could be taken away from their "untutored and often times savage parents," the civilizing process could proceed more smoothly. These federal schools were (and still are) administered by the Bureau of Indian Affairs.

[2] This old law raises interesting issues regarding federal financing of parochial education, especially since there is now much opposition, legal and otherwise, to federal aid for church-operated schools.

Unlike state-operated public schools, the federally operated schools for Indians have not been in the hands of the people they serve. This has brought about some disappointing consequences in the past. It has been difficult for even the best-intentioned outsiders to know what the genuine educative needs of Indian children are. Too frequently the curriculum of the federal schools has offered little to prepare a ward of the government for the stark actualities of life on a reservation.

Funds for the education of Indians have been very limited. Consequently, coverage has been poor. As late as the mid-1950's, for example, about one-half of the Navajo Indian children of school age were not in school. And today the average amount of formal education that Indian adults have had is approximately half of the average amount obtained by American adults in general.

With the conferring of citizenship upon Indians, there has been a trend toward removing the federal government from direct involvement with Indian education. States have the obligation of providing educational facilities for citizens within their borders. The Indians are citizens and thus come under state provisions. Today most of the Indians attend state-operated public schools. Where such an arrangement causes severe financial difficulties, the federal government dispenses monetary assistance to the states. A few federally operated schools for Indians remain, but these schools serve the educational needs of exceptional Indian groups who cannot be educated adequately with state facilities. For example, Chemawa Indian School, located near Salem, Oregon, offers a federally operated, highly specialized program of education for adolescent Navajo and Alaskan Indians who have not been in school before. These Indian youths would present a baffling problem to the typical public school. Few schools have the facilities for dealing with adolescents who have never attended school before, who cannot read, who cannot write, who may not even be able to speak English, but who suddenly arrive at school. At Chemawa Indian School a condensed, somewhat individually tailored program is offered to such pupils.

It appears that the time is not too distant when the Bureau of Indian Affairs will no longer operate schools for Indians and when all Indian children will attend the same schools (state-sponsored or private) that other American children attend.

The Department of Agriculture

There are two major links between the United States Department of Agriculture and American education. The first is the department's attempt

to acquaint rural people with better ways of living and of earning a livelihood. The second is its handling of school lunch programs.

The Department of Agriculture conducts a vast amount of research in
the twin fields of farming and home economics. In cooperation with the
several states, experiment stations throughout the land and research facilities at land-grant colleges are used for testing new and better agricultural
and homemaking techniques and products. From these experiments come

A DEMONSTRATION OF FARM MACHINERY CONDUCTED BY THE EXTENSION SERV-
ICE OF THE DEPARTMENT OF AGRICULTURE.

many educative books and pamphlets. Demonstrations of improved procedures are also offered.

The Department of Agriculture, again in cooperation with the states,
sponsors educative clubs for present-day and future farmers and housewives. Neither the homemakers' clubs nor the children's clubs are limited
to farm people. Urbanites may also belong to these clubs. The club for
children is the 4-H Club. Valuable vocational and homemaking experiences
are gained by youth in 4-H Club activities.

The Agricultural Marketing Service of the Department of Agriculture handles matters dealing directly with school lunch programs. States wishing to avail themselves of these services may procure funds administered through the Agricultural Marketing Agency, provided that the states match the federal funds. The money is used by the states to provide low-cost (and sometimes free) wholesome meals in high-school or elementary-school cafeterias. For very poor children this is often the best, most filling meal they receive during the day.

A school milk program is also administered by the Agricultural Marketing Agency. Elementary schools, high schools, and such nonprofit agencies as child-care centers and settlement houses catering to underprivileged children may qualify for special funds. These funds are used to help defray the cost of milk for the children. Where need is apparent, the children may be given the milk free of charge. (This illustrates the social-work function of American education, discussed in Chapter 3.)

And So Forth

Many other divisions of the executive branch of the federal government deal with educational services.

The Department of State is much concerned with intercultural education. In cooperation with other nations and with the UN, educational, scientific, and cultural projects are encouraged. Americans are sent abroad to study, teach, and offer their services as trained experts. Foreigners are brought to the United States to study and share their ideas with Americans.

The Veterans Administration is also involved in education. It provides funds for the rehabilitation of disabled veterans. It assists veterans in continuing their formal education after the completion of their assignments in the armed services. The average American is familiar, at least vaguely, with the so-called G. I. Bill of Rights and the Korean Bill. Both of these programs have offered money to veterans who wish to continue their education. The Veterans Administration also assists in the education of the orphaned children of those members of the armed forces who have been killed in action.

And so forth. . . . This rapid sketch of the executive branch of our federal government gives an idea of the relationships that exist between the executive branch and the field of education.

Congress and Education: Federal Aid to Education

During much of the twentieth century, a significant as well as emotion-arousing issue has been the question of federal aid to education. The early

1930's offers an illustration. Federal aid to education was thought to be so crucial in 1934 that the American Association of University Women urged study groups to investigate the subject and published a syllabus for them to use. The topic of federal aid was selected as the national theme for interschool debating among secondary-school pupils in the academic year 1934–1935. Several committees and similar organizations, including the National Conference on the Financing of Education (of 1933), have pondered the question.

In the minds of some people, federal aid to education is a novel notion that is both alien to American governmental tradition and an untried scheme. Such an interpretation could hardly stray further from the truth. Congress *does* offer aid to education and has been doing so for a longer period of time than America has had a federal government. Consider a brief list of a few of the consequential laws passed by Congress. Each of these laws has offered financial aid to education in America.

Shortly after the American Revolution, the Continental Congress, operating under the Articles of Confederation, passed a measure dealing with the subdivision and subsequent sale of western lands. The Land Ordinance of 1785 directed that one thirty-sixth of the land should be used to finance education. Later laws, passed after the Constitution was adopted, increased the amount of land set aside by Congress for the support of education.

Beginning with Ohio, Congress has assigned various mineral lands to the states to augment state educational funds. Congress also has passed legislation permitting, under certain circumstances, the payment of royalties to states from profits made in the public domain. For example, sometimes a state receives a percentage of the federal money procured from renting public land for grazing purposes. Occasionally this source of money has been reserved for educational use only.

Land has also been granted to states to stimulate the development of higher education. While a generous Congress during the Civil War years was handing out princely segments of public land to private railroad companies, the Congress also handed out less pretentious pieces of land to states. The latter grants were given with the understanding that the states would establish vocationally oriented liberal-arts colleges. There have been some other, less striking grants of land to states for higher education besides this Land Grant College Act of 1862. Also, there have been laws that provided states with sums of money to continue the operation of land-grant colleges. At the present time the experimental stations of the Department of Agriculture are actually directed by land-grant colleges, and Congress helps pay the cost.

During the twentieth century Congress had passed a series of measures designed to insure that useful vocational education will be offered in public high schools. These measures have set up programs aimed at training youths in vocational agriculture, distributive occupations, and the like. There is federal money for these programs provided the states meet certain minimum requirements.

Courtesy of Texas Agricultural and Mechanical University

BECAUSE OF FEDERAL AID TO EDUCATION, LAND GRANT COLLEGES SUCH AS TEXAS AGRICULTURAL AND MECHANICAL UNIVERSITY HAVE BEEN ESTABLISHED.

Since the Great Depression of the 1930's, Congress has from time to time created special scholarships, fellowships, and loan funds for high-school or college students. For example, in the late 1950's, Congress passed a special loan fund for college students as a part of its National Defense Education Act. But probably the best known of these acts was the "G. I. Bill," described earlier.

This incomplete list is ample illustration that Congress has federally aided the cause of education, and has done so for almost two centuries. Federal aid to education is not hypothesis, but fact. An argument as to whether or not the federal government *should* aid education seems out of place, since this would be arguing after the fact. More to the point is the question of how far Congress should go in its assistance of education in order not to invade the legitimate domain of state or local government with regard to education.

A Case Study in Federal Aid to Education

To see the question in clearer perspective, it would be wise to look at a specific congressional boost to education in some detail. If there were an act that was a prototype of federal aid to education, a study of this act would be illuminating. One could see just what techniques Congress uses when it aids education. One could see also whether federal aid seriously jeopardizes state responsibility for education.

Such an act does exist. The Magna Carta of federal aid to high schools for vocational training was the Smith-Hughes Act of 1917. This act can be looked upon as the classic. Subsequent legislative enactments involving federal assistance to states (in the field of education and in other fields) have copied frequently the approach of the Smith-Hughes Act. Americans who are concerned with the relationship between the federal and state levels of government would do well to familiarize themselves with this model act.

The Smith-Hughes Act created a cooperative program between the federal government and the states for promoting education in agriculture, the trades, and industries. This act grew, in part, out of failures of the Morrill Act (the Land Grant College Act). Senator Morrill had ingenuously assumed that the act of 1862 bearing his name would provide for the higher education of farmers and mechanics. Despite Morrill's intentions, students *not* interested in these modest-status occupations have predominated on the campuses of land-grant colleges. In fact, youths planning to become farmers or mechanics typically did not go to college. All of this added up to the fact that, from a practical standpoint, vocational training for future farmers and mechanics had to be given at a level lower than college.

The Smith-Hughes Act also grew, in part, out of the recognition that vocational education should be national in scope, not local. National prosperity and the standard of living of the entire nation could be at stake. Further, a local community offering expensive vocational training is very likely to be educating future citizens of other states. The American labor force is notoriously mobile, from a geographical standpoint. A New England school may well be educating a future citizen of California, and a "Deep Southern" school may well be educating a future citizen of Illinois. Thus, such states as California or Illinois have reason to be concerned about the educational program of, say, Mississippi or Maine.

The administrative supervision of the Smith-Hughes Act was made the responsibility of a federal board for vocational education, now handled through the Department of Health, Education and Welfare. This federal board had the responsibility of maintaining national, bare-minimum educational and administrative standards for vocational education in the fields of agriculture, the trades, industries, and home economics. Any state had three alternatives with regard to the act. It could ignore the act; under these circumstances, it would receive no funds. It could meet the bare-minimum requirements; it could then qualify for funds. It could surpass the national

Darrel Volesky, Central High School, Independence, Oregon

THE SMITH-HUGHES ACT HAS ENCOURAGED THE TEACHING OF AGRICULTURAL SUB-JECTS IN AMERICAN SECONDARY SCHOOLS.

minimums and have an exceptionally fine program; again, it would qualify for the federal funds. The point is this: states were neither forced to follow this federal law to the letter nor compelled to accept the funds.

What minimums did a state have to meet under the act in order to qualify for the funds? State legislation would have to be passed indicating the state's willingness to cooperate and designating the state treasurer as custodian of the federal funds involved. The state would have to set up an administrative board to supervise the state's vocational-education program and to act as a continuing liaison between the state and the federal board. The state would have to submit the blueprints of its program to the federal board for approval. The state would have to match (from one source or another within its borders) the federal funds allotted to it, dollar for dollar. The state could use the federal funds for public educational establishments only. No federal funds could be assigned to private nonsectarian or church schools. The funds coming from the federal government would be paid on a reimbursement basis only. That is, a state would have to advance its own money for vocational education; then the federal government would recompense the state for the federal share *after* the bills had been paid—provided, of course, that the state had met the minimum federal requirements, and provided that the money had been spent for the purposes specified. The pupils receiving vocational training would have to be fourteen years of age or older. If the pupils were going to school part-time because they were already employed, they would have to be sixteen years of age or older.

The act was explicit with regard to the uses to which the federal funds might be put. The funds could be used for two purposes only: first, the training of lower than collegiate-level teachers of vocational agriculture,[3] trades, industries, and home economics, and second, the salaries of these teachers. No federal money could be spent on equipment, buildings, or salaries of other teachers whose courses contributed to the well-rounded education of the youths enrolled in the vocational courses.

The act also sets up formulas of a somewhat complex variety to determine precisely how much money a state might receive and for what subpurposes. One further point. A state might qualify for *some* of the funds potentially available to it without qualifying for all of the funds. For example, a state might offer no facilities at all for the training of teachers of home economics or for instruction in this subject. Yet the state could receive its share of funds for the other vocational fields mentioned in the act.

Must Federal Aid Cripple State Action in Education?

Notice that the Smith-Hughes Act is a permissive, not obligatory, act. The act attempted to establish national minimums, not maximums. States could have somewhat different programs and still qualify under the act. The Smith-Hughes Act was not thrust upon the states. Participation in the benefits of the act was voluntarily. Within the state, the act was administered by the state. The federal government's role has been to assure that bare-minimum standards will be maintained within each participating state. This is far from octopus-like federal domination.

[3] Technically, the training of directors and supervisors of vocational agriculture was included also.

In actuality, the Smith-Hughes Act was so well received throughout the nation that subsequent acts of a similar nature have been passed to broaden the program of vocational education. A list of these acts would include the George-Deen Act, which enlarged the vocational-education program to cover distributive occupations, and the George-Barden Act, which extended the program beyond the states to territories. (Readers interested in social work will also find a striking similarity between the Smith-Hughes Act and the Social Security Act of 1935, with regard to federal-state cooperation.)

One may look forward in the future to a continuation of the venerable tradition of federal aid to education. New congressional acts will be passed and will continue to offer federal assistance to education when the well-being of the nation demands this sort of help. It is very likely that future acts will follow the permissive, nondictatorial pattern of the Smith-Hughes Act. The trend is obvious and has been obvious for many years, despite fears since Revolutionary days of mailed-fist federal control over the states.

The Federal Courts and Education

Ever since the United States was founded—in fact, even before—a question has arisen again and again. The question is, What agency in our nation shall be the final determinant of what is right or wrong governmentally, of what is in or out of bounds constitutionally, of what is in accordance with or what violates American legal tradition? There have been times when the states have considered themselves the final determinative agency—thus the Virginia and Kentucky Resolutions during John Adams' administration, the South Carolinian ado about tariffs during Jackson's administration, and the Confederate attempt to secede from the Union when Lincoln was elected to the presidency. There have been times when the people considered themselves to be this final determinative agency—thus Shays' Rebellion shortly after the Revolutionary War, the Whiskey Rebellion during Washington's administration, and the picketing of integrated schools in Little Rock and New Orleans during Eisenhower's administration. The Supreme Court of the United States of America has come to consider itself the sole and final determinative agency. In fact, there is a term for this function that the Supreme Court performs: judicial review. Judicial review is the process whereby, through deciding cases brought to it, the Supreme Court also decides whether or not a given activity within the nation is in accord with the intent of the federal Constitution. In other words, the Supreme Court judges the judge. The right of judicial review on the part of the Supreme Court was established during Jefferson's presidency in the *Marbury* v. *Madison* case. In this now famous case, the Supreme Court declared a certain act of Congress unconstitu-

Herbert Lanks from Black Star

THIS IS THE BUILDING IN WHICH THE SUPREME COURT HAS RENDERED MOMEN-
TOUS EDUCATIONAL DECISIONS.

tional, thus establishing the precedent of judicial review. The words of the
decision are relevant: "It is emphatically the province and duty of the
judicial department to say what the law is." [4]

Through judicial review, the Supreme Court has most deeply affected
the direction American education has taken by delineating which practices
it can or cannot engage in. The Supreme Court, thus far in its history, has
offered decisions in only four basic areas of educative practice: it has attempted to define the status of private education; it has attempted to set
forth the appropriate relationship of religious instruction to public education; it has attempted to deal with segregation in public schools and colleges; and it has attempted to point out the limits of academic freedom. A
brief resumé of a few strategic federal cases from two of these four areas
will illustrate the telling effect that the Supreme Court does have on American educational policy.

The Supreme Court and Private Education

Two consequential attempts, separated both by a century of time and
by a continent of space, were made to cripple private education and thus

[4] I Cranch 137 (1803).

destroy it. The first attempt was made in New Hamphire in the second decade of the nineteenth century. The second attempt was made in Oregon in the third decade of the twentieth century. First, a look at the New Hampshire case.

Filled with the naturalistic spirit of the European Enlightenment, Jeffersonians, at the end of the eighteenth century and the beginning of the nineteenth, attempted to wrest control of the colleges from the hands of church groups and to place it in the hands of the states. The Jeffersonians were humanitarians who had a deep faith in the innate goodness of man, a deep belief that a utopian government could be established, and a deep suspicion of dogmatic, doctrine-bound, organized religion. Although the Jeffersonians tried to gain control of several colleges in several states, they were temporarily successful only in the case of Dartmouth College in New Hampshire.

Early in the nineteenth century a rift developed between the president of Dartmouth and his faculty and trustees. The Jeffersonians dominated the state legislature of New Hampshire, and they used this rift as the occasion to change Dartmouth from a private college to a state college. A new board of trustees was appointed, and the college had its name changed to Dartmouth University. The old royal charter of Dartmouth College, granted by the British monarch George III in 1769, was altered to accommodate these changes.

The trustees of the original Dartmouth College, refusing to resign, brought suit against William H. Woodward, secretary of the new Dartmouth University, to recover control of the establishment. The Superior Court of New Hampshire, with Jeffersonian leanings, decided against the former board of trustees. The case, known as *Trustees of Dartmouth College* v. *Woodward,* was appealed to the federal Supreme Court. The Supreme Court decision handed down in 1819 reversed that of the state court and returned the college to the original trustees.

The case is important for two reasons. First, the decision itself rested on the inviolability of a contract against impairment by a state legislature. This decision seemed to say that charters of corporations were contracts and that contracts could not be tampered with by state legislatures. This was a boon to *business* corporations as well as to educational ones. Second, it allayed the apprehensions of private colleges. No longer would they have to fear the possibility that states might appropriate their educational interests.

Now to the Oregon case. . . . In the turmoil of pent-up resentment and cultural sag after World War I, bitter people vented their wrath rather blindly against minority groups, which somehow, by being minority groups, were considered not quite American. This resentment is responsible, in part, for the heavily prejudiced national immigration laws of the 1920's. This same outburst in Oregon—stronghold of fundamentalist Protestantism —took the form of anti-Catholicism. More specifically, in Oregon it took the form of pressing for legislation to outlaw private schools, almost all of which were conducted by the Roman Catholic Church. The Oregon Constitution permits the passage of an act through the initiative process, a process by which the people themselves can initiate an act and bypass the legislature. The process was used by a virulent group of anti-Catholics to pass a compulsory education law in 1922. The act stipulated that, beginning on September 1, 1926, all normal children between the ages of eight and sixteen who had not completed the eighth grade would have to be sent to the local *public* schools in their districts "for the period of time a public school shall be held during the current year." The act was intended, of course, to deal a death blow to Roman Catholic elementary schools in Oregon. It broadly encompassed other private elementary schools in Oregon as well and, indirectly, threatened private secondary schools, which might be next in line for extinction.

The Society of Sisters of the Holy Names of Jesus and Mary, a teaching and social-work order that operated a series of educational establishments, challenged the constitutionality of the act. The sisters were aided by a private, nonsectarian school in Portland, the now defunct Hill Military Academy, the future of which was also in peril. The sisters (and the Hill Military Academy) sought, through court action, to restrain Governor Pierce from carrying out the intent of the compulsory education act.

Pierce v. *Society of Sisters* [5] was decided by the Supreme Court of the United States in 1925. The case hinged basically on the "due process clause" of the Fourteenth Amendment. The Society of Sisters had a going business enterprise, had thousands of dollars invested in structures and equipment necessary to educate children, had valuable good will built up among its patrons, had a trained staff, had long-term contracts with both teachers and parents. The compulsory education law would have rendered useless all of these items of property if put into effect. Amendment Fourteen stipulates that a state cannot enact a law that denies property rights without due process of law. The Supreme Court agreed unanimously with the sisters and ruled that Oregon's law was unconstitutional.

Obviously, the decision permits parents to send their children to parochial schools. But there is a larger implication, too. It encompasses all private schools, sectarian or nonsectarian. "The fundamental theory of liberty upon which all governments in this Union repose excludes any general power of the State to standardize its children by forcing them to

[5] The twin case was *Pierce* v. *Hill Military Academy*.

accept instruction from public teachers only. The child is not the mere creature of the State. . . ." [6]

Taken together, the implications of the Dartmouth and Oregon cases are weighty. Through these cases the Supreme Court has exerted a substantial effect on the development of American education. The United States has swelling public educational systems. However, there is room for private education as well; private schools or colleges, as an alternative to public education, cannot be forced out by state action. If parents prefer to have their children educated in private establishments, they have every right to do so. Had the Dartmouth and Oregon cases been decided the other way, some of the finest schools and colleges—leaders in American education, great because they have the opportunity to be different—might not exist now, because these cases are national in influence.

The Supreme Court and Segregated Schools

A second type of case will serve to illustrate further the effect of the Supreme Court on educational policy. Several states, particularly Southern ones, have segregated the races, especially the Negro and white races, for educational purposes. In a state such as Louisiana, each community would have a dual school system: there would be one set of schools for Negroes, another set for whites. This sort of practice was deemed constitutional because of the Supreme Court's 1896 ruling, in *Plessy* v. *Ferguson,* involving segregated transportation facilities. The court had stated in this case that ". . . equal, but separate, accommodations for the white and colored races . . . are not in conflict with . . . the Constitution of the United States." [7]

The applicability of *Plessy* v. *Ferguson* to higher education was first challenged in the Gaines case of 1938. The state of Missouri, which maintained segregated public schools and colleges, had created a public law school for white students at the University of Missouri, but had failed to make any provisions within the state for law-school education of Negroes. Young Lloyd Gaines, a Negro, sought admission to the all-white University of Missouri Law School, because no public law school for Negroes existed in the state. In *Missouri ex rel. Gaines* v. *Canada,* the Supreme Court of the United States ruled that whatever training a state chooses to furnish within its borders to its citizens must be made available on an equal basis to all, regardless of race.

[6] 268 U. S. 510 (1925).
[7] 163 U. S. 537 (1896).

The Gaines decision, however, did not rule out the possibility of segregated professional colleges. By 1950 the Supreme Court took a stand on the question of separate professional colleges in *Sweatt* v. *Painter*. Herman Sweatt, a Negro, desired admission to the all-white law school of the University of Texas, despite the fact that the state of Texas had instituted brand-new public legal educational facilities for Negroes in the late 1940's. Sweatt, being a Negro, was denied admission to the University of Texas Law School. His case was carried to the federal Supreme Court, which ruled in 1950 that separate facilities are by no means equal facilities.

. . . we cannot find substantial equality in the educational opportunities offered white and Negro law students by the State. In terms of number of the faculty, variety of courses and opportunities for specialization, size of the student body, scope of the library, availability of law review and similar activities, the University of Texas Law School is superior. What is more important, the University of Texas Law School possesses to a far greater degree those qualities which are incapable of objective measurement but which make for greatness in a law school. Such qualities, to name but a few, include reputation of the faculty, experience of the administration, position and influence of the alumni, standing in the community, traditions and prestige. It is difficult to believe that one who had a free choice between these law schools would consider the question close[ly].[8]

So stated the ruling of the Supreme Court, and Sweatt was admitted to the University of Texas Law School.

It became only a matter of time before the same logic would be applied to the lower schools. By 1954 a series of cases, originating in Kansas, South Carolina, Virginia, and Delaware, had come to the attention of the Supreme Court and were decided together under the label, *Brown* v. *Board of Education*. All of these cases contained a common issue. Negro children had to attend separate, segregated schools in their communities; they were not allowed in the schools for white children. Thus, it was claimed, these children were being deprived of the equal protection of the law guaranteed by the Fourteenth Amendment. The Supreme Court concurred unanimously. Separate facilities, kept separate solely on the basis of race, are inherently unequal. The opinion handed down by the Supreme Court quotes from one of the cases in the above series that had been heard in the United States District Court for the District of Kansas.

Segregation of white and colored children in public schools has a detrimental effect upon the colored children. The impact is greater when it has the sanction of the law; for the policy of separating the races is usually interpreted as denoting the inferiority of the negro group. A sense of inferiority affects the

[8] 339 U. S. 629 (1950).

motivation of a child to learn. Segregation with the sanction of the law, therefore, has a tendency to [retard] the educational and mental development of
negro children and to deprive them of some of the benefits they would receive
in a racial[ly] integrated school system.[9]

The Supreme Court concluded that the doctrine of "separate but equal"
had no place in the field of public education.

The Gaines, Sweatt, and Brown cases are samples of how the Supreme
Court has interpreted racial segregation in education. These court interpretations are now intensely affecting the course of American public education.
Despite recalcitrance, despite obduracy, despite vituperations, desegregation
is being accomplished school by school, district by district, county by county,
state by state. These court decisions are bringing desegregation to all levels
of education, from primary to graduate school. The import of such decisions
is summarized eloquently in *Brown* v. *Board of Education.*

Today, education is perhaps the most important function of state and local
governments. Compulsory school attendance laws and the great expenditures for
education both demonstrate our recognition of the importance of education to
our democratic society. It is required in the performance of our most basic
public responsibilities, even service in the armed forces. It is the very foundation of good citizenship. Today it is a principal instrument in awakening the
child to cultural values, in preparing him for later professional training, and in
helping him to adjust normally to his environment. In these days, it is doubtful
that any child may reasonably be expected to succeed in life if he is denied the
opportunity of an education. Such an opportunity, where the state has undertaken to provide it, is a right which must be made available to all on equal
terms.[10]

These cases, concerning the status of private education and segregation,
offer examples of two of the four educational areas about which the Supreme
Court has spoken. As mentioned earlier, the Supreme Court has ruled also
on the relationship of religious instruction to public education and on academic freedom. Several of the federal cases relative to religious instruction
in public schools were reviewed briefly in Chapter 3. While Supreme
Court decisions such as those described above do indeed affect education,
it should be borne clearly in mind that the cases are not decided on educational merits alone. The Supreme Court does not approve or disapprove
educational practices *per se*. Its decisions always rest on the *constitutionality* of these practices. Thus, the cases are argued and settled on constitutional rather than educational issues. Even so, the Supreme Court has
affected the tenor of education throughout the nation.

[9] 347 U. S. 483 (1954).
[10] *Ibid.*

Full Circle

And now we come full circle. This chapter began with a discussion of the constitutional bases of federal involvement in educational matters, and has ended with a discussion of the Supreme Court's interpretation of educational practices in the light of the Constitution. The federal government has a distinct role to play in the field of education. The next chapter will survey the functions of lower levels of government in providing and sustaining education.

The Chapter in Capsule Form

1. This chapter is about the governing and financing of American education by the federal government.

2. While the Constitution of the United States does not mention education specifically, the document is elastic enough so that the absence of the term has not meant the absence of the idea. The federal government is looked upon as having a legitimate legal role in the education of the American citizenry.

3. The executive branch of the federal government deals considerably with education.

3.1 The Department of Health, Education and Welfare is the only cabinet post carrying the term "education" in its title. Within the department are these agencies that handle educational matters.

3.11 The Office of Education performs advisory services and administers certain educational programs.

3.12 The Children's Bureau performs advisory and administrative functions.

3.13 The Office of Vocational Rehabilitation directs rehabilitative programs.

3.14 The department oversees the American Printing House for the Blind, Gallaudet College, and Howard University.

3.2 Many schools and colleges are supported by the federal government.

3.3 The Department of Justice, Bureau of Prisons, provides

educational facilities for prisoners in federally operated correctional institutions.

3.4 The Department of the Interior, Bureau of Indian Affairs, has maintained schools for Indians.

3.5 The Department of Agriculture has educationally oriented extension programs and operates lunch and milk programs for school children.

3.6 Numerous other departments, such as the Department of State, carry on educational activities also.

4. Congress, for years and years, has passed measures extending federal aid to education. A critical problem concerns whether or not Congress, in so doing, damages lower levels of government. The acts thus far passed, such as the Smith-Hughes Act, have not impaired the rightful roles of state and local governments in education.

5. The Supreme Court of the United States, through judicial review, has helped to define the constitutionality of education policies and practices throughout the land, such as:

5.1 The right of private schools and colleges to exist side by side with public facilities.

5.2 The right of all Americans to receive an education on equal terms.

For Supplementary Reading

ALLEN, HOLLIS P., *The Federal Government and Education*. New York: McGraw-Hill Book Co., Inc., 1950.

Some years ago, a Congressionally instituted commission, known popularly as the Hoover Commission, made a comprehensive analysis of the activities of the federal government. This book is the original report on education used by that commission. It is a careful investigation of the issues and problems of education from a federal viewpoint.

EWING, CORTEZ A. M., *American National Government*. New York: American Book Co., 1958, pp. 580–582.

Most textbooks devoted to a political-scientific description of the federal government spend only a few sentences on the subject of education. This book is offered as an example of such a work. Ewing gives a concise summary of the role of the federal government in education. The entire book is useful as a statement of the over-all structure and functioning of the federal government.

FELLMAN, DAVID, *The Supreme Court and Education* (No. 4 of *Classics in*

Education, ed. Lawrence A. Cremin). New York: Bureau of Publications, Teachers College, Columbia University, 1960.

> This booklet, available in pocketbook edition, contains digests of numerous twentieth-century Supreme Court decisions affecting education.

GRIEDER, CALVIN; PIERCE, TRUMAN M.; and ROSENSTENGEL, WILLIAM E., *Public School Administration,* 2nd ed. Baltimore: The Ronald Press Co., 1961.

> This is a standard textbook in school administration. Like so many books on the subject, its emphasis is on local school administration. Running through the book, however, are materials dealing with the federal government and education.

MARDEN, CHARLES F., and MEYER, GLADYS, *Minorities in American Society,* 2nd ed. New York: American Book Co., 1962, Chapters X–XV.

> These chapters offer a perspective on the Negro and the Indian in America. The treatment is sociological.

MORT, PAUL R.; REUSSER, WALTER C.; and POLLEY, JOHN W., *Public School Finance,* 3rd ed. New York: McGraw-Hill Book Co., Inc., 1960, Chapter XVII.

> A trenchant discussion of the federal financing of education.

United States Government Organization Manual. Washington: Office of the Federal Register, National Archives and Records Service, General Services Administration, published yearly.

> This official handbook of the federal government describes the agencies of the several branches of the government. It gives brief summaries of the work of these agencies. Very useful for reference purposes.

5

A Political and an Economic Approach to Education

Part II: State and Local Government and Education

The evolution of colonial education, largely in the service of religion, into the public school system of today is the story of changing conceptions regarding the American democratic society, of the functions of State-maintained education in such a society, and of the role therein of the free exercise of religion by the people. The modern public school derived from a philosophy of freedom. . . .

from Mr. Justice Frankfurter's concurring opinion in *Illinois ex rel. McCollum* v. *Board of Education,* 333 U. S. 203 (1948).

Thinking It Over Beforehand

Who manages our public schools?

How private are private schools?

What state agencies affect educational policy?

What local agencies affect educational policy?

Is it desirable to have wide discrepancies in the financial and academic status of different public schools within a state?

Education as a State Function

The previous chapter described the relationship between the federal government and education. The chapter began by raising the question whether there actually was a federal governance of education. By the time the reader finished the chapter, he might well ask whether there is any governance of education other than federal. The present chapter will offer an answer to this.

Education in America is a state function, primarily, and it is deeply entrenched as a state function for a number of reasons. First, as was pointed out in the previous chapter, there is no direct reference to education in the federal Constitution. Why it was omitted is the subject of a considerable amount of speculation. A shrewd guess is that religion was the major reason. Education was to a large extent in local church hands in the 1780's. The authors of the Constitution may have wanted to stay away from ecclesiastical wrath, knowing full well that the ratification of the Constitution would cause trouble enough without having organized religion needlessly annoyed over the control of education. Whatever the exact reason, education is not specifically mentioned in the Constitution. Because of this, it is included by default in the Tenth Amendment. This amendment leaves to the states the governmental functions not mentioned in the Constitution itself.

There are other reasons why education is a state function. Second, no one has ever challenged in the courts (federal or lower) the *right* of a state to control education. Whatever disputes there have been were over *methods* of control, not the right, as such. Third, the first federal aid to education, the Land Ordinance of 1785, which set aside acreages for the support of schools in the Old Northwest, implied that the particulars of organizing schools and of operating them would be left to the local residents, not to Congress. Fourth, in the Colonial period, education was in the hands of local or Colonial powers, whether secular or sacred. Fifth, even before the federal Constitution was written, several states in the Revolutionary or immediate post-Revolutionary period included in their state constitutions the suggestion that education was an enterprise for which the state should make provision. Sixth, all of these factors were part of a larger reason: they set precedents. Precedent is a reason in itself. Usage or custom is a strong power in determining the organization of government. It is customary for education to be considered a state governmental function— hence, it *is* a state governmental function.

Today all states support systems of public education. When the federal government becomes involved in education, it does so in order to guarantee that the states are handling certain educational situations adequately (for example, equitable educational opportunities for socially or physically handicapped citizens), or in order to advise state and local leaders in education (for example, the research work of the Department of Health, Education and Welfare), or in order to make it easier for the states to perform their educative function (for example, federal aid for vocational education), or in order to fill gaps that have gone unbridged by the states (for example, military colleges). Characteristically, the federal government, whenever feasible, works through the governments of the states in assisting education rather than dealing directly with state-sponsored schools. For example, if Jonesdale High School wanted federal funds for its program in vocational education, it would not apply directly to the federal government. Instead, the matter would be handled through a state board of vocational education (or some comparable body), which, in turn, would have direct dealings with the federal government.

That education is basically a state function and not a federal one means that the United States does not have a system of public education. Instead, there is a design of education that is unique to each of the fifty states. No state has precisely the same arrangement as any other state in every detail. When anyone talks about the "American system of education," he is talking about something that does not exist. There are American systems of education. This being the case, a writer who attempts, as I am, to discuss the state and local government of education in a single chapter finds himself in a most frustrating situation. To do justice to the subject he needs fifty chapters—one for each of the fifty state systems of education. But this sort of detailing belongs in an advanced volume in education rather than in a prefatory one. A single chapter on the subject cannot escape being filled with either sweeping generalities that apply only some of the time to only some of the states, or with tedious lists of minute modifications of educational practices that are similar in all fifty states. The present chapter will err in the direction of expeditious vagueness. Be forewarned. The chapter will describe similar tendencies among the states rather than emphasize variations among them. Each educational generalization may or may not apply to your state.

State Agencies That Directly Affect Education

On the state level there are diverse main branches and twigs of government that affect the orientation of education in the state. Several will be identified in the following paragraphs.

The Constitution of the State

The basic legal document of a state is its constitution. In a broad, general way, it establishes policy for the state. Reference has been made already to the fact that the federal Constitution fails to identify education explicitly. State constitutions are less obtuse. State constitutions ordinarily include some generic allusions, at least, to education as a state function.

People sometimes think that public schools are *local* schools. The public schools of Dallas are thought to belong to Dallas. The public schools of Albany are thought to belong to Albany. The public schools of Oakland are thought to belong to Oakland. The inference from this would be that each community or district controls its own schools, and that therefore education is a local function. The logic may be sound, perhaps, but the conclusion is not supported by fact. The fact is that from a state constitutional standpoint, and therefore from a legal standpoint, education is a state function, not a local one. It becomes a local function only to the extent that the state creates local agencies to carry out its educational task.

The State Legislative Body

The state constitution being a rather vague document, it is necessary for the state legislature to make the laws required to carry out the intent of the constitution. State legislatures pass enabling laws that make it possible for the state to carry out its educational duty as set by the constitution. Typically, the laws are varied and complex, applying usually to the areas of teacher certification, compulsory attendance at school, general rules governing the conducting of schools, the transportation of pupils, the assigning of state-collected money for educational purposes, and the like. It is by no means unusual for legislatures to go so far as to prescribe certain topics that must be included in the curriculum, such as kindness to animals, or state history and government, or the injurious effects of narcotics and alcohol. Whereas the state constitution assigns education to the state, the state legislative body details the techniques for offering and administering education within the state.

The State's Attorney General

Whenever a question arises as to the intent of a state law, the attorney general of a state has the duty of interpreting that law. No matter how carefully a bill has been worded before it becomes a law, questions will unavoidably arise as to precisely how the law will affect a specific situation. The attorney general is the person to turn to for the answer. The opinions of attorney generals can be highly significant and can have a direct bearing on governmental practices within the several states. Not infrequently, educational issues arise, and the attorney general is called upon to determine how the state laws apply with regard to them. Customarily, the rulings of the attorney general go undisputed. Thus, he can have an important effect on the course of education in the state.

State Courts

The agencies that adjudicate legal issues in the states are the courts. If people wish to challenge the rulings of an attorney general, they turn to the state courts. There are, of course, many other reasons for turning to a court, but no matter what the reason, the decision of a court (and this includes federal courts as well as state courts) is the final word, unless, as rarely happens, changes are made in the laws or the constitutions to override unfavorable decisions. This means, for students of education, that when the points in question have educational connotations, the courts normally have the last word. Thus, courts can exert a weighty force on the educational practices within a state.

The Governor of the State

The chief administrative officer of the state is the governor. He executes the laws of the state. He is, in effect, the chief educational administrator in the state, because it is his duty to see that the intent of the state's constitution and the intent of the state legislature's laws concerning education are fulfilled. This duty he delegates in part, as we shall discover soon. Even so, a governor who is vitally concerned about education can have a notable effect on the position and condition of education in his state for several reasons. First, as the respected chief administrative officer of the state, his public pronouncements in behalf of education help set the tone within the state with regard to educational matters. The public usually will weigh his words carefully. Second, it is the governor who, as the principal executive of the state, indicates to the legislature what policies he would like to have enacted as laws. Since education is a big enterprise and requires a great deal of money, he no doubt will let the legislature know what he wants done in this field. Third, as governor, he supervises and advises the various state boards and agencies, including educational ones, and he is usually heeded. Thus, he can have an indirect effect on the educative committees of the state. Fourth, frequently the governor is assigned the task of appointing people to state-level educational positions. (This will be alluded to again below.) His attitudes toward education will be reflected in the caliber and ability of the people he chooses. Fifth, the governor is commonly expected to prepare the budget for the state. His devotion to education will be mirrored in his willingness to assign adequate funds to the state's educational enterprises.

A Variety of State-Level Boards

Numerous boards associated with the executive branch of the state government and having educational functions are found in most states.

One such board is concerned with elementary and secondary education, and is often called the state board of education. Usually the members are appointed by the governor, and their terms are of sufficient length and staggered in such a way that no single governor during one term in office is able to appoint a majority of the board members. This type of organization has the effect of making the board nonpolitical—which is all to the good, since education receives rough treatment when it is used as a political toy or ploy. In general, the state board of education is a policymaking agency for elementary and secondary education in the state. If the state maintains public junior colleges (sometimes called community colleges), these will probably come under the survey of this board, too. The precise amount of power assigned to a state board of education will depend on the state constitution, the willingness of the legislature to grant it power, and the amount of authority delegated to the chief school officer and his staff (to be described below). As a rule, however, the state board of education formulates broad policies that concern such areas of education as the certification of teachers, the administration of school funds, minimum requirements for school buildings, and the curricular course of study.

In the previous chapter there was a discussion of the Smith-Hughes Act. States wishing to participate in the Smith-Hughes program (and subsequent programs that have augmented the original one) are required to have a state board of vocational education. Often the state board of education serves also as the vocational education board, although in some states it is separate.

There may be distinct state boards that determine educational policies for agencies designed to care for so-called exceptional residents of the state. These agencies might include schools for blind children, schools for deaf children, schools for children with other sorts of physical or mental handicaps, and schools within places of detention for juveniles or adults who have overstepped the law.

Then there are boards (or directors or regents or trustees) for the public higher-educational establishments of the state. In a few cases there is a single, unified board for all of the public colleges and universities within the state. More typically, each major higher-educational endeavor will have its own group of directors. These boards are policymaking councils, as are those committees alluded to in the previous paragraphs. It is rare for public junior colleges to be classified on the state level as belonging to "higher education." Thus, as pointed out above, ordinarily the policy for public community colleges is formulated by the state board of education rather than by some directorate of higher education.

A Chief School Officer

A chief school officer, or a commissioner of education, or a state super-intendent of public instruction is found in every state. While there is some logic for suggesting that the governor is the chief educational officer, the title is carried by another state official. The chief school officer works closely with the state board of education, if such a board exists in the state. Usually this officer is a fairly powerful governmental official. His duties tend to include the preparation of record-keeping forms for the use of the school administrators, the preparation of guides and handbooks for the various grade levels, the tabulation of data concerning the state's schools, speaking out for education throughout the state, administering the state's department of education (to be described next), and cooperating closely with the state board of education, the governor, and the legislature to improve the status of education in the state.

Selection of the chief school officer varies among states. Ideally, it is felt, his selection should be entirely removed from the political arena. That a man is a Republican or a Democrat, that he has an agreeable per-sonality, or that he can solicit votes readily will not guarantee in themselves his being a leader in education. The most nonpolitical way of selecting the chief school officer is to have the nonpolitical state board of education (itself appointed usually by several governors) do the appointing. Ideally, his term of office should be indeterminate (like that of a federal Supreme Court justice), making him more or less untouchable politically.

In a few states there is a chief *higher*-educational officer whose rela-tionship to the public colleges and universities is somewhat akin to that of the chief school officer to public elementary and secondary schools. The chief higher-educational officer is a coordinator of the administration and finance of public higher education. He serves also as a public-relations man for higher education. The financing of higher education is one basic reason for the creation of this office. It is usual for state legislatures at each session to pass measures for the financing of the state colleges and uni-versities. Each president of such a higher-educational establishment acts as a lobbyist in behalf of his college or university and presents his requests to the legislature. The result is that the most articulate and persuasive presi-dents, the presidents who are most astute as lobbyists, receive the most generous amounts of money. The colleges with presidents who are less successful at lobbying may suffer. In order to equalize the financing of public higher-educational establishments, some states have devised the plan of employing a nonpolitical, chief higher-educational officer. He makes a single, unified appeal to the legislature in behalf of all the public colleges and universities. To borrow an expression from the Community Chest, he "puts all 'begs' in one 'ask-it!' " The colleges and universities share equitably whatever funds he procures for them. This lessens the financial differences among the public colleges and universities within the state. Indirectly, to the extent that money buys superiority, this lessens the differences in academic excellence among them. Again, most states do *not* have a chief higher-educational officer.

The State Department of Education

The staff of the chief school officer is known as the state department of education. It reviews the credentials of potential school teachers and does the actual issuing of teaching certificates. It keeps the records collected by the chief school officer. It numbers among its members experts in various phases of elementary and secondary teaching and administration who serve as consultants to school personnel throughout the state. It approves or rejects plans for new school buildings. It makes sure that minimum educational standards are maintained throughout the state. It disburses the state funds budgeted for public schools. It approves curriculums and textbooks, and undertakes research activities.

Agencies Below the State Level That Directly Affect Education

Below the state level there are numerous public groups and officers whose functions affect education within the state.

School Divisions

Each state is segmented geographically into school divisions, customarily known as school districts. The term "district," however, has a precise meaning among educationists. For the sake of accuracy, these geographical segments, from a national viewpoint, will be referred to as school divisions. Sometimes school divisions coincide with political boundaries, but more often they do not. And even if political boundaries and school-division boundaries do coincide, the administration of the school division typically will be separate from the administration of the political unit. School divisions are created by the state, and their powers are limited by the state. Their function is to carry out, as a deputy of the state, the wishes of the state constitution and the state legislature on the local level relative to elementary and secondary education. There are five major patterns (or types) of school divisions throughout America, only one of which is common to the several states.

The large city as a separate school district is universal in America. Usually large cities are given a considerable degree of autonomy in educational matters, provided they conform to certain bare minimums as defined by the state constitution or legislature. Frequently, big-city schools will be conducted rather differently from those in other parts of the state—with different courses of study, curriculums, graduation requirements, certification requirements for teachers, and the like—but, of course, within the framework of the laws of the state.

The town as a school division is found in some of the older sections of America, harking back to the educational structure of Colonial Massachusetts. A town is more than a village or little city. It includes the people who live outside the village limits, but who are identified with the village. Theoretically the town is a community of interest, not merely an arbitrary block of land laid out by some geographer or surveyor. Thus, the town ordinarily is a cohesive local unit. As the consolidation of school divisions is becoming more and more common nowadays, there has been some attempt elsewhere in the United States to emulate the town pattern when setting up school districts. More about the trend toward consolidation later.

Occasionally a township or a county will be the school division. While a township is not a county and a county is not a township, these school divisions are similar enough to be considered together as a single type. Both counties and townships are arbitrary political divisions, but at the same time, they do exist, and because of this they are convenient divisions for educational purposes. Usually townships or counties are not communities of interest in the way towns are. The educational result is that people who may have little in common, except the fact that they live on one side rather than the other side of some imaginary surveyor's line, are assigned to the same school system. Usually the township or county division of schools is less satisfactory from the human standpoint than the town technique, because the former tend not to be communities of interest.

The district as the school division is widespread. It is the typical division in the West; in fact, it is a product of the frontier. Usually the school district bears no relationship to any political division, but it does (or, at least historically *did*) bear some resemblance to the town as a school division. School districts came into being in the horse-and-buggy days of the nineteenth century, and they developed primarily around elementary schools.

That school districts came into being before the transportation revolution has meant that they have been geographically small. Children were expected to be able to walk daily to and from the one elementary school in the district. Under these circumstances a school district could not be very extensive, or the children would meet themselves getting up in the morning and coming home from school at night. This is a reason why today there are more school districts than any other single type of local governmental unit in the United States.

Its small size has meant, in turn, that the school district, in most instances, has been also a community of interest. Somewhat isolated people who live within walking distance of one another often form a tightly unified group. This, indeed, is one of the explanations for the difficulty that administrators face when they attempt to erase or combine districts into consolidations.

Courtesy of Marion County, Oregon, Department of Education

THE LITTLE SCHOOLHOUSE SERVING A TINY SCHOOL DISTRICT IS BECOMING PASSÉ TODAY.

That school districts grew around elementary schools has meant that, as the high-school movement waxed strong, separate high-school districts have sometimes come into being. High schools usually draw from a larger area than does a lone elementary-school division. This has made for an overlapping, on occasion, between several elementary-school districts and a "union" high-school district, compounding, of course, the total number of school districts throughout the land. Bear these points in mind when consolidation is discussed later in this chapter.

In some parts of the country, school districts have increased in population as the nation itself has grown. In other parts, school districts have failed to grow in population, and they remain as a rather nostalgic reminder of the past, with their little red schoolhouses, solitary teachers, stark, narrow curricular and extracurricular offerings, and utter economic inefficiency.

Another alternative is for the state itself to be a single school division. This practice is uncommon, but not unknown, in the United States. It bears a resemblance to certain foreign school systems, such as that of France. This pattern places a great deal of power in the hands of the chief school officer of the state and the state board of education.

The Local School Board

Each school division has a local school board. If the entire state is a single school division, the state board of education may serve a dual function and be both the state board and the school board. If the state uses township divisions for its schools, there will be a school board for each township. If the school division is based on the county, there will be county school boards. If the state uses the town as its school division, there will be town school boards. If the state has the district system, each district will have a school board. Cities, as separate school districts, have their own school boards, too. Thus, it will be seen that the school board is ubiquitous. While the local school division is the agent of the state at the local level entrusted with carrying out the educative function, it is the school board that actually handles this function at the local level. If the school division is small in population, the school board itself will be the administrative director of the school. If the school division is sizable in population, the usual procedure is for the board to appoint an educational administrator. The school board in the latter case serves as a supervisory and policy-making board, with the administrator directing the managerial work within the school division. The board delegates its responsibilities for the actual operation of the schools to its administrator. Even so, the board, not the administrator, is *legally* in charge of the school division. Thus, school boards have the last word on the local level.

Duties of school boards are variable, but are likely to include (1) insuring that the state laws relative to education are abided by, (2) hiring and dismissing, or (if the division has an administrator) approving the employment and removal of, school personnel, (3) overseeing the formulation of a school budget, (4) providing means for collecting money for the schools, and (5) planning for the future with regard to building needs, curricular needs, equipment needs, personnel needs, and the like.

The school board is the official liaison between the people and their schools and between the state government and its schools. Thus, like Janus, it faces in two directions. Or perhaps the comparison might better be to the grain of wheat between the upper and the lower millstones. The school board must satisfy the state, or the state may classify the local school division as substandard and withhold funds from it. The school board must satisfy the local citizenry, too, or the local citizenry—neighbors of the school-board members—will use a variety of social controls to bring these members into line. Customarily, school-board members are elected popularly by the citizenry of the local school division. Usually the members run on a nonpartisan ticket. Notice once more that as a general rule, educational officials are kept out of the maelstrom of party politics. Standard procedure dictates that school-board members serve without pay. Whatever the motivations a citizen may have to become a member of a school board, they do not include the desire for income for his services.

The Office of Superintendent of Schools

All school divisions of any appreciable size have superintendents of schools. The superintendent of schools is the chief executive officer in the local school division. He is an administrator whose vocational training has been in the area of school administration. He probably holds a special administrative credential issued by the state department of education. Also, he probably holds a master's degree from some university. His status in the local school division is not unlike that of the president of a corporation: the corporation president is the head executive selected to implement the general policies of the board of directors, to which board he is responsible. Likewise, the school superintendent is selected by and responsible to the local school board, the policies of which he is expected to execute efficiently within the school division.

In states that do *not* have the county pattern of school divisions, there may be county superintendents of schools as well as local superintendents of schools. County superintendents of schools under these circumstances are becoming about as useful as chrome on an automobile; they add to the expense and complexity of the mechanism without adding to its efficiency or ability to function. Historically, county superintendents of schools served to advise and assist minuscule school districts that had no trained administrators and that were managed by local school boards composed usually of lay members. The trend toward the consolidation of school districts has rendered the office of county superintendent of schools passé, unless, of course, the county should become the basic school division. In such a case, the offices of local superintendent of schools and of county superintendent of schools probably would be merged.

The Principal

Each school has a principal who is directly responsible to the superintendent, if there is one. If there is not, as in the case of a tiny school division, the principal is directly responsible to the school board. The principal is the executive officer within the local school. In the business world his position is somewhat akin to that of branch manager of a corporation, the superintendent being the president of the entire corporation.

Darrel Volesky

THAT EDUCATIONAL EXECUTIVE WHOM STUDENTS KNOW BEST—THE PRINCIPAL.

Supervisors

Within the school division there may be specialists who supervise certain narrow aspects of the public-school program. Depending on the size of the school itself and of the school division, a supervisor may be responsible to one of the principals or to the superintendent of schools. The supervisors may be experts in such subfields as primary education, music, health, art, guidance, social work, vocational education, or physical education.

The Teacher

The administrator within the classroom is the teacher. He is responsible directly to the principal of the school in which he is employed, or perhaps to one or more intermediary supervisors, if there are any. The teacher looks like a rather lowly person in the educational hierarchy, but in fact, he is the reason for all of the above officers and agencies. Without teachers there can be no schools. This statement cannot be made with regard to principals, superintendents, school boards, chief school officers, or even legislators. These people are expendable and dispensable educationally. Only the teachers are indispensable if the educative processes are to function.

Extralegal Agencies That Directly Affect Education

A description of the state and local government of education would be incomplete without at least a passing reference to agencies within the state which have no legal control whatever over education, but which, at the same time, can affect education a great deal. I refer to pressure groups. (They will be discussed again in the next chapter.) The wishes of zealots, bigots, prophets, and reformers are heeded at least part of the time in matters pertaining to modifying curriculums, hiring or removing personnel, providing funds for educational purposes, or withholding funds. In fact, any matter that has educational overtones may activate pressure groups. Some social scientists, impressed by the power of pressure groups, suggest that we have in America not three branches of government, but four: executive, legislative, judicial, and pressure.

State and Local Financing of Education

Public schools and colleges sometimes receive money from federal funds or grants. Most of the money needed to operate them comes, however, from sources within the state. The sources of money within the state may be classified as falling into one or another of five major categories.

Tuition Fees

Often state colleges and universities charge students a modest tuition fee each quarter or each semester. Money from this source does not begin to offset the total cost involved in educating a student, but it helps. It is uncommon for public-school pupils to pay tuition.

Gifts

Private benefactors occasionally make grants or leave gifts to public colleges and universities. These may be quite munificent or they may be quite small. There may be conditions attached so that the money must be used only for a single specific purpose, or the money may be available for the general financing of the establishment. It is rare for public schools to receive sizable gifts or grants from private donors.

Earmarked Public Funds

Some money flowing into the coffers of the state or local school division is assigned specifically to educational uses and may be spent only for educative purposes. The precise sources of such funds are highly variable. Perhaps a certain percentage of the excise taxes on gasoline, or liquor, or tobacco must be set aside for education. Perhaps a portion of all revenue from sales taxes must be used for schools. Perhaps interest or royalty from certain public lands must go to education. Perhaps it is an entire tax, such as a specific property tax (and a special property tax is the usual tax in a school division). There are many other possibilities. In each case, the funds received have been dedicated or set apart specifically for the maintenance of educational establishments. They cannot be spent for anything else. A sizable proportion of the money used to finance schools is earmarked.

Appropriations

Education is becoming increasingly costly. As it does so, the above sources of revenue are proving to be insufficient. Therefore, the legislatures, during each of their sessions, find it necessary to take special educational funds out of current general monies for the support of schools and colleges. A general fund is not earmarked, is raised through any source of revenue, and is used to pay for the multifarious operating expenses of the state.

Borrowing

Borrowing money, for which interest must be paid, is a practice of schools and colleges principally for the purpose of financing new buildings and purchasing real estate. Sometimes money is borrowed to defray current operating expenses. In the former case, the loan will most likely be a long-term loan. In the latter case, it will be a short-term loan to keep the school in operation until anticipated revenues arrive. Frequently, state and local laws restrict the extent of borrowing that can be done by a school division or a public college.

Both the state and the school division raise funds for the maintenance of local schools. Often intermediate political units contribute also to the financing of schools. For example, counties may levy taxes or earmark funds to be distributed to local schools. Thus, the financing of public schools may come from numerous sources and levels of government.

Private Education and the Government

The word "private," in the expression "private education," suggests that private schools and colleges are entirely independent of public regulation or public financial assistance. Private education is far from independent of public government, as we shall see. For this reason some education-

Courtesy of the Office of Education, Archdiocese of Portland in Oregon

MOST SCHOOL-AGE CHILDREN WHO ARE ENROLLED IN PRIVATE SCHOOLS ATTEND PAROCHIAL SCHOOLS.

ists do not use the word "private," but substitute the word "protest" when referring to these schools and colleges. Supposedly, private education exists because of some sort of protest against public education—thus the term "protest educational establishments." The protest may be against statism, or against nonreligion, or against the inadequacy of teaching materials or techniques, or against lack of prestige of public schools, or against anything else. An important minority of school children attend private (or protest) schools. Over half of all post-high-school students who are continuing their formal education attend nonpublic establishments, if one includes in this list not only colleges and universities but also such moneymaking ventures as barber colleges, business colleges, drama schools, technical institutes, and trade schools.

Private schools and colleges come under the protection and support of federal, state, and local government in several ways.

In certain instances, educational establishments are chartered by some public governmental agency. If chartering is a legal necessity, the very existence of the private school is dependent upon the willingness of the government to allow it to operate. Not all private establishments that choose to call themselves schools or colleges are governmentally chartered, however.

In the foregoing chapter the Supreme Court case, *Pierce* v. *Society of Sisters,* was mentioned. The case dealt with the question of whether or not private elementary education could be outlawed by a state, and the decision was in the negative. Nevertheless, the Supreme Court in this decision did rule that a state has the constitutional power to oversee private schools. These are the exact words:

> No question is raised concerning the power of the State reasonably to regulate all schools, to inspect, supervise and examine them, their teachers and pupils; to require that all children of proper age attend some school, that teachers shall be of good moral character and patriotic disposition, that certain studies plainly essential to good citizenship must be taught, and that nothing be taught which is manifestly inimical to the public welfare.[1]

This decision has been used by various states as the authority for rigid inspection of private schools to insure that they meet the same minimum standards required of the public schools within their borders.

The federal, state, and local governments even offer financial assistance to private educational establishments. Several state constitutions specifically forbid assigning public money directly to private schools; it is assumed generally that it would be unconstitutional for the federal government to make direct gifts to private educational establishments if they are church-operated. Even so, public money is used to assist private schools and colleges.

The federal government, through research grants, loan funds, and the paying of the tuition of veterans, does help private colleges in particular and, to some extent, other private schools. The federal government also

---

[1] 268 U. S. 510 (1925).

permits the employees of private schools and colleges to participate in the federal social-security program, which involves old-age, survivor, and disability insurance for the employees.

Sometimes the state or a lesser governmental division helps private schools by furnishing textbooks, transportation, and, in a few instances, school supplies. This sort of state aid has been challenged in the courts when parochial schools have been involved. The court decisions have not been entirely consistent. In general, however, the decisions have revolved around whether furnishing these materials and services assists the students as such, or whether this assistance aids the establishment of a religion. If the decision is the latter, the practice is declared unconstitutional; if the former, the practice has been allowed under certain circumstances. When a state or local school division transports parochial-school students or furnishes their textbooks or supplies, the courts have viewed these policies as benefits to the welfare or protection of the children. A parochial-school child is protected from being run over on a busy thoroughfare if he is transported in a public-school bus. A parochial-school pupil's welfare is being benefited if he is given books or supplies with which he may learn the accumulated knowledge of his elders.

States also exempt nonprofit organizations, including schools and colleges, from taxation. This, too, is financial assistance to private establishments, since they escape having to pay what otherwise might be heavy taxes on their assets.

Some Trends in the State and Local Government of Public Schools

During the course of the twentieth century, several trends have become apparent in the area of state and local governing and financing of public schools. Five of these trends have been especially significant.

Increased Financial Role of State Government

There has been a trend toward having the state play an enlarged role in the financing of public schools. This, in fact, is part of a national trend toward centralization in the financing of general-welfare functions of government, whether the function be health, economic security, education, or other.

The bases for the state's increased participation in helping to defray the cost of education are many. (The student should be apprised of the fact that they are the same bases, in general, that are used as arguments by advocates of increased *federal* assistance to education.)

First, wide discrepancies exist in the ability of various school divisions within the state to raise adequate funds to support a respectable educational program for the pupils. A little community composed mainly of sub-marginal farmers cannot possibly support as fine an educational system as can a booming, bustling, opulent industrial or commercial area. The taxes necessary to support even a frugal, minimal program in the former case could be economically killing. (Remember Chief Justice John Marshall's statement that the power to tax involves the power to destroy.) On the other hand, the latter community could probably support a program far above the minimum level with only a nominal tax rate.

Second, the regions of the state having the highest ratio of children to adults are often the areas that are least able to pay for schools. Conversely, the areas with the lowest ratio of children to adults are, as a rule, those that have the highest potential source of tax revenues. The highest ratios of children to adults are found usually in modest residential suburbs and in rural areas. The residential suburbs, by definition, lack taxable big-business properties, which are a prime source of revenue. Rural areas are often farm areas. Farming has been such a precarious occupation in America that the federal government has had to subsidize it for years and years. These areas with high ratios of children, therefore, are likely to lack the economic potential to pay the full cost of educating their children. School divisions having a low ratio of children to adults usually are urbanized, industrialized, commercialized areas that are the centers of wealth in the state. There is no inevitable positive relationship between the need for educational facilities and the ability to afford them.

Third, Americans are famous for being mobile. Yearly a large minority changes its place of residence. Suppose that a child were educated in a poverty-stricken school division that had very low educational standards. His education would in all probability be inferior. He might be little more than a functional illiterate, even though he had gone to school. Then, later, when he matures, he moves to another community. How different would his contribution to the new community be if he had been well educated? His vote, when he goes to the polls, will weigh just as much as that of a better-educated person. A poorly educated person is likely to earn less than the person with a good education. Thus, the former will pay fewer taxes than the latter for the support of public endeavors. In fact, the latter will be required to pay proportionately more taxes if poorly educated residents cannot shoulder their fair share of the taxes. This discussion is sufficient to make the next point. For purposes of self-protection, communities want their future residents to be well educated. A well-educated person is likely to make a greater potential contribution, both tangible and intangible, to the community than that same person with latent talents untapped. The way to insure that future residents will be well educated is to insist that all of the schools in the state come up to at least a certain minimum standard. This, in turn, means that the poorest schools must have sufficient money to pay for minimum standards. If the local school division cannot raise the funds, the funds will have to be supplied from sources outside the division.

Fourth, from a humanitarian standpoint, Americans have a high regard for children. Children are looked upon as our means to group immortality. They are our most prized natural resource. At the same time, we believe that all of the children of our state deserve the finest education that we can give them. No child ought to have to go to a run-down, fifth-rate school because of the accident that he lives in a poor school division. This humanitarian attitude toward children has been a stimulus also for having increased state support for schools.

The increased state participation in the financing of schools has had its problems. One of them is to make sure that a school division will not shirk its rightful financial role when it knows that the state is increasing its allocation to that division. Stated differently, School District *A* is poor and raises paltry funds for education within its own district, so the state pays 60 per cent of the cost. School District *B* is wealthy and raises magnificent sums for education within its district, so the state pays only 10 per cent of the cost. Why should not School District *B* collect fewer funds within its district so that the state will pay 60 per cent of its school expenses, too? Generally the way this problem is averted is that the state uses a financial formula to equalize the cost of education on the basis of ability (which is not the same thing as willingness) of a school division to pay for a minimum educational system within its borders. In this way, some school divisions get proportionately more than others, but a minimum program is guaranteed throughout the state in all schools.

Consolidation

There has been a trend toward the reorganization of school divisions into larger, consolidated districts. Reasons for this trend can be summarized rapidly. First, the transportation revolution has meant that schools no longer have to be within walking distance of the pupils. A child can often cover ten miles in a school bus more quickly than he can walk one mile, even though the bus stops several times along the way. Second, little, one-room schools are inefficient educationally, and they make the per-pupil cost of education very high when compared with schools large enough for each teacher to teach one grade only. Third, population shifts may reduce the size of an already small student population in some school divisions, making it less possible for the division to offer a substantial educational program. Fourth, both elementary and secondary curriculums have been greatly broadened, but enriched course offerings are impractical unless there is a large-enough number of enrollees. Fifth, state legislatures have increased the proportion of the financial burden of education that they bear. As they have done so, they have been less and less willing to permit educationally and financially inefficient, small school divisions to continue operating independently. Education is a state function. Therefore, the state legislatures have the right to reorganize the structure of their educational systems if they see fit.

The movement toward reorganization into larger consolidated districts has developed along with the automobile industry. By the 1920's, the automobile was an accepted adjunct of American life; also by the 1920's, educationists and politicians were beginning to weigh the merits of merging school divisions into larger consolidated districts.

Early attempts at consolidation met resistance. Consolidation, in fact, has developed a bad name in some sections of the United States. Consolidation was new, and there were early, zealous advocates who made mistakes. Mistakes are inevitable when a new invention is tried out, but they

Courtesy of Marion County, Oregon, Department of Education

CONSOLIDATED SCHOOLS ARE BECOMING EVER MORE PREVALENT.

are also a means of learning. They help explain why it is that later generations can have a more complex culture than earlier ones. Later generations stand on the shoulders—often the bent shoulders—of previous generations. The mistakes made by pioneers in consolidation were mainly oversights of a social and economic nature. Comments have been made already about the cohesiveness to be found within some communities. In a tiny neighborhood, the school may be the focal point of that cohesiveness. To close the school and transport the pupils to the new consolidated school may effect a deep social loss, which the people will resent. There is another dimension to cohesiveness also. A person's identification with a particular community has the effect of making him very loyal to it and, at the same time, encourages him to look upon other communities, especially those close at hand, as rivals. A considerable amount of animosity between communities can develop. Now, if two rival communities are assigned to one consolidated school district, what results are likely to occur? Unless the administrators involved are exceedingly adroit, the results can be most disastrous educationally.

The chief oversight of the pioneers in consolidation was the economic value of a farm child to his parents. When children can commute to and from school quickly, they can add to the farm income by doing a host of chores. If they must spend hours riding a school bus, the chores must be left undone or someone else's work must be cut short. Farmers who eke out a precarious living are not anxious to lose the economic contributions of their children.

Contemporary educational administrators who act as planners in the reorganization and consolidation movement are careful to make reorganized school districts follow patterns of community spirit whenever feasible. They put social cohesiveness to work where it is present. They build cohesiveness where formerly it was lacking. They recognize that consolidation need not mean closing little schools and building large ones. The little schools can sometimes be used in the reorganized district, although their function may be changed. For example, a two-room country school that is absorbed into a consolidated district may be used still for the first- and second-grade pupils in the adjacent area. Or a small elementary school may be converted into the junior high school in the reorganized consolidated district. In this way, community allegiance to the school can be retained while, at the same time, smaller communities can be joined to larger ones educationally. Continuing to operate the existing schools also lessens the transportation problem. During the period since World War II, the reorganization movement has been much better received. Yearly there are fewer and fewer school divisions, as consolidated, larger districts become ever more common.

Standardization

There has been a trend toward increased standardization of public schools within the state. This trend toward standardization is traceable to various factors.

First, at each legislative session, state legislatures typically pass a series of laws relating to the governance of schools. This is one of the inevitable governmental "facts of life." Laws become dated and need to be recast. Experience may show that laws are now needed where once there were none, or insufficient ones. Legislators spend months each session developing laws. Some of the laws they develop are of an educational sort, and some of the educational laws place requirements on local schools. Every time a new law *requires* that schools adopt a particular practice, they become more similar than before.

Second, education is identified as an American panacea, a cure-all. When a problem arises, Americans are likely to see its solution in better education of the citizenry: if the citizens can just learn about a particular subject, there will be no problem any longer with regard to that subject. Americans believe in education as the cure-all whether it works or not, and so they use it. They believe that if people only knew how wonderful democracy is and how demoniacal communism is, all sane people would choose democracy and eschew communism. So they pressure their state legislatures into passing laws requiring that all schools *must* include in their curriculums instruction in the benefits of democracy and the horrors of communism. They believe that if people know the history of their state and nation, they will be loyal to their native land. So Americans pressure their state legislatures into passing laws *requiring* all schools to teach state and national history courses. They believe that if children are exposed to the lives of great people, they will emulate those people and grow up to be fine adults. So they pressure their state legislatures into passing laws *insisting* that instruction be given concerning the lives of Frances Willard or some other folk heroes or heroines. And so it goes. The end result is that a great deal of required subject matter must be taught in all schools. This also has a homogenizing effect on education.

Third, as states assume a larger share in the financing of education, they require that schools come up to a certain minimum level regarding such particulars as courses of study, the length of the school day and school year, the keeping of certain records, and the qualifications of teachers. If schools do not meet the minimums, state funds are withheld. Few schools dare resist this sort of pressure to conform.

Fourth, educators themselves have contributed to the standardization of secondary schools and colleges by instituting accrediting agencies. The first such agency was the University of Michigan, which, in 1871, began to admit without entrance examinations capable students who had graduated from those Michigan high schools that were deemed acceptable by the university. Since 1871, agencies have been developed that have become regional and, in a few cases, national in scope. These accreditation agencies have judged secondary schools and colleges on the basis of such criteria as preparation of their teachers, quality of instruction offered, adequacy of educative materials, length of the school term, and, in the case of some high schools, the performance of their graduates in college. Only those schools and colleges meeting the standards established by the accreditation association have been accredited. Because the reputation and prestige of an educational establishment will suffer unless that establishment is accredited, the movement toward accreditation has tended to be a movement toward the homogenization of educational practices throughout the nation.

Increased Scope of Activities Associated with the Local School Division

Once upon a time the work of the local school division revolved almost entirely around a one-room elementary school in which little children learned to read, write, and cipher. As public secondary schools emerged, existing school divisions or unified districts or consolidated districts have accommodated themselves to offering an advanced public-school education. During the twentieth century a still more advanced type of public education is becoming attached to the school district: the public junior college or community college. It is not unusual for the junior college to be housed in the same facilities as those used by the local high school, and for the two faculties to be merged. In California, for example, a person who has been certified to teach on the secondary level is also certified to teach in a public junior college in that state. The thirteenth and fourteenth years of schooling are defined frequently as belonging to secondary education. From the administrative standpoint, this may mean that the superintendent of schools of a large school district will be not only the official responsible for elementary and high-school education; he may also have the function of college chancellor.

As schools in America have become youth centers of a social-work variety (a trend described in Chapter 3), the administrative duties connected with public education have increased greatly. The nonacademic life of the pupils has become more and more the province of the schools. Provisions for these other facets of students' lives have appeared as a result. Consider some illustrations.

Many schools in America are in the restaurant and vending businesses. A school without facilities for preparing and serving hot lunches to the pupils is thought to be obsolete. Many have school stores or some counterpart (perhaps vending machines) to sell anything from pencils and ink to apples and soft drinks. The schools may also operate book-rental agencies if textbooks are not furnished free of charge to the students.

Schools operate limousine services, in the form of school buses, to bring pupils from their doorsteps to the schoolyard and back again daily. Numerous school divisions have a staff of medical experts to insure that the physical well-being of the students is not neglected. Some large divisions even hire psychiatrists.

Courtesy of Superior Coach Corporation

MANY SCHOOLS NOW HAVE TRANSPORTATION FACILITIES FOR THEIR STUDENTS.

The growth and popularity of the extracurriculum has brought organization after organization into being. These organizations must be supervised and their activities scheduled and coordinated. During the last century the public grew to expect educational establishments to furnish spectacular sports exhibitions for the community. This habit began first on the collegiate level; it is now deeply entrenched on the senior-high-school level, and is beginning to make inroads into the junior high school. A glance at the sports section of a newspaper will offer ample evidence. School administrators find themselves almost in the position of fight promoters as they arrange interscholastic sporting events.

All of these services and activities have multiplied many times the administrative and supervisory work that must be performed in the operation of an up-to-date school division.

More Nonteaching Specialists

Related to this last trend is another. There has been a tendency toward the employment of an increasing proportion of nonteaching specialists in the educational field. States, lesser political units, and local school divisions hire more and more specialists whose positions are administrative or supervisory rather than directly educative. In industry or the military many of these people would be called staff appointees. This is part of a much larger governmental trend in America toward bureaucracy. Specialized staff positions in education that would have been undreamed of a century or so ago are rife nowadays. To illustrate, in a sizable state department of education one probably would find such nonteaching educational specialists as: fiscal specialists, public-relations specialists, publication specialists, clerical specialists, research specialists, statistical specialists, legal specialists, language-arts specialists, nature-studies specialists, social-studies specialists, art specialists, music specialists, health and physical-education specialists, kindergarten specialists, driver-training specialists, transportation specialists, school-building specialists, reorganization and consolidation specialists, school-lunch specialists, handicapped-children specialists, able-children specialists, occupational specialists, agricultural-education specialists, home-economics-education specialists, trades- and industries-education specialists, distributive-education specialists, adult-education specialists, vocation-rehabilitation specialists, educational-media specialists, and textbook specialists. Counterparts for at least some of the above positions are found likewise in larger school divisions. Sometimes the administrators and their staff specialists seem to be moving in the direction of outnumbering the classroom teachers!

Public education is big business. No wonder education is the most expensive of all state-sponsored governmental activities. No wonder, also, that education has become far more than a log with an instructor at one end and a pupil at the other. Ours is a complex technological age, calling for a great deal of specialization, even in the field of education. This, indeed, is one of the hallmarks of our age.

The Chapter in Capsule Form

1. Education in America is first and foremost a state function.

2. Each state has its own system of education, which is somewhat unique. There is no American system of education.

3. Several state-level agencies and officers help to define and direct education.

3.1 The constitution of the state sets the legal basis for education within the state.

3.2 The state legislature defines more precisely the pattern of education in a state.

3.3 The attorney general of the state interprets the laws pertaining to education.

3.4 The state courts also interpret the laws pertaining to education.

3.5 The governor, as the executive head of the state, is also a leader in state-sustained education.

3.6 Several state-level boards, especially the state board of education, help to implement education matters.

3.7 The chief school officer is the executor of education at the state level.

3.8 The state department of education functions as the staff of the chief school officer.

4. On a lower than state level, there are other agencies and officers that help to define and direct education.

4.1 Geographically, there are local school divisions that contain the actual school facilities. States differ in the way they are divided into geographical school divisions. The school division puts into effect the policies of the state-level educative agencies.

4.2 The local school board is the semi-executive, semi-legislative committee governing the local school division.

4.3 A large school division usually has a trained person as its chief administrative officer, the superintendent of schools.

4.4 Each school plant typically has an administrator, called a principal.

4.5 A school division or a school plant may have one or more supervisors who are specialists.

4.6 At the base of the administrative hierarchy are the classroom teachers.

5. Not only is there an official administrative framework of education within the state, but there are also unofficial agencies, known as pressure groups, that influence and direct education within the state.

6. Within the state itself, some of the money for the financing of the current expenses of public education comes from tuition fees and gifts. Most money for public education, however, comes from earmarked

funds and appropriations. Schools also borrow money—usually to enlarge or remodel physical facilities.

7. Private education comes under governmental influence, just as public education does, but to a lesser degree.

8. Among the trends in state and local governing and financing of education are these:

8.1 The financial contribution of the state toward defraying the cost of education has been on the increase.

8.2 School divisions are being reorganized and consolidated into larger school districts, which are more defensible from both a financial and an educational standpoint.

8.3 Differences in educational standards among schools within the state are lessening as uniformity increases.

8.4 The administrative work of the local school division is growing in quantity as new services and activities are added to the schools.

8.5 Education, as the most expensive and one of the vastest functions performed by the average state, is becoming more and more a bureaucracy that employs increasing numbers of nonteaching specialists.

For Supplementary Reading

ANDERSON, WILLIAM; PENNIMAN, CLARA; and WEIDNER, EDWARD W., *Government in the Fifty States*. New York: Holt, Rinehart, and Winston, Inc., 1951, 1960, Ch. XXI.
   A summary statement of tendencies in the governing and financing of state educational systems. The authors are political scientists.
The Book of the States. Chicago: Council of State Governments, published biennially.
   See the articles on education. This reference book is used commonly by political scientists.
DAHLKE, H. OTTO, *Values in Culture and Classroom*. New York: Harper & Brothers, 1958, Part III.
   Dahlke offers a sociologically oriented picture of the power structure of education.
MORT, PAUL R.; REUSSER, WALTER C.; and POLLEY, JOHN W., *Public School Finance*, 3rd ed. New York: McGraw-Hill Book Co., Inc., 1960.
   Several chapters in this authoritative volume deal with state and local roles in the financing of education.

Mort, Paul R., and Ross, Donald H., *Principles of School Administration,* 2nd ed. New York: McGraw-Hill Book Co., Inc., 1957.
  Of the many textbooks on the subject of school administration, this one is recommended as one of the best. Much of the book is applicable to the state and local levels of educational administration.
Pate, James E., *Local Government and Administration.* New York: American Book Co., 1954, Ch. XX.
  This book, written by a political scientist, gives a political-scientific slant on the state and local government of education.
Thurston, Lee M., and Roe, William H., *State School Administration.* New York: Harper & Brothers, 1957.
  One of the very few books that are addressed specially to the administration of education at the state level.

Each state will have numerous pamphlets, bulletins, and other printed matter about education within its borders. These are available through the state's department of education. For specific details concerning the educational organization of a given state, consult these publications.

Two other excellent sources of information about education within a particular state are various publications of the National Education Association and the Office of Education of the Department of Health, Education and Welfare. The latter's *Biennial Survey of Education in the United States* contains authoritative statistics.

6

A Sociological Approach to Education

The Fourteenth Amendment, as now applied to the States, protects the citizen against the State itself and all of its creatures—Boards of Education not excepted. . . . That they are educating the young for citizenship is reason for scrupulous protection of Constitutional freedoms of the individual, if we are not to strangle the free mind at its source and teach youth to discount important principles of our government as mere platitudes.

from *West Virginia State Board of Education et al.* v. *Barnette et al.*, 319 U. S. 624 (1943).

Thinking It Over Beforehand

What makes one community different from another?

Why are schools in different communities not alike?

Are the attitudes of the public important in determining the quality of education?

Are opportunities for a *full* formal education distributed equally among all of America's children?

How is social class related to education?

An Above-Average Suburb

When the twentieth century began, Ashburn, population about 200, was a tiny agricultural hamlet fifteen miles away from the heart of a city of 100,000 people. The hamlet's business center contained a combination general store and post office, a feed store, a church, a Grange hall, and a school. The school was housed in a two-storey frame building, the lower floor devoted to the elementary grades, the upper floor to an embryonic high school. The community was a farm community; without farming there would have been no Ashburn.

Today the nearby city approaches the half-million mark in population. Since World War II there has been a steady migration of people from this city to its suburban areas. Real-estate promoters and others have brought some of these migrants to Ashburn. The result has been that by 1960 there were 10,000 people living in Ashburn.

Once upon a time, back in the 1920's and 1930's, people moved into suburbs in order to escape the high cost of city living. A person earning modest wages could supplement his meager earnings by becoming a "spare-time farmer." He could procure a few acres in the suburbs, build a tarpaper shanty, raise several dozen chickens, have a cow or a goat, cultivate a vegetable patch, and grow some cane or tree fruits. His cost of living would be lower in the suburbs than in the slums, or near slums, of some city. By working on his miniature farm every morning before going to work, every evening after coming home, and on weekends and holidays, he and his family could raise their standard of living a step or two. A few of these people had moved into the Ashburn area during the Great Depression.

But the situation has recently undergone deep changes. The migration to Ashburn after World War II has been made up of an entirely different sort of suburbanite. These new suburbanites are junior executives, successful professionals, and prospering merchants. Their place of employment is the big city. They sought, however, to escape from the confines of city life. They wanted to capture a different way of life for themselves than the one they had in the city. They anticipated that living costs would be higher in Ashburn than in the city—and they were right. Their incomes are high enough to permit them to gain those supposed benefits that come from suburban living. The houses that they have purchased in Ashburn are new and excellently constructed. According to 1960 standards, their homes are in the $40,000 to $70,000 class. Their ample garages usually house two or three cars, one of which, almost invariably, is a late-model station wagon and the other (also almost invariably) a late-model compact European car. Several of the residences have private swimming pools.

No longer are there any farms in Ashburn. Some of the farmers have remained in the community, but they have become real-estate promoters, having divided their farms into tracts. Other farmers sold their farms and fled to new farms beyond the periphery of the sprawling city.

A major reason why the farmers have left is that taxes have mounted. The new arrivals in the community, while wanting to capture somewhat the idyllic rural way of life, at the same time wanted to retain all of the ease of the urban way of life. This has meant that the new residents have demanded and obtained such urban comforts as paved streets, cement sidewalks, adequate street lights, effective sanitary services and facilities, playgrounds and parks, police protection, and superior schools. All of these items cost a considerable amount of money, and have meant that taxes have skyrocketed since World War II. Taxes for such services and facilities as the above are based usually on property holdings. Under these circumstances, the farmers could not possibly operate exorbitantly taxed acreages at a profit. Not only have the farmers moved away, but so have the "spare-time farmers." No longer can one avoid high living costs by residing in Ashburn.

The character of Ashburn itself and of its residents has changed completely. Replacing the farms are acres upon acres of commodious tract homes. The general store–post office is gone. In its stead are neon-lighted, sparkling, giant shopping centers with their chain grocery store, chain drug store, chain variety store, and a series of shops for dry cleaning and shoe repairing. The farmers and "spare-time farmers" are gone. In their stead are substantial, fairly high-status suburbanites.

The new adult migrants who come to Ashburn are usually married and in their thirties or forties when they arrive. They bring with them, typically, a family of school-age children. This means that the school-age population of Ashburn has greatly increased since World War II. The adults coming into the community are highly educated, the junior executives and merchants often being products of university departments of economics or business administration. The professionals have become professionals after years and years of advanced study. The wives of these men usually are college graduates, too—several of them having majored in education. They want their children to receive excellent schooling. Having received a great deal of education themselves, they can recognize superiority and inferiority in education when they see it. They are willing to tax themselves heavily in order to procure the sort of schools that they feel their children should have.

Some of the finest school buildings in the state are located in Ashburn. There are three beautifully constructed, excellently equipped elementary schools. There is an equally superior junior high school. The senior high school is as praiseworthy as the others.

Education in Ashburn

The impact of the new residents upon the schools of Ashburn has been both direct and definite. It can be summarized thus:

First, instead of the earlier interest in a Smith-Hughes type of "practical" education, today the demand is for a rigorous academic curriculum that will equip a student to enter easily an "Ivy League" type of college. And most of the graduates do attend college.

Second, where once the Parent-Teacher Associations spent their energies planning money-raising ventures, today the PTA's are concerned with pupil progress, pupil reports, adequacy of library materials, and effectiveness of school methods and equipment.

Third, where once the school board watched every nickel and dime in order to keep costs at a minimum, today it is dedicated to excellence regardless of cost. The members of the school board, themselves highly educated, have an understanding of what it means to have a school staffed by competent people. The school board knows that one gets what one pays for, by and large, in hiring a person, and it wants only the best. By state standards, salaries are high in the Ashburn school system. Some of the most capable teachers and administrators in the state are employed there. The board has little difficulty in finding teachers. Applicants far outnumber openings on the staff. Competent, adequately trained people want to teach at Ashburn.

Fourth, where once the teachers were among the very few well-educated people in Ashburn, today they are no better educated than most of the other adults in Ashburn. In fact, some of the adults are better educated than the teachers. These adults, as parents, are somewhat demanding of the teachers. They know whereof they speak when they talk about education. Elusive answers or vague statements filled with pedagogical clichés are most unacceptable to them. These people can talk about the problems of educating children at every grade level. They read with interest the sections on education in weekly news magazines. They are familiar with the writings of James Conant and Martin Mayer. They expect the teachers to know as much as they do—if not more—about education. They are most critical of poor teaching and full of praise for able teaching.

Fifth, where once the schools in Ashburn catered to several types of students, today they have taken on much of the flavor of the nonparochial private school. Nonchurch private schools typically cater to a single social stratum of the society rather than to all of America's children. The backgrounds of their students are homogeneous for the most part. The families of their students are secure financially, having incomes well above the average. The curriculum of the nonchurch private school is likely to be much more rigorous academically than that of the average public school. These are characteristics of the schools in Ashburn, too.

A Below-Average Village

Rose of Sharon began, like Ashburn, as an agricultural village. Unlike Ashburn, Rose of Sharon remains an agricultural village. Located in the arid Southwest, Rose of Sharon came into being when water was brought to the parched desert soil by means of a governmentally sponsored reclamation-irrigation project. Without water the area would revert again to a wild state occupied by sagebrush, cactus, jack rabbits, and rattlesnakes.

The unincorporated town of Rose of Sharon has a population of approximately 1,000 inhabitants. Community ties extend beyond the limits of the village, some five miles in each direction. The farmers in this ten-times-ten-mile surrounding area consider themselves residents of Rose of Sharon. They do their banking, transact their business, have their hair cut, fight their influenza germs, repair their teeth, attend church, belong to social organizations, and send their children to be educated in Rose of Sharon. There are half as many farm residents as townsmen. The larger community of Rose of Sharon, which includes the farms as well as the village, is comprised of some 1,500 residents.

The economy of Rose of Sharon centers around farming. The principal agricultural crops are fruits and vegetables, which find their way eventually to the grocery stores of the nation. These crops demand intensive care, and necessitate the hiring of many field laborers. The mild climate of the Southwest and the human control over water makes it possible for agricultural activities to continue almost twelve months of the year. This, in turn, makes it possible for the community to support a permanent group of agricultural laborers who live in Rose of Sharon, rather than using itinerant field labor. The village of Rose of Sharon is the shipping point and trade center for the farms. It contains the usual array of stores and offices, as well as the homes of the business people and agricultural laborers.

Rose of Sharon is known as a very religious community. There are several churches in the village. Most of them range from inflexible and conservative to schismatic and dissentient. These pietistic groups are the dominant churches of the community. They have a puritanical effect on the life of Rose of Sharon.

The people of the community are socially heterogeneous rather than homogeneous. Nearly one person in five is Mexican, ethnically speaking; the others are of more direct European ancestry. Residents follow several different occupations all of which carry different prestige ranks. They are also marked by differences in income. Some people are more successful at their occupations than others. This, too, creates differences in income. The people differ in the amount of formal education that they have received, which in turn may somewhat affect occupations, income, and prestige. The level of living of different residents varies, as well. These differentials have formed the basis for social cleavages in Rose of Sharon. There are four fairly discrete social levels in the community, a condition that makes for social-class stratification. Diagram IV suggests the hierarchy of social classes in Rose of Sharon.

Class I is spoken of as "The Top People." It represents approximately 10 per cent of the community. Class I is composed of the successful farmers and businessmen. As a group, the members are clannish. They prefer engaging in social activities attended only by members of Class I. At the same time, members of Class I have a considerable amount of civic consciousness. They belong to the leading civic and social organizations, in

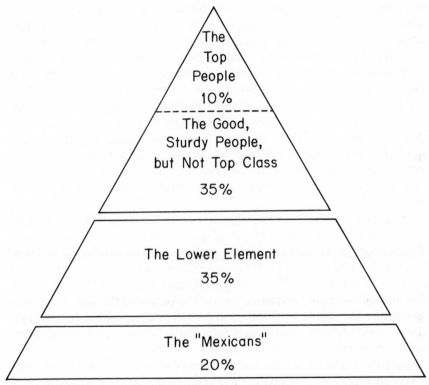

The
Top
People
10%

The Good,
Sturdy People,
but Not Top Class
35%

The Lower Element
35%

The "Mexicans"
20%

DIAGRAM IV.   HIERARCHY OF SOCIAL CLASSES IN ROSE OF SHARON.

which they play leadership roles. These people are the officers of the men's luncheon clubs, the women's clubs, and the lodges. All of the members of the local school board belong to Class I. The adults in Class I are not highly educated. Most of them attended, but did not complete, high school. They have achieved their social and economic status by means other than education for the most part—principally through inheritance. Members of Class I are active in church work, especially in laic roles of leadership, including the superintendency of the Sunday schools and presidency of the women's and missionary societies. These people have pleasant, well-furnished homes similar to the unpretentious ones seen in the mass-circulation house and garden magazines.

Class II is referred to by people not in this class as "The Good, Sturdy People, but not Top Class." Some 35 per cent of the community belong in this category. Occupationally these people are the less successful farmers and those people who work for the local businessmen, such as clerks in stores, attendants at service stations, mechanics in garages, and the like. As a group, these people are not well educated. Half of the adults in Class II did not attend school beyond the eighth grade. There are no college graduates in the group. These people are members, rather than officeholders, of the various civic, social, and religious organizations. They are also the people who do the backbreaking labor when a club or church has a dinner, a bazaar, or a sale of baked food. These people are very religious and are faithful communicants of pietistic churches. They place great emphasis on appearing respectable and on living exemplary lives as defined in puritanical terms by their churches. The homes occupied by the "Good, Sturdy People, but not Top Class" are modest in appearance and furnishings. Typically, their homes are old and the furnishings are old but comfortable. Class I and Class II, together, control the social life of Rose of Sharon.

Class III is called by those who are not of this class "The Lower Element." Thirty-five per cent of the people of the community are in this classification. All of the wage earners in the group are agricultural laborers. None of the adults in Group III completed high school, and most did not complete eighth grade. Their limited formal education helps to explain their limited social and economic status. The people in the first two classes do not like the people in Class III very well; they consider them riffraff. The "Lower Element" participates rather little in the social organizations of the community. It is isolated socially. Members of clubs do not want people from Class III in their clubs. Farmers who hire people to do squat labor find it distasteful to accept these same people as their equals in clubs or other social organizations. Some of the people in Class III attend the same churches as members of Class I and Class II, but when they do, they are treated as being of a lower order and are not listened to in decision-making matters. The other members of Class III who attend church go to those churches that are attended exclusively by members of Class III. The homes occupied by these people are very modest and of low standard. Some of the homes are unpainted shanties. The furniture is not unlike the houses themselves in appearance.

Class IV, the one remaining group, is composed entirely of people of Mexican ancestry, and is referred to as "The Mexicans." Twenty per cent of the residents are "Mexicans." They are looked upon by all of the other residents as being an inferior, foreign element, although several of the "Mexican" families have been in the United States longer than several of the other families. The "Mexicans" are employed as agricultural laborers, just as members of Class III are. This, indeed, is why the upper classes avoid close association with members of Class III. The Class III people are like "Mexicans" occupationally. The "Mexicans" do not attend the same churches as the other residents of the community, nor do they participate at all in the civic and social clubs and organizations of the community. The "Mexicans" are ghettoed and live together in one corner of the village. This district is called derisively "Mexican Town." Housing in this ghettoed area is shabby. It is considered an insult among the non-"Mexicans" to be told that one's house looks like a house in "Mexican Town," although several of the Class III homes fit the description. The "Mexican" adults are poorly educated: none has finished high school, and most have not gone beyond the fifth grade. The "Mexicans" are even more rigidly insulated from the social life of the community than members of Class III. The Spanish language is the tongue most used by the "Mexicans." The children learn Spanish before they learn English. In fact, the children rarely learn to speak English without an accent because of the isolation of the "Mexican" group from the English-speaking residents. The latter teach their children to avoid the "Mexican" children.

Education in a Divided Community

Just as the social make-up of Ashburn affects education, so, too, the social make-up of Rose of Sharon has educational consequences.

There is relatively little appreciation for education in Rose of Sharon. Most of the leading citizens (Class I) are not college educated; indeed, some of them are not even high-school educated. Yet they occupy enviable positions in the community. This has the effect of making all members of the community question the value of higher education. The people of Class I expect their children, by and large, to follow in their own occupational footsteps. The Jones Grocery Store someday will become the Jones & Sons Grocery Store. The successful farmers will make certain that their sons "get the right start" in farming. These plans for their children are not oriented toward education.

Members of Class II do not look upon education as a means of social advancement, either. Saving money, getting a store, or getting a good farm, and thus being like the Top People, are far more significant. The people in Class III cannot afford to keep a child in school for many years. Their children usually do not do well in school because they cannot grasp academic materials easily. Why learn that one should say "I am he" when everybody knows that one says, "It's me"? What possible use is there in learning to recite "By the shores of Gitche. . . ." (whatever the word is)? Who would ever use $\sqrt{a - b} = c$? Besides, the family must start the children contributing to the family income as soon as possible. Usually the children in Class III drop out of school at an early age and go to work in the fields. Only token attempts are made by the community to force these children to return to school until the legal minimum age for leaving school has been reached.

Members of Class IV, largely left out of community life, accept their lot fatalistically. The "Mexican" children do even more poorly in school than the children from Class III. The difference between their cultural backgrounds and the school environment, and the discrimination against them, even though they attend the same school as the other children, alienate these children. They drop out of school at a young age and go to work. No vigorous attempt is made to keep them in school.

The school board is in the hands of farmers and businessmen from Class I. These people have not used education as the means of gaining their social and economic positions; thus, they have little appreciation for the value of an education. They try to keep school costs as low as possible. "Frills" mean property taxes, which are highly distasteful. Schools are looked upon as a necessary evil. The law requires that schools be provided, but schools consume precious tax dollars that would not have to be collected otherwise. The result is that the salary scale for teachers in Rose of Sharon is among the lowest in the state. Teachers do not want to work at Rose of Sharon when they are able to receive higher pay elsewhere. The rate of teacher turnover is high, and the quality of teaching is low. Some of the least-qualified teachers in the state teach at Rose of Sharon. Several of the teachers hired by the school board have emergency certification only. (These teachers do not qualify for standard teaching credentials; they have been certified temporarily by the state because of a shortage of teachers.) This sort of teacher can be hired more cheaply than others.

The school buildings are aging wooden structures in bad repair. Actually, they are dangerous; a fire could level them quickly. But no one is interested in sinking tax dollars into school buildings. The school equipment also is poor in quality and amount.

The curriculum of the elementary school meets minimum standards only. There are no special music, art, or physical-education teachers. There is no orchestra, no glee club, no well-organized athletics program. The curriculum of the high school is a stripped program, too. The required courses are taught, but there are few elective courses. To be sure, there is a vocational program in agriculture and in home economics since these subjects seem reasonably practical, but advanced courses in mathematics, nature study, art, or foreign languages are not offered.

The austerity of the Protestant churches of the community affects education in Rose of Sharon. The minor vices of dancing and entertainment are labeled as immoral by these churches and are prohibited. The schools have neither extracurricular social dances nor dancing as a part of the physical-education instruction. Even the use of motion pictures as visual aids to teaching is frowned upon, but is permitted if the films are documentary ones only. Dramatic presentations by the pupils (such as school plays) are taboo because of their unsavory association with the legitimate stage.

The power of the churches is demonstrated also in the hiring of teachers. Teachers are expected to be active participants in church activities if they hope to be hired for more than one year. Through indirection and subterfuge, applicants for teaching positions are queried about their religious beliefs, and only supposedly orthodox Protestant teachers are chosen for the positions.

The teachers quickly realize the power structure of the community, and in grading the children on their schoolwork, they bear this structure in mind. Typically, the best grades are assigned to the children in Class I, whether or not they merit them. Rarely, if ever, are failing grades assigned to children in Class I. On the other hand, low grades are usual for children from Classes III and IV. These low grades help destroy any interest in school on the part of these latter children. Children from Classes III and IV are underrepresented at high school; customarily, they drop out before they are ready for high school.

Schools and Their Communities

By no stretch of the imagination can Ashburn be said to typify the American suburb. Likewise, by no stretch of the imagination can Rose of Sharon be said to typify the American village. There are many sorts of suburbs and many sorts of villages. And there are other communities that are neither suburbs nor villages. Nevertheless, Ashburn and Rose of Sharon do illustrate a relationship between sociology and education. Sociologists are interested in identifying the major activities of human social life and in seeing how these activities are interrelated in the ongoing life of the community. The schools are a part of the fabric of American life. They are interwoven with the rest of the social life. Using Ashburn and Rose of

Sharon as starting points, the rest of this chapter will identify some of those factors of community life that have sociological implications for education.

Communities Themselves as a Factor

Early in this century, sociologists used to think in terms of two polar types of communities, from the ecological standpoint. One type was urban, the other rural. Even as sociologists taught courses in rural sociology or urban sociology, two significant trends in American life were taking shape. One of these was the urbanization of all American life. The cultural revolution described in Chapter 3 has made a hard-and-fast dichotomy between rural and urban cultures untenable. Rural people demonstrate the effects of the cultural revolution on their lives fully as much as urban people do. America's current mass society is a technologically oriented, urbanized, mass society, whether the mass man lives in a rural setting or in an urban setting. The second significant trend has been that of suburbanization, or an outward movement of urban residents and functions into once rural hinterland areas. Suburbanization itself may, indeed, be but a phase of a much greater movement toward merging individual cities into tremendous urban regions. Already the development of urbanized regions may be seen on the east coast between Washington, D. C., and Boston, Massachusetts, on the west coast in southern California, and also in several other sections of the nation.

Today sociologists think in terms of three sorts of ecological settings: urban, suburban, and rural. They realize full well that this division is more functional than categorical, because of the spread of urbanization to all areas of America. Educationists also find it helpful to make use of this threefold division of communities. Approximately one-third of the American people live in each of these three ecological areas.

Urban Communities and Their Schools

For centuries cities have been characterized by the diversity within them. The city is a mosaic of social worlds. It is the center of law and of lawlessness, the center of wealth and of poverty, the center of conservativism and of Bohemianism. Its people are old-line Americans and immigrants representing all races and racial admixtures, following all sorts of religious faiths. The city, in a very real sense, is a series of communities rather than a single community. Sociologists have known for years that cities are composed of what are called natural areas. Amid the heterogeneity of the city, like people and functions have a tendency to cluster together. Cities have "automobile rows," "secondhand-dealer rows," warehouse areas, industrial districts, shopping centers. Cities also have slums, foreign districts, apartment-house areas, modest residential zones, opulent residential districts.

If all children in a single city were to attend the same school, the urban school would be exceedingly cosmopolitan. But cities are divided, typically, into geographical school districts. Because a city is a mosaic of natural areas—of social worlds—school districts within a city are as heterogeneous as the people themselves. Within a city there are slum schools and high-status schools. There are schools with students from foreign homes and schools with students from old-line American homes. There are schools with children whose fathers are common laborers and schools with children whose fathers are in genteel occupations. Urban schools range from "blackboard jungles" to exclusive, country-club-like establishments.

The process of suburbanization has had a selective effect in its siphoning of people from the city. Suburbanites are more likely to be old-line Americans than first- or second-generation. Suburbanites are more likely to be Caucasion than Negro or Mongolian. Suburbanites (with exceptions, to which we shall allude later) are more likely to be middle status or high status than low status. These facts mean, in effect, that non-Caucasians, new Americans, and low-status people are overrepresented in the city. Despite its heterogeneity, the city is not a true cross-section of the American population. This, too, has its educational implications. The people in Rose of Sharon who might be in Class III or Class IV are heavily represented in the urban schools. They bring with them to the schools their many educational problems, some of which will be mentioned in subsequent sections of this chapter and in the chapter to follow.

While cities are centers of wealth, urban schools are not so well financed as one might at first assume. In fact, some cities are hard pressed to support their schools. There are many reasons for this; here are three. First, when higher-status people move from city to suburb, they no longer are available to be taxed. The low-status people who are overrepresented in the city have modest quantities of taxable goods. Thus, a significant source of revenue is not present to be taxed. Second, the very heterogeneity of the city works against concerted action to improve the condition of education. It is difficult to rally people to a cause, especially one that will cost money, when the people live in separate worlds. Third, the services required of urban governments have grown immeasurably. For example, excellent transportation facilities are needed to bring suburban commuters to their daily work in the city, and police facilities are needed desperately to cope with the so-called growing urban crime problem. Often the people who pay the least urban taxes demand the most tax-supported urban services. Urban schools must compete for tax dollars with other costly governmental demands.[1] Urban schools face great financial problems.

Suburban Communities and Their Schools

Suburbia, U. S. A., has been so caricatured since World War II that many Americans have become convinced that a suburb like Ashburn is well-nigh typical. Suburbanization is not a new phenomenon in American life, and suburbs are heterogeneous when compared with one another.

Courtesy of Glenn Arbogast & Associates, Architects, Los Angeles

A LARGE-SCALE SUBURBAN MOVEMENT HAS NECESSITATED THE CONSTRUCTION OF MANY NEW SCHOOLS SUCH AS THIS ONE IN PALOS VERDES, CALIFORNIA.

There are suburbs in which the wealth of the residents is obvious in the beautiful homes they occupy, and there are suburbs in which far-from-pretentious, half-finished, amateur-built houses predominate. There are planned suburbs, and there are unplanned suburbs. There are new suburbs, and there are suburbs that have grown out of former villages. There are residential suburbs (sometimes called "bedroom communities"), and there are industrial suburbs. There are suburbs in which the breadwinners are organization men, and there are suburbs in which the breadwinners are low-status laborers. This means, of course, that any attempt to make sweep-

[1] By way of illustration, almost two-fifths of the school children of Boston attend schools that were built before the outbreak of World War I. One school still in operation was built in the 1840's. The high cost of other municipal services is part of the reason for Boston's reluctance to improve its educational facilities. See "Boston's Backwardness," *Time*, LXXXII, No. 14 (Oct. 4, 1963), p. 116.

ing statements about suburbs is fraught with danger because of their variability. Recognizing the danger, we shall be rash and attempt to identify some tendencies even so. An implied "for the most part," "more or less," or "in the main" must accompany each of our statements, however.

There is a higher rate of home ownership in suburban communities than in urban areas. This has the effect of giving the adults more of a sense of permanence than tenants in cities have. The feeling of permanence, in turn, encourages parents to show concern about the schools in which their children may spend all of their school years.

The income of suburban families is higher, on the average, than that of urban families. The 1960 federal census reported that over one-sixth of the families in central cities had yearly incomes of $3,000 or less, whereas fewer than one-tenth of the families in fringe areas outside central cities had incomes as low. One-sixth of the urban families in central cities had incomes of $10,000 or more, whereas almost one-fourth of the families in the fringe areas had incomes in this bracket. These statistics suggest that suburban families can pay higher taxes for the support of schools than can urbanites. With many qualifications, some of which will become apparent in other sections of this chapter, there is a tendency for the suburban schools to spend more money per pupil for education than urban schools do.

Income and education are related factors, although they do not correlate perfectly. By and large, the people in upper-income brackets have more education than the people in low-income brackets. Suburban adults, as a group, are well educated by current American standards. If these adults have children who are in school, the adults often show a considerable degree of interest in school affairs and procedures. There is a tendency for suburban schools both to utilize the latest educational procedures, techniques, and materials and to stress academic excellence. The latter is especially true on the secondary level. In Ashburn all of these suburban educational tendencies were writ large.

Rural Communities and Their Schools

The word "rural" brings to mind the countryside. But sociologists use the word to include both small communities, such as Rose of Sharon, which are not adjacent to urban centers, and the open country. Only a minority of the rural people actually live on farms. The rural, nonfarm people are businessmen in small towns or at crossroads, people who commute to the city to work, operators of farms or farm laborers who do not live on farms, and retired people. Economically, therefore, the rural population is diverse.

The rural population is a shrinking population. One of its chief characteristics is its small proportion of young adults. Young people leave rural areas to go to the city, and they never return as residents. Technologically advanced agriculture certainly has been a principal reason for this phenomenon. The transportation revolution has taken its toll also. In a certain sense, the crossroads store has become like the urban corner delicatessen—a place to shop between trips to the major business districts or central cities. Opportunities for employment are very limited in rural America.

Rural schools have the reputation of being stark, deplorable, and inferior. This was particularly true before the consolidation of rural schools became prevalent. It is still true, however, that the average adult rural resident has received fewer years of formal education than his urban or suburban cousin. These averages demand explanation. Highly educated people, such as physicians, lawyers, engineers, business executives, college professors, and other similarly trained people usually seek employment in urban areas. There would be little or no chance for them to find positions in rural areas, because there are few rural jobs that require much education. Well-educated people, therefore, are lacking in the totals from which rural averages are calculated.

Rural schools have some problems that are unique to them. One such problem stems from the fact that many of the children educated in rural schools will move to the city after they have left school. This raises a basic curricular question. What is the best sort of education for a rural child who someday may become an urbanite or a suburbanite? Another issue is the thorny, prickly, still unresolved problem of attempting to provide educational facilities for the children of itinerant laborers. While mechanization has reduced the quantity of laborers needed to harvest agricultural products, there are some crops, such as berries and other fruits, that must still be harvested by hand. Annually, as beans, broccoli, and berries ripen in the spring, thousands of people follow the harvest from area to area, state to state, and region to region as migrant field laborers. Their children spend a few days in one school, a few more days in another school, and a few more days in yet another. The decentralization of education in America— one of the strong features of American education—places extreme hardships on these wanderers and on the schools that receive them temporarily. No adequate answer has been found for this rural educational problem. Some mild attempts have been made to alleviate the conditions to some degree, such as Colorado's summer schools for the children of migrants. Rural areas also have a problem of recruiting well-qualified teachers. Teachers tend to prefer urban or suburban areas, with their more cosmopolitan atmosphere, to the bland life of the American village. This problem, however, is lessening as urbanization increasingly spreads to rural areas and as rural provincialism declines.

Two types of American migrants: the pioneer and the itinerant. An adequate education for children of itinerants continues to be a problem.

Despite problems and shortcomings presented by rural schools, there are some educationists who thoroughly believe that the finest public schools in America can be found among the excellently administered rural schools. Their reasoning is based on several facts. The best rural schools are not overcrowded. They maintain a close working relationship with the adults of the community. Their curriculums are tailored to the genuine educational needs of the children they teach. Their courses of study are truly useful and have a telling effect on the students.

Population as a Factor

The size of a population directly affects schools. Stated more tersely, tiny populations mean tiny schools; large populations mean large schools. It is very difficult for little schools to offer well-rounded educational programs; often it is necessary to have two or more grades in one elementary-school classroom, and the teacher must divide his time between the different grades. The chances for rich educative experiences may possibly be hampered when children in the same classroom are studying entirely different materials at the same time. The physical-education program may be difficult to administer when, for example, there are not enough boys in the same age group to have competing teams for baseball, soccer, or touch football. Small high schools are even more perplexing than small grade schools. Usually all elementary-school children are subjected to the same set of courses. High-school students, on the other hand, have varying educational interests, which are expressed through their selection of different elective courses. A small high school, such as that of Rose of Sharon, may be unable to offer many, if any, elective courses. A high-school education becomes extremely expensive when there is only a handful of students in an elective class. And a high-school education becomes inadequate if all students are forced to take required courses only and cannot pursue their interests in elective courses. The community of Ashburn at the turn of the century had a small elementary school and an even smaller high school which faced problems similar to these.

As described in the previous chapter, there has been a rather steady trend toward the consolidation of school districts in order to overcome the chief educational and financial difficulties faced by tiny schools. When several small school divisions are joined, they can have one or more efficient elementary schools and a high school that can offer expeditiously an adequate variety of courses to fill the educational needs of several different types of students.

But on the other hand, schools and school systems can be so big that they are unwieldy. This situation happens sometimes in huge metropolitan areas. For example, the City of New York, the population of which is less than one-fourth that of France, employs more people in school administration than can be found in the entire French nation. A Gargantuan school system can become an impersonal education factory in which superintendents and school-board members do not know their teachers, in which the public does not know many (if any) of the school personnel, and in which the school administrators and specialists do not know the pupils. This sort of system could become thoroughly corrupt and could continue to be corrupt for some time, the general public being completely unaware of the situation.

Several years ago President Franklin D. Roosevelt appointed an advisory committee to analyze the problems of American education. The committee's conclusions should come as no surprise to the reader at this point. It reported that, whereas the little rural schools (such as those in

Ashburn at the turn of the century and in Rose of Sharon) were the least satisfactory of all schools, the great metropolitan schools were also highly unsatisfactory because their awkward, clumsy bigness made them almost unmanageable. The report concluded that the healthiest public schools were to be found in the less populous cities and especially in the well-to-do, autonomous suburbs of metropolitan areas. The present Ashburn school system fits into this last category.

Related to size is another population consideration—population shift. Even the person who has not been introduced to the study of sociology knows that populations change in size because of one or another of four causes: migration into an area, migration out of an area, births, and deaths. Americans are very mobile people. There has been a great deal of population movement ever since Colonial times. One of the principal phenomena of this sort nowadays is the suburban movement discussed earlier. The onslaught of a sizable migration of people into an area can alter the entire make-up of a school system, as has been demonstrated above in the description of the Ashburn schools. But, just as in-migration affects schools, so does out-migration. Sometimes people leave a community in such large numbers that the community becomes a virtual ghost town. The schools must adjust to this sort of change also.

Fluctuations in the birth rate have educational implications. America, since 1940, has witnessed a significant rise in the birth rate, which has been described popularly as a "baby boom." This so-called baby boom has had crowding effects on educational establishments. New buildings have been needed. Teacher shortages have been acute. Taxes for educational purposes have risen.

The rise in the proportion of children in the American population may be seen in these figures, drawn from federal census reports:

Census Year	Percentage of Population Under 15 Years of Age
1900	34.4
1910	32.1
1920	31.7
1930	29.3
1940	25.0
1950	26.8
1960	31.1

The severe depression of the 1930's, the obvious decrease in the proportion of children in the population through 1940, and World War II had the combined effect of discouraging schools from spending more than minimum amounts on buildings and equipment. American schools were not ready in the postwar period for what some educationists call the "tidal wave" of students that inundated first the elementary schools, then the high schools, and now the colleges. Furthermore, many college students in the pre-World War II years were reluctant to become teachers. They thought they saw the handwriting on the wall in the form of demographic statistics which read that teaching was an overstaffed, declining occupation. We know now how wrong they were. Shortages of teachers since World War II have been severe.[2]

Both the lack of space and the insufficiency of teachers have stimulated some school districts to seek unusual solutions to this educational enigma. One answer has been for a school to offer a double, or "split," session daily. Some of the pupils come to school in the morning, the rest in the afternoon. In this way the equipment and personnel of the school can serve twice as many pupils. Another answer has been to use teacher aides— untrained people who do the routine chores in the classroom, such as taking roll or handing out papers—to free the teachers for full-time teaching. The teacher aides are somewhat similar to nurses' aides in hospitals. Nurses' aides do the routine washing, dressing, and feeding of patients so that registered nurses can devote full time to the medical treatment of patients. Adequate relief of the educational difficulty occasioned by an increase in the birth rate has not been found yet, although there are a few signs that on the elementary and secondary levels the situation is improving.

Still another population factor is the death rate. A long-range trend has been for the American death rate to decrease as average life expectancy has increased. This population characteristic, too, has educational significance. Adult education is one of the most rapidly developing fields of education in contemporary America. Current statistics from Los Angeles indicate that in that area one high-school diploma in eight is issued by an adult school.

Minority Status as a Factor

Minority status is another social factor that affects American education. Some people, by virtue of being different, are somehow considered deficient. This is especially obvious with respect to race. Most Americans belong to what commonly is referred to as the "white" race, although the term is not very accurate, since Caucasian skin color varies from light tea

[2] For the sake of accuracy, the reader should be aware of the fact that shortages have fluctuated from discipline to discipline, from level of education to level of education, and from region to region.

to pinkish tan, but not white. Less than 20 per cent of Americans are statistically referred to as "nonwhites." Often, nonwhites are classified by the dominant white group as being inferior.

America's way of life is based on lofty and challenging ideals, including an ideology to the effect that all men are brothers under the skin, that all men are created equal, that everybody should be given an equal chance in

Courtesy of Polk County, Oregon, Extension Service

ADULT EDUCATION IS OF GROWING IMPORTANCE IN AMERICA.

life, that God is color-blind, that liberty and justice should be equally available for all. Yet these grandiose ideals get enmeshed in preconceived notions, prejudices, and myths that are passed down from generation to generation and function in the aggregate as a conflicting ideology. The dilemma caused by the collision of our elevated democratic and religious ideals on the one hand with our adverse folk thinking on the other is a topic that Americans do not enjoy discussing. It is easy to bring emotional temperatures to the boiling point quickly by broaching the subject. Many Americans prefer preaching rather than practicing the ideals of respect for human dignity regardless of race. Despite our humanitarian ideals, and, in fact, despite governmental moves to realize these ideals through the protection of civil rights for all Americans, some people in America find themselves functionally in the category of second-class citizen.

In Rose of Sharon the people of Mexican ancestry were categorized as belonging to one of America's lesser "stocks and breeds." The children of Mexican heritage and the "white" children attended the same school, but the "Mexican" children did not do well in their schoolwork. The home background of the "Mexican" children and the use of a foreign language exclusively in the home made adjustment at school difficult for them, particularly when the teachers and the "white" pupils accepted community stereotypes.

At certain times and in certain places in America, various racial minority groups have been forced by law to attend separate schools. Interestingly enough, children of "white" immigrants have not been segregated purposely in this fashion. In the year 1907 Congress created a commission to study immigration. The commission made an elaborate report, which included an investigation of the education of children of immigrants. The commission studied thirty-seven American cities to gather information about the educational status of these children. It found that over half of the schoolchildren surveyed in these cities had foreign-born fathers. In two cities, Chelsea and Duluth, the percentage of pupils who fell into this category was almost 75. Certainly the educational problems that some of the children of white immigrants have posed have been as great as, if not greater than, those posed by nonwhite children. Language barriers, cultural differences, economic differences, and variant family backgrounds have been present. Despite these difficulties, America's public schools have met the problems of educating children of white immigrants without resorting to segregated educational facilities.

Logically, it seems farfetched that nonwhite children, who are just as human as white children, who are just as educable as white children, and who have created no more of a Sisyphean labor educationaly than have white children, should have been shunted into segregated schools. The logic seems especially forced when one surveys the accomplishments of the American public schools in the acculturation of white immigrant children in unsegregated establishments. That nonwhite children should be made the exception educationally is singular under the circumstances.

At one time or another and at one place or another in America, children categorized as Japanese, Chinese, Korean, Mexican, Negro, and Indian have been assigned to segregated schools. A few comments about these minority groups follow.

Chapter 4 described both the former segregated educational facilities for Indians and the Supreme Court action to end educational segregation of Negroes. The majority of American Negroes lives in the Southeast. The educational integration of Negroes and whites in previously segregated states is occurring despite several complexities. The Supreme Court decisions of the 1950's regarding the desegregation of schools, in part, have increased the hostility of some whites toward eventual integration of the races. These decisions, in part, have placed a political weapon in the hands of white demagogues. At the same time, these decisions, in part, have made the young southern Negroes less willing to accept the sorry lot of their parents and grandparents. The Southern educational scene at the present time is as unstable as nitroglycerine, and as explosive. There has been some integration of schools—mostly in border states—and in most cases integration has taken place without violence. In a few cases there have been explosions involving high state and federal officials, white rabble-rousers, white mobs, federal troops, and aggressive Negroes. Barring an amendment to the Federal Constitution, the long-run prospect is educational integration in public schools, with no child being denied admission to school solely on the basis of ancestry. But this probably will not be realized immediately, what with emotions and feelings now running as high as they are, both among some Negroes and among some whites.

People of Oriental extraction are found mostly in the western United States. In 1906 the board of education of the city of San Francisco took steps to segregate Orientals. This board, fearful of what sensationalistic newspapers were calling the "yellow peril," passed a ruling stating that Chinese, Korean, and Japanese children could not attend the same schools as the other children of San Francisco. The government of Japan became incensed that the ninety-three children of Japanese ancestry, scattered throughout twenty-three schools for whites in San Francisco, should be humiliated in this fashion. President Theodore Roosevelt, considering it ridiculous to risk international conflict over what he called San Francisco's "wicked absurdity," informally had the order of the school board rescinded.

The population of Mexican ancestry is concentrated in the southwestern portion of the United States. In the past, such states as Texas and California have, on occasion, purposely segregated Mexican-American children from other children in schools. Among the various reasons given, the one most stressed was that of the language barrier. Numerous Mexican-American children start school without a command of the English language. It has been argued that under such circumstances a different type of instructional program is needed for the non-English-speaking child. Current research, including language studies involving military personnel during World War II, points to the conclusion that a child learns a new language best if he is placed immediately in a situation in which he is forced to speak the new language from the start. This, of course, is the way a baby learns to speak in the first place. Apparently, the integrated school is superior to the segregated one for teaching English to the pupil who cannot speak English when he enters school. One might add that many a child whose parents migrated from Europe and who could not speak English has gained

Leland Harriman

"GHETTOING" CREATES EDUCATIONAL SEGREGATION IN NORTHERN CITIES.

[194]

fluency in English by attending a nonsegregated school, as the history of public education in America shows.

State court cases in both California and Texas in the 1940's declared the educational segregation of Mexican-American children on the basis of ancestry to be illegal, thus anticipating the federal Supreme Court's ruling with regard to segregated schools for Negroes in 1954. The Texas courts, nevertheless, have permitted segregation at the first-grade level if the segregation is based entirely on inability to speak English and not on the ancestry of the child as such. Perhaps more important, educationally, than the fact of segregation has been the fact that so many of the Mexican-American families have been itinerant agricultural laborers. Probably the education of the Mexican-American child has suffered more from the latter situation than from the former.

Action on both the state and federal levels is beginning to make enforced educational segregation passé. The consequences of segregation still remain with us, however. Separate educational facilities usually have been inferior. It is easy to demonstrate statistically that racial minority groups in America have not been so well educated as the majority group. For example, back in the year 1940, the urban native white population, age twenty-five or over, in the state of Mississippi ranked higher in median years of schooling attained than any like-age adult racial group in any residential category in any other state. Yet, Mississippi as a whole, a state in which the Negro population is nearly equal in size to that of the whites, ranked close to the bottom nationally in median years of schooling attained by adults age twenty-five or over. One of the chief reasons for the latter situation was the low caliber of educational facilities available to Negroes in the segregated schools of Mississippi.

It must be borne in mind that the low educational attainment of non-whites is not caused by school policies alone. This low educational attainment is traceable to the entire intricate Gordian knot of community prejudices and practices which forces second-class citizenship on some Americans, which makes it impossible for some minority groups to compete fairly with members of the dominant group, and which has, especially in the past, destroyed the will to strive for anything beyond social inferiority.

In the discussion about Rose of Sharon, it was pointed out that the people of Mexican ancestry were ghettoed. Commonly throughout the United States, minority groups (racial or otherwise) are shunted into segregated residential areas. In small communities that have integrated schools, ghettoing, as such, does not keep the children from the minority groups out of the schools attended by the other children. However, if the community is a big city with several schools, ghettoing segregates pupils even though the city or the state does not try purposely to maintain segregated schools. In a city such as Chicago, which has a large Negro population and in which Negroes have been ghettoed for decades, several schools are attended predominately by Negroes. A child normally is expected to attend the school situated in his geographical school division. If, because of ghettoing, all of the people in the school division are, say, Negro, then it follows that all of the children who attend the school in that division will be Negro. Even the small-sized metropolis of Portland, Oregon, which does not have many Negroes in its population, has several elementary schools in which, because of ghettoing, the majority of the children are Negroes. This type of geographical segregation is now under fire in several states and is being challenged severely.

Social Class as a Factor

An obvious and simple truism is that human societies are composed of people. Usually the people who comprise a society vary among themselves; the more complex the society, the more chances there are that the members of the society will be heterogeneous. Even small societies evidence dissimilarities among their members; differences, as such, are not necessarily of consequence. But if a society prizes some of these differences and deprecates others, those characteristics that are received either favorably or unfavorably become important socially. Those members who possess the desired characteristics will be in an advantageous social position. Conversely, those members who possess the disliked attributes will find themselves in disregard. Lines of distinction will be drawn between people. A hierarchy of stratification will emerge. The hierarchy will be based on the values assigned to socially significant dissimilarities among the members of the society.

This phenomenon of stratification, with accompanying status differentials, is not confined to human beings. Such lower animals as chickens, goldfish, and communal insects (wasps, bees, ants, etc.) practice it also. Social stratification among human beings is worldwide. Even the supposedly classless society of the Soviet Union has social stratification. So, too, one finds typically that people in American communities are divided into social levels or classes, and that the status of some people carries more power and prestige in the community than that of others. Not all communities have the same number of social classes, nor are the criteria of class differentiation identical from community to community, nor would a person belonging to a particular class in one community be assigned necessarily to that same class in another community. Yet, common to most communities are a recognition of a hierarchy of classes and the social conditioning of the behavior of the residents because of the class system.

Stratification unquestionably affects education. Some people purposely use education as a social escalator—as a means of changing their social class. The bright youth coming from a low-status home who, somehow, can graduate from college, who can gain social polish by associating with students capable of teaching him the folkways appropriate to the higher class to which he aspires, and who can prepare himself for a learned occupation, can move upward into a higher-level social class. This does happen. It is stated sometimes that one of the important functions of the college in American life is to assist in the metamorphosis of the lower-status student by teaching him to behave like a person of higher status and by giving him an opportunity to contact those people who may aid in his social mobility. Probably the college extracurriculum is more important than the curriculum in serving this function. Canby develops the idea thus:

> From a commonplace family in a commonplace town, with no prospect ahead but a grind of money-making and association with other stuffy nobodies, the youngster whose parents had invested in a college education, might hope to pass by his own native abilities into the brave, translunary world of great cities and gilded corridors of their privileged sets. For if he could once place himself in the right college group, his own would take care of him, provided that he did not too egregiously disappoint them in his later career. From henceforth he would be not Jones of Columbus, but Jones of "Bones" or some other tight-ringed fraternity.[3]

Numerous studies of the social-class background of public-school teachers indicate that many people have improved their class position by entering teaching. A significant number of people wanting to be teachers come from low-class (but not bottom-class) families. Entry into the vocation of teaching elevates these people to a higher social stratum.

But an education does not invariably guarantee social mobility. Evidence mounts, at the present time, to the effect that social-class factors as well as minority status, when coupled with inferior educational facilities, impede social mobility. Mention has been made already of the heterogeneity of urban schools. The quality of education received in poorly staffed, inadequate, urban slum schools that cater heavily to lower-class children and to children from depressed minorities may actually decrease the chances a child has for someday changing his status. Wretched educa-

---

[3] H. S. Canby, *Alma Mater; the Gothic Age of the American College* (New York: Farrar & Rinehart Inc., 1936), pp. 71–72.

tional offerings in deficient rural schools seem to have the same effect on children.

The factor of social class has other educational implications also. Children from middle-status and high-status homes are far more likely to do well in school, to receive good grades, to complete high school, and to go to college than are children from low-status homes. The situation in Rose of Sharon illustrates this general principle. The Class I and Class II children received higher grades and continued their formal schooling longer than the children in Classes III and IV. This phenomenon happens all over the nation, regardless of the native intelligence of the pupils. A distressingly high proportion of drop-outs from school comes from low social classes.

Social class makes for a selective factor in school enrollments. The various social classes are fairly evenly represented, proportionately speaking, on the elementary level. This is less true on the secondary level, and least true on the collegiate level. By the time pupils get to high school or college, the higher social classes are heavily represented and the lower social classes are underrepresented proportionately. Who will be educated? High-status people are likely to receive more education than low-status people, and the situation continues from generation to generation.

Social class has a bearing upon the quality and amount of pupil participation in school activities. By and large, children from a high class have more money at their disposal than those from a low class. Also, children from a high class are less likely to have to work after school or on weekends or vacations. This gives them more time for school-sponsored activities. Further, the prestige of the families of children from a high class is ascribed to the children. Their classmates (particularly on the junior-high-school level and up) tend to look up to them. Conversely, children from a low class find themselves shunned more and more by the other students as they enter adolescence and as students learn adult stereotypes. Student-body officers and officers of school clubs usually come from the higher classes in a community. In fact, children from a high class are much more likely to be members of school clubs. Likewise, extracurricular athletic, musical, dramatic, and purely social activities are engaged in to a greater extent by high-status children than by low-status children.

School boards commonly are made up of high-status people. Low-status people are underrepresented or, more frequently, have no direct representation whatsoever on the boards. In consequence, the wishes, goals, needs, and viewpoints of the high-status people are the ones that are implemented through the school boards. Remember that the people from Class I in Rose of Sharon controlled the school board. This, in turn, means that

From an advertisement used by Equitable Savings &
Loan Association, Portland, Oregon

WHAT IS THE PROBABILITY THAT THESE CHILDREN WILL RECEIVE AN ABOVE-
AVERAGE AMOUNT OF FORMAL EDUCATION?

[199]

the school policies are largely geared to children from higher classes, thus creating a gulf between low-status children and the school policies.

Parents' Appreciation of Education as a Factor

Very closely related to social class and, indeed, overlapping it is the factor of the parental attitude toward education. In Rose of Sharon the people who controlled the social life of the community had little regard for education. They tolerated rather than respected it. The result was an inferior school system. On the other hand, the suburbanites in Ashburn had a high regard for education. The result was a fine school system.

Usually, higher-status people prize education more than do lower-status people, and usually higher-status people control school policies. The schools reflect the attitudes of these people—which has a snowballing effect: higher-status people assist in the administration of school policy; school policy reflects the attitudes of the higher-status people; these people like schools that accomplish what they expect the schools to accomplish, and they react favorably toward the schools; the schools, glad to receive the approval of the higher-status people, try all the harder to please them, and so it continues.

When parents have a high regard for education, they transfer their feelings to their children. This attitude, in turn, becomes a motivational force, encouraging the children to do acceptably in school. Parents who are well educated want their children to be well educated also. Parents who themselves were good students expect their children to be the same. If their offspring have difficulties at school, these parents are quick to recognize the existence of difficulties, quick to confer with teachers about overcoming them, and quick to want to help their children. This makes for close cooperation between home and school, parents and teachers.

It is usual for people who have similar interests to associate with one another and to encourage their children to play together. If these people happen to be parents who esteem education, their children become surrounded by such attitudes. A child's parents expect him to do well at school. He plays with other children who come from a similar environment and who have been encouraged also to do well at school. The situation is something like being in a maze of mirrors. Everywhere one turns one sees the same thing, finds the same attitude. There is no escape. The same analysis holds true for the child whose parents think that schools are a waste of time or that schoolteachers are snobs whose function is to give "A" grades to rich children and "F" grades to poor children. Children are conditioned by their parents' attitudes and by the attitudes of their play-mates, who, in turn, are conditioned by their own parents.

Parents who have an appreciation for education are far more likely than other parents to confirm and buttress at home what the teachers are attempting to do at school. The child from such a background finds that the same activities and accomplishments that solicit favorable reactions from his teachers solicit identical reactions from his parents. And so, too, for unfavorable reactions.

In a community such as Ashburn, in which the majority of parents esteem education, the attitudes generated by the parents are transmitted to their children, and these attitudes strengthen the work of the schools. In a community such as Rose of Sharon, in which the majority of parents have a low regard for education, these attitudes also get passed on to the children and sap and weaken the school system.

The Occupational Structure as a Factor

The occupations represented in a community have a bearing on education. People who have gained access to their occupations through schooling are far more interested in education than people who have not used education as a stepping stone to enter their occupations. Thus, in Ashburn, the men followed occupations that they had prepared for in school and college. These men were concerned about education in Ashburn. They wanted Ashburn's schools to be as adequate as the ones they had attended. By contrast, most of the employed people in Rose of Sharon had not used education as a means of access to their occupations. The work of the agricultural laborers does not demand formal schooling. The farmers and tradesmen, while certainly using some of their schooling in their occupations (arithmetic, for example), failed to recognize the worth of education and thought of such factors as hard work, thrift, and inheritance as the chief source of admittance into their occupations. These people were little interested in having excellent schools in Rose of Sharon.

Parents have an influence, sometimes overt, sometimes subtle, on their children's choice of occupation. This influence can be seen, at least in part, in the well-documented fact that sons usually follow an occupation that is either identical or similar *in type* to that of their fathers. For instance, sons of learned professionals usually become learned professionals or enter another occupational category that carries similar prestige, such as managerial work. Sons of unskilled laborers usually become either unskilled laborers themselves or laborers of a fairly similar sort, such as operatives.

The schools of a community or a school division will reflect both the occupational status of the parents and the occupational goals of the children. In a community where most of the parents are laborers and where most of the children will probably become laborers also, the drop-out rate from school will be inordinately high. The quantity of children doing well in difficult academic work will be low. The proportion of students completing high school will be small. The demand for such courses as advanced algebra, physics, or Latin will be slight. The quota of youths going to college will be woefully minute. The high school in this sort of community or school division is likely to emphasize terminal courses rather than college-preparatory courses, manual-arts courses rather than academically oriented courses, industrial courses rather than cultivational courses.

In a community such as Ashburn, quite the reverse would be expected. The children from the homes of learned professionals and well-educated businessmen will do acceptable work in academic subjects.[4] The drop-out rate will be low. Virtually all of the children will go to high school and graduate. Well over half of the high-school graduates will go to college. Then, eventually, they will enter occupations similar to those of their parents. The high-school curriculum will be oriented toward preparing students for college. Terminal courses of the home-economics, bookkeeping, vocational-agriculture, and auto-mechanics variety will be at a minimum. There will be a substantial enrollment in the nature-study courses (physics, chemistry, biology, etc.), the mathematics courses, and the foreign-language courses.

Wealth as a Factor

A homespun half-truth is that the physical appearance of a community's schools is a reliable index to its economic status. Shabby schools spell poverty. Beautifully appointed, well-kept schools bespeak wealth in the community. However, it should be obvious by now that the situation regarding the appearance of school buildings is not that simple. The other factors that have just been discussed and that are to be discussed in this chapter would be meaningless otherwise. Yet, at the same time, wealth *is* a significant factor in determining what schools will be like. Not only does money influence the size and shape of school buildings, but, more important, it can even affect the educational achievement of students.

---

[4] It must be stressed that the native intelligence of children whose parents are in genteel occupations is *not necessarily* higher than that of children of laborers. In both groups there will be a range in the distribution of intelligence-test scores, and the two ranges will overlap to a great extent. Social factors are fully as significant as native intelligence in accounting for differences in school achievement.

The financing of local schools was discussed in the previous chapter. It will be recalled that not all of the money for the support of a local school comes from the immediate school district. A sizable proportion is derived from state sources. Thus, the character of the schools is at least partly a reflection of the financial status of the entire state.

There are some serious discrepancies in the quality of education received by citizens of various states. Again recognizing full well that factors other than wealth may be at work, those states in which the average per-capita income is below the national average usually offer the lowest quality of education to their schoolchildren, and those states in which the average per-capita income is above the national average usually offer the highest quality of education to their schoolchildren.

Here is an illustration. The average per-capita incomes in Massachusetts, Illinois, and California are well above the national average. The average per-capita incomes in Georgia, Arkansas, and South Carolina are below the national average. Men registering through selective service are given a basic academic achievement test known as the Armed Forces Qualification Test. Those whose scores are too low are rejected from duty in the armed services. Between July, 1950, and June, 1951, a time when the United States was facing military difficulties in Korea, the percentage of rejections for the above-mentioned states were these:

State	Per Cent of Rejections for Failing Armed Forces Qualification Test [5]
Massachusetts	3.7
Illinois	5.2
California	7.1
National average	16.4
Georgia	30.2
Arkansas	39.2
South Carolina	56.0

[5] Source: *NEA News,* April 9, 1954.

What does this illustration mean? It means, for one thing, that the opportunity to procure an adequate education is much less in poor states than in wealthy states. Children are cheated when a state has too little money to furnish effective educational systems. There is another meaning here, too—one with national implications. States that can afford excellent educational facilities contribute more than their fair share of draftees to the armed services, while states that have scant sums for education do not contribute their fair share. This, in fact, is one of the arguments used in behalf of extending federal aid to education. The preamble to the Constitution calls upon the federal government to provide for the defense of the nation. Provision for the general defense is inadequate when an alarmingly high percentage of potential draftees from some states must be rejected because their education has been deficient.

Some of the money for the support of schools comes from the local school divisions. When the people of a school division are affluent, they can tax themselves more heavily for the support of schools than poor people can. The differences between the excellent school system in Ashburn and the stinted school system in Rose of Sharon were caused partly by finances. Rose of Sharon is not a wealthy community. The large number of agricultural laborers and the modest way of life of the people in higher categories are indicative of this. The residents of Rose of Sharon could not raise substantial sums for educational purposes even if they did decide to support their schools less grudgingly, and even if they did aspire to a better-endowed school system. The residents of Ashburn are more favored financially; they can afford to have choice schools.

It costs a great deal of money to have well-designed school furniture, a well-equipped playground, an auditorium technically adequate for staging various sorts of activities, a gymnasium full of appropriate athletic apparatus, classrooms with sufficient lighting, heating, and teaching facilities, a library stacked with tiers of intriguing reference works, a competently trained teaching staff, and a number of other hired people, such as a school nurse, social worker, and guidance counselor. Poorly financed schools lack many of the supplies and services that well-financed schools can procure. Poor school districts have schools that are usually inferior to those of wealthier divisions.

Community Pressures as a Factor

Special-interest groups, the predilections of the residents, the general orientation of the community—all have effects on education. In Rose of Sharon, for example, the churches influenced school activities. The churches opposed those educational activities that they defined as sinful. The school people found it expedient to accede to the demands of the churches.

Often there are pressure groups at both the community and state levels that are weighty enough in their influence to sway or modify educational practices. Throughout American history, religious groups have been highly successful in this regard. The same is true regarding politically oriented pressure groups. The latter, with distressing recurrence, define patriotism according to their own narrow, preconceived notions, and then set about trying to fit all people into the Procrustean mold of their stereotype. These groups may attack textbooks, courses of study, or teachers for supposed sins of either commission or omission. Especially vulnerable are teachers of social studies. The same zeal may be used to establish or erase one or another school activity, including such trifles as the biological or geneological qualifications of children permitted to hoist or lower the American flag on the school's flagpole. In politically distraught times, such as the early 1950's or the early 1960's, when there has been a great deal of publicity given to the fear of the infiltration of America by inimical alien ideologies, these politically oriented pressure groups become particularly ardent.

There are moral or ethical pressure groups, too, that have had mild success in regulating educational policies and practices. For example, such a group may press for inculcating upon the younger generation the immorality of consuming alcoholic beverages. Many states, as a result of prohibitionist urgings, require that the evils of alcohol be denounced in the schools.

One should not dash to the faulty conclusion that pressure groups are necessarily a thorn in the flesh of educationists. A few pressure groups are of great assistance to educationists in improving the schools. Most pressure groups are difficult to cope with, however.

There are times when pressure groups become dominated by frenzied members who refuse to recognize that a person can oppose the tactics or strategy of the pressure group without opposing the cause as such. If the pressure group is a narrow-minded religious one, the person who dares to oppose it is likely to be branded as being against *all* religion. If the pressure group is an illiberal political group, the person who dares to oppose it is likely to be branded a traitor to his nation. If the pressure group is a hidebound moralistic one, the person who dares to oppose it is likely to be branded a licentious libertine. Few vote-conscious legislators or position-conscious school administrators have the crocodile skin or the financial independence necessary to ignore the assaults of pressure groups. The result is that schools are very likely to knuckle under to the wishes of such groups.

The predilections and orientation of a community have their effects on school practices and policies, too. Communities, such as Ashburn, that place high value on a rugged, academically centered curriculum, have schools that mirror this attitude. Very frequently a community will be avidly interested in athletics. Merchants, alumni, and provincial residents bask in the publicity and prestige of having their Saturday's heroes, from high school or even junior high school, win first place in the conference. This sort of "rah-rah" people is eager to have sufficient funds budgeted for athletics, even though funds for some of the other school enterprises must be pared to accommodate these expensive neogladiatorial contests.

Darrel Volesky

SCHOOL ACTIVITIES OFTEN MIRROR COMMUNITY INTERESTS. THESE GIRLS ARE CHEERING THEIR TEAM.

This sort of townspeople influences both the hiring and firing of teachers of physical education. They want coaches who can produce winning teams. Indeed, these predilections make for inequities in teachers' salaries, athletic coaches receiving inordinately higher salaries than the other teachers.

There are all kinds of interests that communities can have. If these interests have educational implications, they may very well affect the educational policies in these communities.

Teachers as an Ameliorative Factor

If teachers find community forces in operation that seem to detract from the mission of the school, should not the teachers attempt to change these forces? If Rose of Sharon falls short of being an ideal community, should not the teachers help to reframe and rebuild the social life of the community? Surely teachers are not passive entirely.

The vast majority of schoolteachers,[6] as a group or individually, rarely instigate major controversy or become outspoken champions of unpopular viewpoints in controversies. Despite occasional adverse publicity, schoolteachers have a reputation for being conservative. This conclusion has been confirmed by some limited research as well as by unscientific commonsense observations. The average teacher, it appears, does not challenge the status quo openly and publicly. There are numerous reasons for this conservatism, some of which stem from the public's image of the role of the teacher, others stem from administrative controls, and some can be traced to the teachers themselves.

Every occupation carries with it a set of expectations concerning the behavior of the people who follow the occupation. In important occupations, these expectations apply not only to the person's working hours, but also to his leisure hours. The surgeon is an example. Let him be rash, hasty, or erratic, and let him show poor judgment in other facets of his life, and he will undermine his career as a surgeon. Potential clients will be afraid to have him perform an operation on them. The public has a stereotype of the schoolteacher as well. He is seen as a sober citizen who lives a virtually impeccable life. If the teacher were not such a person, it is argued, little children with their impressionable minds might be in danger under his tutelage. A child might be led astray and his life ruined if his teachers were to set a poor example for him. Teachers, like clergymen, are expected to live twenty-four hours a day the image they display during their working hours. There have been school boards in the past that have included in their teachers' contracts certain personal "moral" requirements such as no dating, no Bohemian conduct, and, on the positive side, the requirement that the teachers attend church regularly. While most "blue laws" have not been sustained when challenged in the courts, the public continues to

[6] This discussion does not include college professors. There are some differences, both in degree and kind, between schoolteachers and college professors which make the following analysis inaccurate if it is applied to higher education.

expect its teachers to live more flawless lives than those of the majority of the community. Teachers, for the most part, apparently accept the stereotype and tend to avoid those activities, including crusades for distasteful causes, that would bring them more notoriety than respect.

The public is kept well informed about what happens daily in school. In fact, the public has a running account of school events in the form of reports and sometimes distorted tales that the pupils bring home to their parents. Schoolteachers are at a disadvantage when the major source of information about them comes from juveniles. Let something unusual or unsavory happen at school, and the public will know about it and believe it in short order. If the incident is in the least bit spicy or questionable, a group of indignant parents probably will be telephoning members of the school board, the superintendent of schools, or the principal and demanding immediate remedial measures.

The teacher who ignores the image the public has of teaching or the parents' image of him probably will not remain a schoolteacher. The mild teacher, the teacher who never risks offending the public, the teacher who conforms to the stereotype, is most likely to be secure in his position. These factors encourage conservatism among schoolteachers.

The formal administrative organization encourages conservativism among teachers also. In general, the members of school boards are successful people who have gained the esteem of their fellow citizens and therefore show little interest in wanting seriously to disrupt the very social order that has brought them the status they now occupy. School-board members may want minor modifications in educational procedures, but they are not usually interested in a thorough overhauling of the social structure of the community. Typically they are satisfied with the status quo. The schoolteacher who dares to challenge openly and flagrantly the community practices would find himself almost certainly in disfavor with the school board.

The administrative officers of a school division—superintendent, principals, and supervisors—are employed, in part, because of their ability to direct others. They are judged by the school board and by the public largely on the basis of their capacity to keep the teachers in line. A schoolteacher who is a rebel or a reformer may jeopardize the position of the administrators, who, therefore, usually take a dim view of the teacher who advocates publicly that there should be pronounced changes in the social life of the community and who proceeds to carry out his beliefs. It is the exceptional administrator who would be willing to endanger his own position by supporting such a teacher.

But this discussion of administrative characteristics is theoretical, for the most part. The majority of teachers do not object to school-board views or administrative policies and procedures. They accept willingly the situation as it exists, and they try to cooperate fully with the formal agencies of school government. If they tire of one school district, they resign and accept a position in another school district. This, too, encourages conservatism on the part of the teachers.

Most public-school teachers are women. In our culture, women are not expected to show too much aggressiveness in their behavior. Elizabeth Cady Stanton and Carry Nation, of the last century, and Margaret Sanger and Anna Garlin Spencer, of this century, are looked upon as anomalies. Few parents would want their impressionable offspring to be instructed at school by contumacious women. Sedate parents act as a sedative upon women teachers.

Whereas most teachers are women, most administrators are men. Our culture has a tradition of male domination. Even though this tradition has been changing, most men in administrative offices are not favorably disposed toward women in less authoritative positions who flagrantly question policy within the school or elsewhere. These factors help to keep the schoolteacher a quiet, conservative human being.

Most teachers are of humble parentage, and teaching as an occupation supplies these people with only a moderate income. Teachers, as a group, lack that financial self-sufficiency which is almost a prerequisite to being the leader of an unpopular movement, unless the leader is zealous enough to risk becoming a martyr. Most teachers cannot afford to risk a loss of income for a cause that might prove to be nothing more than a will-o'-the-wisp. Humble parentage, also, does not usually make a teacher desirous of being a crusader. Instead, it seems to encourage schoolteachers to imitate the most conservative behavior of the citizens of higher status, to whose ranks they aspire. Probably such teachers hope, by doing so, to gain admittance to a higher class than that of their parents. As teachers behave in this fashion, they internalize the conservative ideologies and viewpoints of the higher classes. In time, these points of view become their own, and they find no basis for quarrel with the status quo.

A generation ago educationists used to talk about the ameliorative role of the school. This role referred to the supposed duty of the elementary and secondary schools to remake the social order and construct an improved way of life. The public's image of the teacher, the administrative image of the teacher, and the teacher's image of himself make this ameliorative role of the school dubious. The conservatism of the average teacher in the elementary school or the high school is a strange basis for social reconstruction. The average teacher shows little interest in wanting to change the community in which he teaches.

Standards for Teachers as a Factor

Public-school teachers must be certified. Certification usually is a state function, not a function of the local school division. Yet, the points of view of the people in the several communities of a state are reflected, at least obliquely, in state standards for certification. Legislators are far from immune to the wishes of their constituents, and, of course, legislators make the laws that govern the certification of teachers.

Since World War II there has been a shortage of teachers. The people, through their legislators and other governmental leaders, have used two basic methods to meet the shortages. One has been to raise both standards and pay for teachers. This course of action has had the effect of attracting the best-qualified teachers of the nation to those states with high standards and high pay scales. In the West, California offers a key illustration of this approach. The other method has been to assume that the teacher shortages are caused by artificial barriers that restrict easy access into teaching. If standards were lowered, more people could qualify as teachers. If there were no standards at all, all people could qualify as teachers. Hence, the way to overcome teacher shortages is to reduce standards until the teacher supply equals the demand. As a matter of practice, when this second arrangement is used, little effort is made to raise salaries for teachers. In the West, again, Idaho has exemplified this latter plan.

Schools are greatly affected by the relative competency of teachers and administrators who serve them. Thus, practices regarding the certification of teachers have their effects on the schools of a community. When teacher shortages exist, when there are more vacancies than there are teachers to fill them, some communities are forced to hire the most inept of the certified teachers. Some communities, like Rose of Sharon, may prefer actually to hire the bottom-rung teachers because they can be procured at lower salaries.

Here is a place where differences in communities appear. Which communities procure the best teachers, and which communities employ the more inept teachers? All of the community factors discussed earlier in this chapter have a bearing here. State certification sets minimums only; a community may demand higher standards than those set by the state. If the community is willing to pay for a teacher who more than meets minimum standards, if the community offers an atmosphere conducive to attracting and retaining effective teachers, it can get them. Notice that Ashburn had no shortage of teachers. Teachers practically waited in line for the opportunity to teach in one of Ashburn's schools, since Ashburn is a community in which informed parents believe in the value of education and are eager for their children to have an excellent one. Also, Ashburn is a community that is willing to pay the price for quality in schools and in teachers. In contrast, Rose of Sharon is a community that the best-qualified teachers avoid. The academic climate of the community is inferior, and the pay scale is too low to encourage the most competent teachers to take a serious look.

There is an old-fashioned, tattered platitude to the effect that teachers are humanitarians and therefore ought to look only at the challenge of teaching and pay no attention to surroundings, salaries, or any other benefits. Few teachers subscribe to this view. They consider it a veneer advanced by a community to cover up its own niggardliness. The laborer is worthy of his hire. By and large, communities get what they deserve, according to the criteria they set for attracting and selecting teachers—even though the pupils, unfortunately, may suffer as a result when the criteria are substandard.

The Chapter in Capsule Form

1. The chapter began with a brief description of two very different communities and the effects that sociological factors have on the schools in each community.

1.1 Ashburn, a rather high-status suburb composed of progressive residents, has excellent schools.

1.2 Rose of Sharon, a somewhat backward and socially divided community, has inferior schools.

2. The description of Ashburn and Rose of Sharon was used as the springboard for a discussion of some social factors that influence the quality and quantity of education.

2.1 The type of community—urban, suburban, or rural—bears a relationship to the type of school system found there.

2.2 Population size and population shift are closely linked with education.

2.3 Untoward attitudes regarding race and other criteria of minority status often interfere with the educational progress of children belonging to minority groups.

2.4 Social class greatly affects education. The orientation of the school system usually is more favorable to higher-class pupils than to lower-class pupils.

2.5 Parental attitudes toward education condition pupils and are a motivating force for good or bad, from the educational standpoint.

2.6 Schools reflect the occupational status of parents as well as the occupational aspirations of the pupils.

2.7 Wealth of a community and of a state often has a direct bearing on the quality and quantity of education offered.

2.8 Education in America is especially vulnerable to the influences of pressure groups and other similar outside forces.

2.9 Teachers usually do not challenge seriously the social conditions existing in a community, nor are they encouraged to do so.

2.10 Schools are greatly affected by the caliber of teachers and administrators who serve them.

For Supplementary Reading

BARTKY, JOHN A., *Social Issues in Public Education.* Boston: Houghton Mifflin Co., 1963.

A "problems" approach to education, presented briefly and simply, which provides easy reading.

BOSSARD, JAMES H. S., and BOLL, ELEANOR S., *The Sociology of Child Development,* 3rd ed. New York: Harper & Brothers, 1960.

This is the outstanding volume on the subject of child sociology.

CONANT, JAMES B., *Slums and Suburbs.* New York: McGraw-Hill Book Co., 1961.

An important study gives account of schools in large cities and in satellite communities.

"Crucial Issue Splits a Town," *Life,* LIV (April 26, 1963), pp. 73–84.

This article is a tabloid presentation of pressure-group action in a school district. See also "Letters to the Editors" on page 25 of the May 17, 1963, issue for reader reactions to the article.

GRAHAM, GRACE, *The Public School in the American Community.* New York: Harper & Row, 1963.

A carefully written, well-documented sociological analysis of education in America.

HAVIGHURST, ROBERT J., and NEUGARTEN, BERNICE L., *Society and Education,* 2nd ed. Boston: Allyn and Bacon, 1962.

This is one of the best current textbooks in educational sociology.

POUNDS, RALPH L., and BRYNER, JAMES R., *The School in American Society.* New York: The Macmillan Co., 1959.

An overview of American social trends and their relationship to education is presented.

WARNER, W. LLOYD; HAVIGHURST, ROBERT J.; and LOEB, MARTIN B., *Who Shall Be Educated?* New York: Harper & Brothers, 1944.

An analysis of inequalities in educational opportunity that has become a classic.

7

A Psychological Approach to Education

A teacher works in a sensitive area in a schoolroom. There he shapes the attitude of young minds. . . .

from *Adler* v. *Board of Education of New York,* 342 U. S. 485 (1952).

Thinking It Over Beforehand

How does one transfer training?

In what ways are children similar to and different from one another?

What happens inside an individual as he learns something?

How does one make a person *want* to learn something?

What, basically, are the differences between a teacher-made test and a standardized test?

Psychology and Education

No social science has so profoundly affected the thinking, the activities, and the procedures of educationists as has psychology. Psychology holds an almost undisputed first place for having contributed most heavily to the academic field of education. That it is closely related to education is beyond question for most people. As a result, those who are trained today as schoolteachers have, on the average, a better background in the psychology of education than in any other single social-scientific foundation of education. The typical educationist knows the subject of psychology much better than any other social-scientific discipline. It is no accident that educationists in small colleges are called upon sometimes to teach courses in psychology.

Educationists, however, are utilitarians when it comes to psychology.

They are interested in those psychological findings that they can apply directly to their teaching. Schoolteachers pick and choose from psychology those principles that are useful to them. The value judgments of educationists deeply influence what they appropriate from theoretical psychology and what they consider the tenets of educational psychology. Teachers have preconceived notions about how they want learning to progress in the classroom and about what a teacher should know with regard to his pupils and what pupils should know about themselves and others. They have preconceived notions about how a teacher should teach. The educationists select from the larger field of psychology those insights that advance their notions. Because of these facts, the psychology of pedagogy at its weakest sounds like the folk wisdom and common-sense truths of a *Poor Richard's Almanac*. Educational psychology at its finest is extremely useful for guiding teachers in the teaching processes.

Knowledge for What?

The *raison d'être* of formal education is to teach materials so meaningfully to pupils that they will be remembered. The *raison d'être* of spending quantities of money on education is to offer materials so tellingly that the pupils will be adequately prepared to cope with their environment. The *raison d'être* of employing tens of thousands of people as teachers is to have materials presented so lastingly that pupils will cherish deeply and protect fully the values of their elders. This reminds us of the two universal principles of education discussed in Chapter 2. The people who support education want the pupils to transfer what they have learned in school to life beyond the schoolroom. They want both the pupils and the society to benefit. Transfer of learning is the pivotal point of the psychology of education.[1]

Unless knowledge gained through the educative processes makes a difference in the lives of its recipients, education seems scarcely worth the effort, time, or money. Education, defined in simplest terms, is the modification of behavior. But unless behavior is indeed modified, the attempt to

---

[1] I recognize that there is room for debate about the central concern of educational psychology. It is my studied conviction, however, that Mursell is correct when he writes, "That transfer is possible in some sense and to some extent is bound to be the working credo of every teacher. . . .

"If there is no such thing as transfer, if a learning experience can have no effect beyond the situation in which it occurs, then teaching is stultified. So it becomes very necessary to understand the nature of transfer of training and the conditions which bring it about, and to see how such an understanding bears upon our work." J. L. Mursell, *Psychology for Modern Education* (New York: W. W. Norton & Co., 1952), pp. 290–291.

educate will be fragmentary. An educated person is one whose behavior is different from that of the uneducated person precisely because of his education. This means that mere verbalization is insufficient as the mark of an educated person. The educated person not only knows but practices what he has learned. That is, his behavior has changed.

Many people can verbalize an idea or ideal, but do not make use of it in their daily lives. Their education has fallen short, is less than complete. Until behavior is altered, education is segmented and far from whole. The ideas and ideals to which a person is exposed must be integrated into his daily living for education to be complete. In other words, learning must be transferred if education is to be called effective.

The supercharged, self-dubbed patriots who become both ardent and eloquent in their praise of the American heritage are examples. They can mouth platitudinously by the hour the virtues of our cherished democracy. They can recite the gallantry of yesterday's heroes. Yet, these same people, when faced with the knotted difficulties of current life in America, may be willing to use the most un-American tactics to preserve what they consider to be the American way of life. They would snatch away hard-won liberties in order to trap those with whom they disagree and whom they brand as heretics. They would curtail the right of freedom of speech. They would deny the right to be treated as innocent until proven guilty in a duly authorized jury trial. They would withhold the right of equal protection of the laws. These people, certain of the worthiness of their own goals, would sacrifice heterogeneity in thought and action—indispensable ingredients of the American way of life—for the deadly homogeneity of the anthill. Thus, they would destroy in practice the very ideals that they extol in theory.

Another example is the person whom the sociologist, Edwin Sutherland, has called the white-collar criminal. Such a person usually considers himself to be, and is thought to be, an upright, conscientious, respectful, and respectable citizen. Such a person may take a leading role in civic affairs and even win a "citizen of the year" award. Yet, this same person may advertise his products misleadingly, may sell nostrums which he knows to be useless or even harmful to a gullible public, may swindle his customers in financial transactions, may misrepresent himself when filling out income-tax and other forms, or may handle other people's money craftily in deceptive business ventures.

Numerous behavioral-scientific studies,[2] and the history of religion in Western civilization as well, might be cited as further illustration. There are people who can recite scriptural passages pertaining to kindness to one's fellow man and peace on earth, good will toward men. And these

[2] Such as T. W. Adorno, *et al., The Authoritarian Personality.* New York: Harper & Brothers, 1950.

people seem to sincerely believe in what they quote. Yet, as the studies alluded to above show, and as the bloody history of religion shows, the more ardent and certain a person is about his positive religious convictions, the more likely he is to display hostility and prejudice when confronted with fellow humans who are not of his persuasion. The person who claims to have a deep faith may be the very one who is most willing to persecute, chastise, and vilify God's "less enlightened" human creatures, thus creating hostility, ill will, and animosity toward his fellow man.

These illustrations point to the fact that the ability to verbalize in one situation is no guarantee that a person will apply his knowledge in other situations. But unless learning is transferred, education will have been less than efficacious. Unless behavior is modified, the exposure to new materials will have been less than availing. Unless words are put into deed, the exertion will have been less than productive.

Certainly the subjects taught at school are thought to be important for the survival of both the individual and the group, or else they would not have been included in the curriculum. As we have demonstrated earlier, the indispensable lore and wisdom of a society are inculcated in youths in the curricular offerings of that society's schools. Certainly in America we are committed to a series of complex educational systems because we consider formal education essential for both the well-being of our citizenry and the welfare of our society. We have remarked already that public education is usually the most costly enterprise undertaken by a state. Under these circumstances, it is not too much to ask that the recipient of an education behave differently from an uneducated person—that education make our people approach life in a more discriminating manner than the way in which they might approach it if not exposed to schooling—that pupils transfer what they have learned when they leave the cloistered confines of the school.

This means, then, that an exposure to history must result in more than a pupil's being able to recite dates, such as:

> In fourteen hundred ninety-two,
> Columbus sailed the ocean blue.

This means that an exposure to the multiplication of factors must result in more than the pupil's being able to repeat a table of numbers. This means that an exposure to grammar must result in more than a pupil's being able to identify the principal parts of a verb.

This means, further, that if education really is worthwhile, the pupil's entire outlook will be different. This means, further, that the pupil's behavior will be modified, which means that learning will be transferred.

What is needed, then, is for the pupil to so absorb the materials to which he has been exposed in school that his consequent overt behavior will be changed. And this is the crucial question to which educational psychology is addressed. How can learning be conducted so that one might reasonably expect that a *transfer* of learning will result?

Psychological Insights into Teaching

Educationists want the contributions of the school to be so important to the pupils that the latter will transfer what they have learned to other phases of their lives. Educational psychology is devoted to identifying those patterns and processes of teaching that will contribute to the transfer of training. Without attempting to offer at this point a neatly packaged recipe, we shall summarize in the remainder of the chapter some of the salient ideas that relate to the crucial issue of the transfer of training. In order to teach meaningfully, so that the behavior of the students is likely to be modified, teachers need (1) to understand the pupils they teach, (2) to understand how learning takes place, (3) to understand how to motivate students effectively, and (4) to understand how to measure adequately the progress of their pupils. Each of these understandings is subject matter for psychology. Some fragmentary introductory comments concerning each of these four follow.

On Understanding Children

If teachers are expected to accomplish the society's educational goals, they must have a clear understanding of their pupils. They must know what to watch for in children. They must know how children differ from one another. On these subjects psychology has much to offer. Psychologists have studied thoroughly the pattern of growth and development of children. Psychologists have identified major similarities and differences in children. Psychologists have discovered techniques of working with children who have problems. All of these insights are helpful in preparing teachers to be effective instructors. The greater understanding the teachers have of their pupils, the easier it is for them to present scholastic materials tellingly, so that a transfer of learning will be effected.

Child Growth and Development

One way for teachers to understand children is to become acquainted with studies of child development. Such studies show what children in general are like physically, socially, mentally, and temperamentally at each grade level. They show how children change in these characteristics. They show how much variability can be expected in these characteristics. Fortunately for educationists, abundant and excellent summaries of child growth and development, which trace the "normal" child from birth through adolescence, are readily available. Materials for these summaries are gained primarily by the use of one or another of three methodological techniques.

Darrel Volesky

ALL FOUR OF THESE BOYS ARE THE SAME AGE AND ARE IN THE NINTH GRADE.

One such technique is to study a random sample of children who belong to a particular category—for example, eight-year-olds. This is called a cross-sectional study of children. It is a very convenient technique for identifying the range of differences in a supposedly homogeneous group, for identifying central tendencies among children in the same category, and for identifying what a person might reasonably expect of children in that category. Let us say, to illustrate the cross-sectional approach, that you are a junior-high-school teacher of boys' physical education. How much phys-

ical exertion can a boy at the threshold of adolescence stand without harm-
ing himself? What will these boys look like? How well do they comprehend
team play involving adherence to strict rules? Do they fatigue easily? How
well coordinated are they? How easily are they controlled, from a disciplinary standpoint? How childish and how adult are they in their behavior?
Questions such as these are very important, because the answers to them
ought to affect the physical-education program designed for these boys.
Answers to this type of questions are important to other teachers also.
For example, the teacher of chorus must know if he can expect the average
fourteen-year-old boy to sing soprano, bass, or neither. And furthermore,
how might such a boy with a high voice react if he were asked to sing
soprano? Would this assignment so humiliate him that he would develop
a hatred for music and, perhaps, for school in general? Cross-sectional
studies are very valuable to teachers as a basis for planning courses realistically.

A second methodological technique is to follow the development of a
group of children over a period of years. This approach is known as the
longitudinal study. It is more difficult than the cross-sectional approach,
because of the sociological fact that Americans are highly mobile. Rarely
does the same group of children beginning the first grade together remain
together throughout all of their public-school years. Despite the technical
difficulties involved, longitudinal studies are better than cross-sectional
studies, because the children are compared to *themselves* at different times
in their development; the cross-sectional approach compares one set of
children to a completely *different* set. Longitudinal studies help emphasize
the vitally important fact that the rate and time of change in children are
variable. These studies demonstrate differences as well as similarities.
Differences in children are exceedingly significant educationally. Here is
an illustration from the junior high school. Girls are considerably more
mature in appearance and actions than boys during their junior-high-school
years. But *some* boys are more mature than *some* girls. The junior-high-
school-age girl who still has a child's body, or the junior-high-school-age
boy who looks like a man, may feel very uncomfortable within his age
group. The teacher who is aware of the fact that the rate of change varies
in children—that the little girl will overtake her peers in time, and that the
boy will be physiologically advanced only temporarily—can convey these
facts through his attitudes toward the children involved and toward the
other children as well. Longitudinal studies help to emphasize individual
differences in pupils.

A third methodological technique is to study a single individual over
a period of years. This approach is known as the individual study of the
child. This system is appropriate for gaining an understanding of the

behavior of a particular child. Individual studies are valuable as a means of identifying the uniqueness of each child, and as a basis for teaching each child most effectively.

In all three of these approaches to the study of children, the intent, from the educational standpoint, is to contrive means for understanding children so well that teachers and schools can adjust their educational programs for maximum results.

Similarities and Differences in Pupils

Every schoolchild is a composite of his heredity, his environment, and his unique experiences. These three forces mold him into what he is. In some respects, every child is like *all* other children, in some respects every child is like *some* other children, and in some respects every child is like *no* other children.

Every student is equally a representative of the species *Homo sapiens*. His sex, his race, and his physique have no bearing here in regard to how much a human being he is. The pupil may be male, Mongoloid, fat, and stocky. The student may be female, Negroid, tall, and lean. Both are equally human beings. We as human beings share our humanity with all other living human beings. In this respect, everyone is like everyone else.

Most students are born whole—that is, with two eyes, both of which have reasonably acute potentials for vision; with two ears, both of which detect readily a wide range of sounds; with two arms terminating in hands with five digits each; with two legs terminating in feet with five digits apiece; with a sensitive brain and nervous system; and with the physical potentials for articulate speech. Obviously, this sort of detailing could be continued, but these items are sufficient to illustrate the point that most people have that equipment that we take for granted as characteristic of the human species.

But some children are deficient in this equipment. Some children are born blind, or become blind, or have very faulty vision, making them different enough so that they cannot be dealt with at school in the same way that "normal" children can be treated. Some children have hearing losses. Some children lack arms or legs, or cannot use these appendages in "normal" fashion. Some children have seriously impaired mental equipment. Some children cannot speak articulately, for a variety of anatomical reasons. The pupils who are abnormal in one or more of these ways may have to be taught somewhat differently from the majority of the students. In certain cases of deficiency, it is common procedure to place the pupils in separate classes or even in separate schools, in order that the teaching-learning processes may be modified expediently to accommodate psychological and anatomical inadequacies. Teachers find it highly useful to know about the physical status of their pupils in order to adjust their teaching accordingly. It is the exceptional pupil, of course, who varies sufficiently in one or more of the aforesaid ways to demand specialized educational attention.

Some pupils are like some other children, yet at the same time they are different from most other children. This has been suggested already in the preceding paragraph, which dealt with anatomical features. When one adds environmental (sociological) factors, it is obvious that the statement can apply to everyone. The community in which the child lives is the same community in which other children live. Most children, however, live elsewhere. And, as the previous chapter demonstrated, communities are variable. Likewise, the subcultural group in which a child finds himself (for example, Class I in Rose of Sharon) is the same group as the one with which some other children in the community are identified. But most children are not of that same subcultural group. Even such a broad category as membership in the American society and culture, while shared by numerous children, excludes most of the children of the world. Knowledge about social, economic, and cultural differences is of value to the teacher as he decides how to present effectively his classroom materials to his pupils.

Each child is different from all other children of the world in certain ways. Unless he is an identical twin, triplet, or the like, the exact combination of genes that have gone to make up the contents of his chromosomes will be different from that of all other human beings. Furthermore, in his socio-cultural environment, he will have things happen to him in such a way that the experiences will be unique. His future behavior, by consequence, will show idiosyncrasies. This happens in the case of identical twins also. Twins may look alike, but their experiences are never totally identical. Teachers find it useful, for educational purposes, to identify, recognize, and adapt instruction to the uniqueness of each pupil. A cliché of educationists is that teachers should "provide for individual differences" in the classroom.

Many school systems have what are known as cumulative records. Pertinent data about each child are placed in a file, which is handed from teacher to teacher who instructs the child. As significant data become known, they are placed in the child's cumulative record. Cumulative records include physiological, mental, academic, emotional, social, and temperamental facts about each child. A teacher who has a particular child in his class for the first time can gain quickly an understanding of his pupil by reading in the cumulative record what others have discovered about the child.

Courtesy of Occidental Life Insurance Company of California

ARE TWO HUMAN BEINGS—OR THREE—EVER COMPLETELY IDENTICAL?

Guidance

The guidance movement, while having roots in earlier centuries, has been primarily a twentieth-century phenomenon. It is an extension of what has been said already about understanding children. This movement is an attempt to assess individual pupils in order that they may in turn understand themselves. It is an attempt to encourage pupils to find in school those materials that will be most rewarding in their lives. It is an attempt to help teachers and administrators deal with pupils and adjust school programs and policies so that the educational goals of the society may more readily be realized.

As usually conceived, guidance is a specialized service that is placed in the hands of an expert designated as a counselor (or some similar title). The counselor is a combination of parent, priest, and prophet. Pupils turn to him for fatherly advice, bare their souls to him, ask him about what the future has in store for them. The counselor, thus, is a specialist in problem solving. This service is performed best as an extension of the classroom teacher's work. Teachers are parent-priest-prophets, too, but they do not have the time or (usually) the background to be full-time guidance workers. The role of the counselor in the educational setting is to augment the limited counseling done by the teachers.

Imagine a pupil who has no friends at all in school. He is *in* the class, but not *of* the class. Or imagine a child who is a Frankenstein's monster. He is in trouble perpetually. Or a pupil who cannot read, even though he is in the fifth grade. He seems bright enough—except when it comes to reading. Or a pupil who is made up of equal quantities of ability and laziness. He could earn the highest grades in the class, but he is almost failing. Or a pupil who has been ready to discontinue his schooling for several years. He remains in school only because the strong arm of the law insists that he wait until age seventeen to drop out. Or a student who cannot grasp algebra or physics, yet who expects to become an optometrist. He has made an irrational vocational choice. Or an exceptionally promising pupil who has no plans for college. His family is poor and cannot afford to support him after he completes high school.

These examples are not fantastically extreme. Teachers face similar problem students frequently enough that educationists have come to recognize the need for guidance specialists. If a teacher had only one or two pupils per class, he might have the *time* to handle these pupils. But teachers have swollen classes, and it is a full-time job just to handle the teaching processes. Time, though, is only one consideration. Unless a person has *training* as a counselor, he can do far more damage than good in advising people, especially when the cases are snarled and knotted, as they usually are. The fact is that the majority of teachers are not proficient as solvers of problems that reach beyond their immediate academic work. The high-school teacher of mathematics, for example, ought to be sufficiently prepared to advise students regarding careers in mathematics. This same teacher doubtless could offer only "advice to the lovelorn" to eccentrics and social deviators. This does not mean that teachers are second-rate; it means, rather, that there is need for specialists who have both the *time* and the *training* to study pupils.

By studying pupils, the counselor serves three groups. He serves also the mission of the schools. The first group is the pupils themselves. A pupil who is helped by a counselor may begin to understand himself better. This

Darrel Volesky

GUIDANCE COUNSELORS HELP PUPILS FIND THEMSELVES AND PLAN THEIR FUTURES.

helps the student orient himself. Schooling is usually more meaningful for the pupil who knows where he stands.

The second group served by the guidance worker is the teachers. He helps teachers perform their instructional role more effectively. By passing information about pupils on to the teachers, the counselor helps them understand their pupils better. The counselor, from his background of training, can offer hints to the teachers about how best to handle certain pupils in order to make schooling most beneficial to everyone concerned. The counselor is also what sometimes is called a "resource person" to whom teachers may turn for further information about child growth and development which they themselves cannot find readily.

The third group served by the guidance worker is the school planners. The counseling of students often sheds light on the condition of the school's program and policies. Principals, superintendents, and members of school boards can gain knowledge derived from the counselor's intimate work with students. They can get clues as to where the program and policies of the school are sufficient or deficient, and where they can be improved.

[225]

Behind the guidance movement and the other studies of children is the desire of educationists to have schools make so much difference to students that the students will lead more effective lives—to their own advantage and to the advantage of society as a whole.

Understanding Children and the Transfer of Learning

Industrial psychologists have discovered that when factory workers are recognized by their managers as human beings with human feelings and emotions, morale generally increases. This finding applies equally to education. When a person—child or adult—believes that other people care, he usually is much more receptive to those people. Thus, a step toward effecting transfer of training is for the members of the school staff to show an interest in the pupils, to make the pupils feel that they are important, to make them sense they are wanted. Basic to all of this is an understanding of children.

The human organism usually takes over two decades to mature fully. During this slow period of maturation the child changes greatly. Physically this is very obvious, if one compares, for example, the proportionate size of the head to the total size of the body of a baby and to that of an adult. It can be seen, without technical measuring equipment, that the infant's head is much greater in its proportionate size to the rest of its body than is true with regard to the head of an adult. Not only are there changes in appearance as one matures. There are changes also in the ability of the child to manipulate his body. The preschool child, as an illustration, will be clumsy in his use of scissors. Often he will be unable to make the scissors cut accurately, if at all. On the other hand, the twelve-year-old probably will handle scissors deftly. And the human world—the world of folkways, mores, culture, societal interactions—changes as drastically for the child as do the above characteristics during his period of growth. A thorough knowledge of the physiological, temperamental, emotional, behavioral, social, and cultural changes that occur in children as they grow from infancy to maturity is an invaluable aid in understanding not only children in general, but also each child.

Teachers must understand children's patterns of growth if they are to teach realistically what the children can grasp and comprehend and manipulate successfully. When the materials taught are beyond the child's grasp, little transfer will result. Materials senseless to the child may remain senseless if introduced at the wrong time. Knowing children and what they can and cannot do is of great importance for effective teaching, teaching that will leave its indelible mark on the future behavior of the children.

If a transfer of training is to be effected, it is essential for members of the school staff to know and respect the desires, notions, dreams, and needs of each child. This knowledge, in turn, may be used in such a way that the work of the school may coincide with the delicate yearnings and gossamer ambitions of each child. Obviously this means not only knowing children thoroughly, but also knowing each student thoroughly. The significant role of the counselor comes into play at this point. What teachers may not understand, the counselor, through his training, may supply.

Children's aims are often temporary and transitory. A child may want to stand up and stretch tightened muscles. He may want to look through the window at the screaming fire engine as it speeds by. He may want to give vent to hostility aroused earlier in the day. He may want to change activities because he has become bored. He may want to share a delightful anecdote with his friends while he is supposed to be busy at his lessons. These short-range aims are often the causes of minor disciplinary problems in the classroom. The insensitive teacher will probably try to suppress all of these transitory aims. The sensitive teacher is more likely to try, when it is feasible, to direct, convert, or even ignore these transitory aims; sometimes they can be made to coincide with the work of the classroom.

More important for the purposes of transfer of training are the deeper aims and needs of children. These may vary from mild ones to ones of such complexity that expert asisstance not usually represented on school staffs may be required. A child may need to feel wanted and loved. He may need to be noticed by other people. He may need to be babied. He may need to be granted more independence. He may need to be shown courtesy. He may need to feel appreciated. He may need genuine encouragement. He may need to share his life more fully with other people. He may need to develop an embryonic philosophy of life in order to accept the sordid conditions that are his fate. He may need to be understood. The insensitive teacher is likely to overlook these deeper needs and thus fail to meet them. The sensitive teacher is more likely to be aware that children, too, have needs, to try to identify them, and to attempt to meet them to the extent that they can be met within the confines of the classroom setting.

All children carry with them into the schoolroom their desires, notions, dreams, and needs. Effective transfer of training calls for a recognition of these yearnings. Effective transfer of training calls for a respect for the owners of these wishes. Effective transfer calls for a linking of the aims of the children with the work of the school, to the extent that such a linkage is feasible and beneficial. An understanding both of children in general and of children as individuals, therefore, is a requisite to an effective transfer of learning—and psychological studies of children are indeed useful in this regard.

On Understanding Learning

One of the most important subfields of psychology is the one concerned with learning. There is no subject of a psychological nature that is of greater significance to educationists than learning, because education involves the acquisition of new behavior, which is the essence of learning. Without learning there could be no education. But the scene gets involved. While learning has been well studied by psychologists, it is an area that is still not fully understood. People have talked, written, and studied about learning for millenia. (Aristotle, for example, had his say about learning.) Doubt still exists, however, as to precisely how learning takes place. Lest this statement disturb the reader, let him bear in mind that learning is a vast and intricate process. Knowledge about learning is somewhat similar to knowledge about our solar system. Astronomers know a great deal about the solar system, but they do not know everything. This same statement may be made concerning the current status of psychological knowledge about learning.

Educationists are not interested equally in all phases of learning. They are interested especially in those aspects of learning that are of benefit to the goals of education, of society, and of learners. Two sorts of learning are of particular importance to educationists. One is perceptual learning, which is rather mechanical. The other is that which comes through reasoning, known as conceptual learning. While the two are not entirely discrete, it is useful for heuristic purposes to distinguish between them.

Perceptual Learning

Numerous pioneers in both psychology and educational psychology dealt to a considerable degree with the idea that the act of learning centers around a stimulus and a response. Stated in very simple terms, a stimulus, often from outside, affects the individual, the individual makes a response, and the stimulus becomes associated with the response. The individual thus learns that this stimulus and this response belong together. When the stimulus is repeated, the individual responds again in the same way. In time the response becomes habitual. Eventually the individual comes to the point of anticipating the response each time he becomes aware of the stimulus. For example, a child sucks a lemon (stimulus). The lemon tastes acid and makes his mouth water (response). Through association the child learns that lemons and watering of the mouth belong together. Ultimately, just the sight of a lemon may make him salivate.

Much animal learning is of this sort. Dogs, for example, show evidence of perceptual learning. They learn to associate such commands as "heel," "down," "go to bed," "speak," and "roll over" with certain responses.

Human beings, as well as lower animals, learn perceptually. Many skills, such as writing, printing, throwing a ball, typing, reading, playing an instrument, doing gymnastic tricks, and reciting the multiplication table, seem to involve stimulus-response-association perceptual learning. Try an experiment, with yourself as the subject. As you read the remainder of this paragraph, analyze what is happening. In all probability you do not need to sound the words as you read them; you simply know what each word is. Each set of letters is a stimulus to you which solicits a particular response inside you. Each word rekindles the previous association that you have made with it. All of this goes on quite automatically. The words that I am using are so familiar to you that you know what they mean without really thinking. It is a rather mechanical process. To the extent that this analysis is correct, the skill of reading may be said to be learned perceptually, through the association of particular sequences of letters (stimuli) with particular ideas (responses).

Some educationists and psychologists have become so impressed by perceptual learning that they *theorize* that all learning is basically mechanical and that the learning process can be compared to a machine. Here is an illustration. Let a vending machine that dispenses candy bars represent the learner. Let the candy bar represent the response. Let the coin inserted into the machine plus the pulling of any levers and turning of any dials represent the stimulus. A coin plus a certain turning and pulling of dials and levers result in the machine's dispensing one sort of candy bar. A coin plus a different set of turning and pushing of dials and levers brings forth another brand of candy bar. And so on. One element has been omitted from this metaphor. A mechanic must adjust the machine in such a way that the stimulus will cause the desired response. This is where association comes into the picture. The learning process of association is the mechanic. Association adjusts the vending machine so that a particular combination of coin and dial and lever manipulation brings a particular candy bar. Now the picture, while vastly simplified, is reasonably complete. Along comes a stimulus (coin plus lever and dial manipulation). The learning process of association (mechanic) has adjusted the learner (machine) in such a way that a certain response (candy bar) results. To apply the metaphor, the combination 5×8 is presented to the advanced student of arithmetic. The pupil's mental equipment has been adjusted through association. The pupil responds mechanically, "Forty."

Perceptual learning and its several accompanying theories are the rationale for drill, for workbook-type assignments, for practice, for having pupils memorize isolated facts, for repeating and repeating scholastic materials. Perceptual learning has been used to a considerable extent in the teaching of such subjects as arithmetic, spelling, and the grammar of a foreign language.

Perceptual Learning and the Transfer of Training

The relationship between perceptual learning and the transfer of training has been a subject of interest for some time in certain educational circles. There is a widely held view, backed by somewhat impressive research, to the effect that if a stimulus is associated deeply with a response, the connection between the two will be remembered long. This is the basis for the suggestion by some educational psychologists that overlearning aids the transfer of training. Overlearning involves continuing to practice a response after it has become associated with a stimulus. Let us say that a person wants to memorize a poem. He stops reciting the poem the first time he can remember it perfectly. Probably he will begin to forget the poem soon. On the other hand, if he recites the poem over and over again after he can say it perfectly, he will be able to recall the poem for a much longer period of time, in most instances.

One of the pioneer protopsychologists, the Germanic philosopher, Johann Friedrich Herbart, seems to have sensed a relationship between the retention of materials and an effective association of stimuli with responses. Herbart's followers, condensing his views, made a list of the "five formal steps" of learning:

1. *Preparation* (reminding the pupil of those materials he knows already, which will correlate with the new material he is about to learn)

2. *Presentation* (actually teaching the new material to the pupil)

3. *Association* (showing the pupil how this new material relates to what he has learned previously)

4. *Generalization and abstraction* (analyzing specific cases involving the new material, to demonstrate how these cases fit a general framework or principle)

5. *Application* (showing the pupil how the newly learned generalizations can be applied to other situations)

A more recent student of the educative processes, Henry C. Morrison, also recognized the relationship between retention of materials and an effective association of stimuli with responses by developing what is known as the Morrison method of teaching. His scheme has five steps, too:

1. *Exploration* (finding out what the student knows already)

2. *Presentation* (introducing the new subject matter)

3. *Assimilation* (studying the new material under the supervision of the instructor)

4. *Organization* (having the student put together the materials he has learned)

5. *Recitation* (having the student present what he has learned to his classmates in order to demonstrate his thorough understanding of the material)

Accompanying these five steps is Morrison's mastery technique, which also makes use of stimuli-response associations. The Morrison mastery technique is a cycle of test-teach-retest-reteach-retest until mastery is achieved.

The purpose of overlearning, the purpose of the Herbartian five formal steps, and the purpose of the Morrison schemes are the same. They are aimed at insuring that stimuli and responses will be so strongly associated that they will not be forgotten. They are aimed at insuring that the materials learned will be available for later use or transfer.

Conceptual Learning

The second type of learning that is of profound importance to educationists is conceptual learning. Whereas perceptual learning is "how-to" learning, conceptual learning is "why-to" learning. It relies on reasoning. There is still debate as to whether or not lower animals are fully capable of conceptual learning. Beyond doubt, however, is the fact that human beings learn conceptually. Perceptual learning can be explained in simple terms of stimuli, responses, and associations. Conceptual learning, however, is far more difficult to explain.

As a means of grasping quickly what conceptual learning is, try to solve this problem.

Joe Doodlebug is a strange sort of imaginary bug. He can and cannot do the following things:

1. He can jump in only four different directions, north, south, east, and west. He cannot jump diagonally (e. g., southwest, northwest, etc.).

2. Once he starts in any direction, that is, north, south, east, or west, he must jump four times in that same direction before he can switch to another direction.

3. He can only jump, not crawl, fly, or walk.

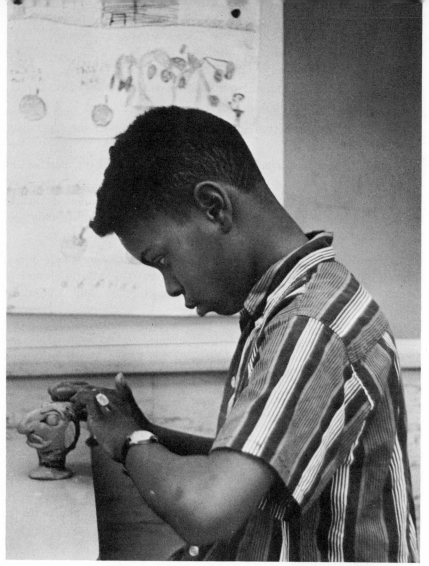

Leland Harriman

IS THIS BOY LEARNING PERCEPTUALLY OR CONCEPTUALLY?

4. He can jump very large distances or very small distances, but not less than one inch per jump.

5. Joe cannot turn around.

Joe has been jumping all over the place getting some exercise when his master places a pile of food three feet directly west of him. Joe notices that the pile of food is a little larger than he. As soon as Joe sees all this food he stops dead in his tracks facing north. After all his exercise Joe is very hungry and wants to get the food as quickly as he possibly can. Joe examines the situation and then says, "Darn it, I'll have to jump four times to get the food."

Joe Doodlebug was a smart bug and he was dead right in his conclusions. Why do you suppose Joe Doodlebug had to take four jumps, no more and no less, to reach the food? [3]

As you attempt to solve the problem, examine closely the learning which is occurring within you. You may call upon your repertoire of previous perceptual associations to see if any will fit. You may rely on trial and error as you hop the bug about in your mind. You may reconstruct the problem mentally or on a sheet of paper. You may go back and read the problem again, weighing each detail for its possible clues. You may try to apply what you know about bugs, or any other jumping creatures, to the problem. You may follow what has come to be called the scientific method: (1) assess the facts, (2) hypothesize, (3) select the soundest hypothesis, (4) try it out, (5a) if it works, solve the problem, (5b) if it does not work, try other hypotheses until the problem is solved, (6) then recheck to be sure that you were not in error.

You may have an illumination, which is much easier to identify than to describe. An illumination is an insight. Here is an illustration. On the ceiling of a cage housing a chimpanzee is a bunch of bananas. The ape is too short to reach the bananas. In a corner of the cage is a box. If the chimpanzee were to stand on the box, he could reach the bananas. The ape jumps at the bananas several times without success. All of a sudden the chimpanzee walks over to the box, picks it up, puts the box under the cluster of bananas, crawls up on the box, and gets the bananas. This sudden awareness of a solution to the problem is called illumination.

Conceptual learning requires thinking—often a considerable amount of it. It involves taking notice of details. It involves comparing the present situation to similar situations in the past, and contrasting the present with past situations. It involves recapitulating or acting out events mentally. It involves looking for contradictions, challenging tangential facts, applying past experience, and "talking things over with oneself." It involves the ability to use abstractions. Because of all of these concomitant factors, conceptual learning is more complex than the perceptual learning of stimulus-response-association.

Just as theories have developed about perceptual learning, so, too, have *theories* developed about conceptual learning. Here is one of the simpler ones. All learning is the result of problem solving. Through trial and error at first, then later through the application of past experience, or at any time through illumination, the individual copes with new situations. He learns by finding solutions to new problems as they arise.

[3] This problem is taken from *The Open and Closed Mind* by Milton Rokeach (New York: Basic Books, 1960), who adapted the problem from its creator, Ray Denny.

Conceptual learning and its accompanying theories have affected educational practices as much as perceptual learning and its theories have. Teachers who encourage their students to ask questions, who themselves ask questions calling for more than memorized facts, who encourage experimentation, who build on the creative impulses of children, are putting conceptual learning to work. Such subjects as art, creative drama, English composition, social problems, and literature can draw heavily on the conceptual learning capacities of pupils.

Conceptual Learning and the Transfer of Training

There is an intimate relationship between conceptual learning and the transfer of training. Indeed, conceptual learning relies heavily on transfer of training for its very existence. Conceptual learning occurs usually when past learning is *brought to bear* upon a new problem—which is, of course, the pith and substance of transfer of training. In order to solve the problem of Joe Doodlebug's reaching his food in just four jumps, it is certainly in order to transfer all previous knowledge one has of a similar sort to this problem. Any problem calling for reasoning may elicit both a recall of past knowledge and an application of that past knowledge to the problem at hand. It is, in fact, difficult to divorce transfer of training from conceptual learning. Those teachers who are especially anxious to have their students transfer their training purposely exploit conceptual learning to the fullest degree.

Many contemporary textbooks on the methods of teaching emphasize the importance of challenging students with problems that force them to review previously learned materials, to select from what they have learned the materials relevant to the present problem, and to apply what they have learned to the present problem. All of this involves the transfer of what has been learned in the past to a current situation.

Caveat

Two warnings are in order at this point. The first is that learning is not an either-or proposition between perceptual learning and conceptual learning. Both sorts of learning exist side by side and have relevance for teaching. Further, there is no hard-and-fast, clear-cut dividing line between the two kinds of learning. Without a considerable amount of perceptual learning the pupil may have few or no resources to rely on in solving a conceptual problem. And who is to say that no conceptual learning goes on when, for instance, a child walks through a heavy spider web? Both the response and the association could involve on his part conceptual learning of a problem-solving variety. While all teachers make use of both perceptual learning and conceptual learning, the materials being taught and the value judgments of the teachers will determine how much each teacher emphasizes each.

The second warning is that learning is an enormous topic. The foregoing discussion has not come close to fathoming it. The intent of this prefatory inquiry has not been to make the reader proficient in the field, but rather to make him aware of the interest that teachers have in the subject of learning. Since teachers deal with learning every day, they need to understand the subject thoroughly.

On Understanding Desirable Motivation of Pupils

Another interest of educationists concerns how to motivate pupils so that they will be eager to learn the subject matter being offered to them and will remember and apply what they have learned. With regard to this interest, educationists select cautiously from the field of psychology. The value judgments of the educationists are greatly involved in what they choose. Not all psychological findings about motivation are considered appropriate to the schools. For example, it is a known psychological fact that an animal can be motivated by electric shocks. The lowly angleworm can be taught always to turn right or left by giving it a shock when it turns in the wrong direction. This fact is of little use to educationists. A pupil could be taught the multiplication table by giving him an electric shock every time he gave a wrong combination. Indeed, he could learn the multiplication table if given a shock each time he recited correctly. This knowledge is of little value to educationists because of the larger consequences. What would the pupil's attitude toward mathematics be if he were given a jolt each time he gave either a correct or an incorrect answer? Would he so hate arithmetic that he would never want to use it? Would he transfer this hatred to all schoolwork? This psychological fact is too risky to try educationally.

Here is a second example. A psychologist can so starve an animal that it will be highly motivated to learn how to perform some trick in order to get food. A rat can be starved into learning how to run through a maze quickly to get food. A pigeon can be starved into learning to peck certain combinations of objects over and over again to get food. Children could be taught spelling by starving them for a week and then rewarding them with crusts of bread when they spelled words correctly. But what about the larger consequences? Again, this psychological fact is not worth trying educationally. Not only is it too risky; it is also inhumane.

Educationists appropriate from the psychologists those motivating techniques which are most likely to make children ardent learners and which, at the same time, are most likely to insure that the children will transfer their learning to situations beyond the classroom. Bearing this in mind, let us get an insight into educational motivation by sampling a few of the motivational techniques advocated by educational psychologists.

Desirable Motivation Is More Likely to Occur in a Democratic Atmosphere

As you study the field of education, you will hear educationists say over and over again that the classroom should be managed democratically. The term "democracy," while used often in America, is a difficult term because it has, not one, but several meanings. For instance, there is Hamiltonian democracy, which emphasizes rule for the people. And there is Jeffersonian democracy, which emphasizes rule for the people and of the people. Then there is Jacksonian democracy, which emphasizes rule for the people, of the people, and by the people. As used by educationists to describe a way to manage the classroom, democracy generally means something similar to the Jacksonian variety.

Within a classroom, concomitant learnings accompany the learning of subject matter. That is, the circumstances surrounding the learning of the schoolwork are learned, also. In fact, these circumstances may be remembered far longer than factual subject matter. The concomitant learning of attitudes is of such significance that educationists are highly sensitive to it. Some educationists would say that the attitudes learned at school are more important than detailed facts. The pupil who leaves school without mastering the conjugation of the irregular verb "to do," for example, is seen by some educationists as being less of a problem to the society than the pupil who leaves school with utter contempt for his peers.

Democracy is viewed primarily as a concomitant factor. It is defined, from the teaching standpoint, in terms of attitudes. When applied to the classroom, a democratic atmosphere involves respect for every member of the class. The quality of learning may suffer if a pupil feels rejected by the teacher and by his peers. If learning is to be of high quality, the pupil needs to feel wanted, appreciated, accepted.

When applied to the classroom, a democratic atmosphere involves a chance for pupils to participate in decision-making. This does not mean that the teacher abdicates his rightful managerial role. It does mean, however, that the teacher can take his pupils into his confidence, can listen to their serious suggestions, can turn over to the students those phases of classroom management that they can legitimately handle. Pedagogical jargon has even been developed to describe this condition, including the terms "belongingness" and "togetherness." These terms hint at the identification which the pupil makes between himself and the class when he helps to prescribe the direction the group takes. This sort of participation promotes his willingness to learn what is being studied by the class.

When applied to the classroom, a democratic atmosphere involves also the opportunity for each pupil to be heard without fear of being ridiculed, or punished in some other way. As a child learns conceptually, he needs to have the opportunity to ask many sorts of questions. He needs also to have the opportunity to try out his ideas in the stone crusher of other people's minds. The atmosphere of the classroom has much to do with whether or not he will feel willing to submit himself to those mental activities.

The purpose of motivating with a democratic atmosphere is to make the pupils feel at ease, to make them identify themselves with the classroom and the school, to make them feel important so that they will enjoy learning and will want to explore the new, so that the lessons learned at school will make a real difference in their lives.

Desirable Motivation Is More Likely to Occur When Materials Are Presented Vividly and in Terms That the Pupils Comprehend

Here is another sort of identification at work. When the subject that the pupil is studying comes alive for him, when he finds himself in the midst of the activity, too, and when he understands adequately what he is studying, pupil and subject matter seem to fuse into a single unit. To clarify the point, notice what happens when a person watches an eery motion picture or television story intently. Notice how tense he becomes when the villain creeps toward the hero. Notice how he shudders when there are weird shrieks. Notice how he grows apprehensive when the hero or heroine becomes alarmed. Why? The viewer is not only watching the performance; he is also living it. It is so vivid and the conditions so similar to those that he himself has undergone, or can visualize, that he identifies himself with the story.

When this sort of identification can be brought about in the classroom, motivation runs high. Pupils come closer to associating themselves with their schoolwork when the lessons are tied to experiences that they have had already.

History, for example, can be very dull when it is taught as little more than a series of nonsense-syllable names and dates. History can be alive and can sparkle with reality when it is presented as a vivid cavalcade of human activities. The study of history can make a difference in the lives of the students when it is presented in terms of their own experiences. The American humorist and critic, Finley Peter Dunne, had his literary spokesman, Mr. Dooley, make this point potently clear when he wrote:

I know histhry isn't true Hinnessy, because it ain't like what I see ivery day in Halsted street. If any wan comes along with a histhry of Greece or Rome that'll show me th' people fightin', gettin' dhrunk, makin' love, gettin' married, owin' the grocery man an' bein' without hard coal, I'll believe they was a Greece or Rome, but not before . . . histhry is a post-mortem examination. It tells ye what a counthry died iv. But I'd like to know what it lived iv.[4]

Alert teachers know this, and they attempt to capitalize on it by teaching vividly and meaningfully.

This factor of motivation is part of the underlying reason for using aural, tactual, and visual aids. When students can hear with their own ears, touch with their own bodies, see with their own eyes, and at the same time relate these experiences to their own backgrounds, they are motivated to learn and remember more than they might otherwise. This factor is part of the underlying reason for making schoolbooks so handsome, lively, intriguing, and appealing that students do not want to put them down. Schoolbook publishers are very alive to this factor.

Educationists are keenly alert to ways of presenting their school subjects so tellingly and so replete with meaning that the students find it difficult to keep for being drawn in and identified with the subjects.

Desirable Motivation Is More Likely to Occur When the Source of Motivation Is Within the Learner Himself

The statement, "The best motivation is self-motivation," is quoted often by teachers. It is far easier to teach a child effectively if he is already primed and has motivated himself. If a child really wants to learn something, he will exert the labor needed for the task with little persuasion. Notice how the pre-adolescent boy who wants to be as good as or better than the other boys in some sport will willingly practice hours and hours. He will spend months tediously bouncing a ball, or tossing a ball through a hoop, or throwing a ball, or hitting a ball. But these activities do not seem tedious to him, because he *wants* to do them.

Teachers are eager to capture this same zest for learning in the classroom. This is why some teachers, particularly those who teach one of the primary grades, advocate teaching around the interests of pupils. For instance, let us say that a stray cat walks into a second-grade classroom. The pupils probably will show a considerable amount of interest in it. They may ask a variety of questions about this cat in particular and all cats in general. Here is an opportunity, some educationists say, for capitalizing on the self-motivation of the pupils. The children, with little prodding, will investigate materials about cats (nature study), will write simple themes and give simple reports about cats (written and oral composition), will find out about community agencies that care for stray cats (social studies),

[4] Finley Peter Dunne, *Mr. Dooley at His Best.* (New York: Charles Scribner's Sons, 1938), p. 201.

These trees are on Mr. Green's farm.

Mr. Green takes care of them.

They are good to have on a farm.

Mr. Green takes care of the farm.

He wants to have a good farm.

What work is he doing here?

Eleanor Thomas, with Ernest W. Tiegs and Fay Adams, Stories about Linda and Lee, *rev. ed. (The Tiegs-Adams Social Studies Series), p. 89. Copyright, 1960, by Ginn and Co.; used by permission of the publishers.*

CONTEMPORARY SCHOOLBOOKS PURPOSELY ARE DESIGNED TO CAPTURE THE IN-
TERESTS OF CHILDREN.

will draw pictures of cats (art), will learn songs about cats (music), will learn to use and spell words related to cats (vocabulary studies), will make mathematical computations that involve cats (arithmetic).

Obviously, teachers cannot always wait for abandoned cats to crawl into their classrooms. So they do what they consider to be the next best thing. They arrange the learning situation in such a way that the pupils will feel self-motivated to learn the school materials. There are many ways to arrange the learning situation so that children become self-motivated. A few example are these: carefully planned bulletin board or other displays in a classroom; a field trip; a guest speaker who talks on an appropriate topic; a story that makes use of some local, state, or national news event; an educational motion picture; a discussion that seems to the pupils to be unstructured, but which has been thought out beforehand by the teachers. Any of these may pique the curiosity and interest of students.

Supposedly, one reason for having elective courses at school is to provide students with the opportunity to pursue those self-motivated interests for which class work is available. Supposedly, also, one reason for assigning reports, projects, and the like is to encourage the students to follow those interests that already have been ignited within them. Before leaving the subtopic of self-motivation, it might be pointed out here that disciplinary problems in the classroom are fewer in number when children are self-motivated.

Desirable Motivation Is More Likely to Occur When Pupils Are Guided in Their Learning

It is frustrating, from the learner's standpoint, not to know where he stands with regard to what is being learned. "Do I understand this?" "Am I handling this correctly?" "Have I shown any progress?" "Is this how I should solve the problem?" "Do I know this well enough to go on?" "What is my score?" "What does the score mean?" Questions of this sort are frequently asked by students. If they go unanswered, motivation probably will decrease. Learners want and need to know whether the efforts they have invested are paying them dividends.

Teachers motivate their pupils by guiding them critically. The suggestions of teachers regarding how the pupils can improve their work give clues to the students as to what is correct or incorrect. When pupils do not know that they are making mistakes, or why they are making mistakes, or where the mistakes are, the learning that occurs is not desirable learning, from the educational standpoint. Likewise, when pupils do not know that their work is correct, or in what way it is correct, the learning that occurs is below standard. Usually, motivation is also below standard in such cases.

Many educational-psychological studies have shown that both effective learning and motivation are higher when the learners are apprised frequently of the results of their learning. Trial and error is changed to trial and success through careful and recurrent tuition. Clumsy errors may impede learning if the student is left to his own devices and receives no critical help from the instructor. (At this moment, for example, you may feel frustrated because you still have not been able to get Joe Doodlebug to his food in four jumps, and you do not know whether you are attacking the problem correctly!)

A Current Illustration of Guided Learning: Programmed Instruction

A recent development in educational circles is a movement referred to by such labels as programmed learning, auto-instruction, machine teaching, or automated instruction. This movement developed partly from knowledge about testing techniques (to be discussed later in this chapter). It developed also from knowledge about individual differences in learners, about how learning takes place, and about the motivation of learning.

Programmed learning is based on the fact that the rate of speed at which individuals learn a subject is highly variable. Some people learn a body of subject matter much more rapidly than others. Programmed learning is based on the fact that new material is learned as it is related to what is known already, as it is used, and as it is applied again and again. Programmed learning is based on the fact that learners want and need to know how they are progressing if learning is to be effective. The quicker a student can find out whether or not he is handling the materials correctly, the more swift will be his progress. If he is blundering, he needs to know about his mistakes as soon as possible so that he can take steps to rectify them. If he is dealing unerringly with the materials, he needs to know this, too, in order to gain confidence to forge on. Programmed learning is based on the fact that there must be constant testing if a pupil is to know at all times the accuracy of his learning.

In programmed instruction the subject matter is broken into tiny fragments. Every detail, principle, generalization, precept, concept, example, term, idea, and symbol (which, taken together, comprise the course of instruction) is divided into its smallest parts. These minute components are then strung together piece by piece in their most logical order, in their most easily learned order. The smallest division of these particles of subject matter is known as a "frame." The frame is the basal unit of instruction. One frame at a time is presented to the learner. The frame is often short, containing perhaps two to three dozen words at most. Sometimes the material included in a frame reviews material already covered. Sometimes the material included in a frame presents the learner with a wee portion of a new subject matter—if so, usually in conjunction with what has been learned already. Sometimes the material included in a frame calls upon the

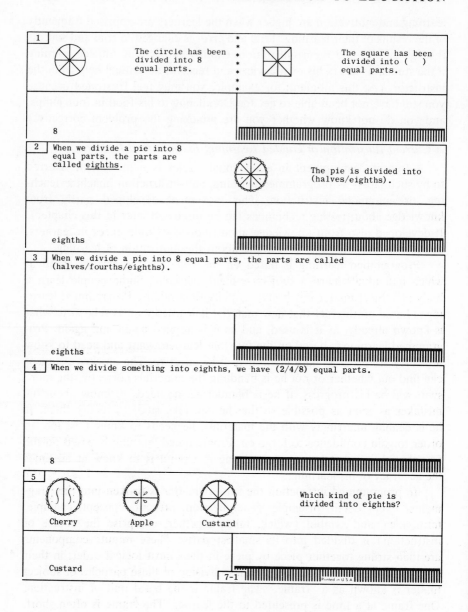

Page 7–1 from the TMI-Grolier course, Elementary Arithmetic Series: Fractions: Basic Concepts, *a product of Teaching Machines, Inc., distributed by Teaching Materials Corporation, a Division of Grolier, Inc. Used by permisison.*

A PAGE FROM A PROGRAMMED TEXTBOOK.

learner to apply what he has learned. A frame contains not only subject matter but also questions about the material being learned. This, indeed, is a fundamental characteristic of programmed instruction. The learner is constantly tested on what he is learning. The type of question used is variable: perhaps it is of the multiple choice variety; perhaps it calls upon the learner to fill in blank spaces. As soon as the learner completes the answers to all questions contained in a single frame, he is shown whether or not his responses were accurate. This, too, is a fundamental characteristic of programmed instruction: the learner immediately finds out which answers are right and which are wrong.

When a learner gives a wrong answer, there are several techniques of dealing with him in programmed learning. One commonly used technique is to permit him to continue to the end of the particular segment of subject matter that he is trying to learn. If, by the time he has completed this segment, he still gives poor answers, his instructor will have him repeat the entire series of frames devoted to this portion of the material. Another commonly used technique is to have the learner take a detour.[5] The detour is comprised of a set of frames that presents again—probably in a slightly different form—the material that is troubling the student. The detour completed, the student is shown once more the frame that he handled incorrectly earlier. If the student's answers are now correct, he goes on. If the student still shows difficulty in dealing with the material, he may take the same detour again, or another one. In this second technique the student does not study new material until he demonstrates competence in dealing with the material leading up to it.

Programmed learning is sometimes known as machine teaching. There are teaching machines that are designed to present programmed instructional material to students. These machines display one frame at a time for study, contain some kind of device for recording answers, and indicate the correctness of the student's answers *after* the student has recorded his own answers. While teaching machines are rather commonly used in auto-instruction, they are by no means its core. Teaching machines are useful for presenting programmed instruction, but they are not indipensable. Programmed learning may be carried on without machinery—with programmed textbooks, for example. You will find a sample page from a programmed textbook on page 242.

Programmed learning is too new for its ultimate place in the educational scene to be fully defined at present. (It was popularized in the late 1950's.) Some pioneer studies suggest that auto-instruction is most mean-

---

[5] The technical term for the detour is "branch." The process is called "branching."

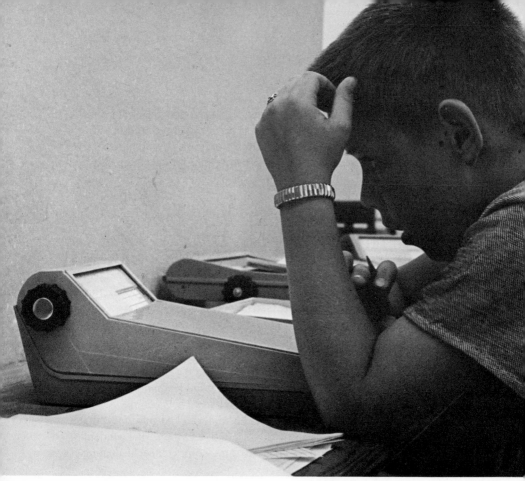

Courtesy of Teaching Machines, Inc.

PROGRAMMED INSTRUCTION IS USED WIDELY AT THE PRESENT TIME. THE MA-
CHINE IS A MIN/MAX III, A PRODUCT OF TMI-GROLIER, DISTRIBUTED BY TEACHING
MATERIALS CORPORATION.

ingful to students when it is used in conjunction with other instructional
techniques, such as classroom discussions or the reading of standard books.

Motivation and the Transfer of Training

Teachers, in order to teach effectively, need a thorough understanding
of how to motivate pupils in such a way that they will find their formal
education a rich, rewarding experience and will readily transfer their
learning. The foregoing discussion of motivation has given a hint as to the
many techniques studied by educational psychologists for motivating pupils
in a desirable way. Later, when you enroll in courses dealing with methods
of teaching school subjects, the matter of desirable motivation will be
treated with more than the cursory attention accorded it here.

[244]

The immediate rationale for the use of motivational techniques is to make learning more effective. This effectiveness is easiest to measure when defined in short-run terms. Are the students eager to learn? Do the students apply themselves to the subject they are learning because they *want* to do so? Is the hum of the classroom the roar of chaos, or the noise of the spinning wheels of productive industry? In the long run, learning is effective only if it makes a difference in the lives of the students—only if it can be transferred to future situations. The conscientious teacher is interested not only in the willingness of his pupils to expose themselves to new materials, but also in how his students will make use of what they are learning in later years. Thus, the conscientious teacher, while seeking to motivate his students, wants the resultant learning to make such a difference in the lives of his charges that they *can* and *will* apply their knowledge when future situations call for it.

The teacher uses democratic procedures in the classroom not simply to encourage in his pupils a sense of "belongingness." Certainly the pupil's feeling of identification with the group is important in its own right. But there is more involved. The teacher, by using democratic techniques in the classroom, hopes that the learning experiences will affect the learner so profoundly that they will be remembered, used, and transferred later.

The teacher tries to present materials vividly and meaningfully to the students not simply to ensnare their attention. Certainly it is desirable for the pupils to pay attention to what they are learning. But there is more involved. The teacher, by presenting the materials vividly and meaningfully, hopes that the learning that occurs will be of sufficient caliber to be remembered, used, and transferred later.

The teacher capitalizes on the self-motivation of the pupils not simply to make the learning situation less painful to all concerned. Certainly it is important to have pupils interested in what they are learning. But there is more involved. The teacher, by capturing the already titlated enthusiasm of the pupils, hopes that new materials learned under these circumstances will be remembered, used, and transferred later.

The teacher apprises his pupils of their progress frequently not simply to give the students an evaluation of their work. Certainly a knowledge of the quality of his learning is of significance to the pupil. But there is more involved. The teacher, by offering frequent tuition to his pupils, hopes that the learning will be of sufficient character to be remembered, used, and transferred later.

While the effective motivation of learning may serve immediate purposes, it serves long-range purposes, too. Teachers attempt to motivate their students so that the knowledge gained by the pupils will be lasting, will be remembered, will be applied to circumstances outside the school-room—will be transferred.

On Understanding Pupil Progress

If teachers are to satisfy the educational goals of their society, they must have an adequate understanding of techniques for measuring and appraising their pupils' improvement. The measurement and evaluation of pupil progress have become indispensable elements of American education, and teachers cannot perform their educative role fully unless they comprehend them well. Measurement and evaluation are used for several purposes in schools. They are used to inform teachers, pupils, parents, and all other interested persons about how well the pupils are progressing. They are used to decide promotion and retention policies from grade to grade. They are used to determine the conditions under which pupils will be graduated. They are used to construct standards for admission into some schools, curriculums, or colleges. They are used for the broader purpose of understanding child growth and development. They are used by guidance workers for counseling purposes. They are used to help teachers better understand their pupils.

Educational psychologists have devoted a great deal of attention to two categories of testing devices for schools. One is the sort of test composed by the teachers for ascertaining how well their students have grasped the lessons taught them. The other is the sort that measures such factors as potentials, capabilities, abilities, and achievements of pupils. The former category is referred to usually as "teacher-made tests." The latter is often given the name "standardized tests." The work of educational psychologists in developing both of these categories of measuring and evaluating devices has been of sufficient significance to merit further prefatory comments here.

Teacher-Made Tests

Evidence suggests that informal oral questioning of pupils is a very ancient practice. It may come as a surprise to learn that written examinations for the purpose of evaluating pupil progress are not much more than a century old in America. Written essay examinations were introduced into American schools scarcely a decade before the outbreak of the Civil War. The practice seems to have been adopted first by the schools of Boston. Since the introduction of teacher-made, written essay tests, the educational cauldron has been frothing, foaming, and fuming.

By the early years of the twentieth century, the American scene was highly complex with regard to written tests. Examinations of an essay variety had become an accepted ingredient of the teaching processes on all levels of education. At the same time a science of mental measurement was beginning to develop. This measurement movement cast serious doubt on both the validity and the reliability of essay examinations as measurements of pupil progress. A series of studies between 1890 and 1920 demonstrated the woeful inadequacies of essay-type examinations. These studies pointed out that scores on essay examinations had little meaning. Several equally competent teachers would grade the same essay examinations differently. Some teachers always scored papers higher or lower than other teachers, regardless of the caliber of the students' work. Such irrelevant factors as the mental and physical well-being of the grader affected the scores that he would assign to the essay tests. Even the attitude of the teacher toward his pupils was reflected in his grading of such tests.

A countermovement developed, beginning actually in the nineteenth century, but not becoming obvious until the twentieth. This countermovement sought, on the one hand, to retain the idea of teacher-made tests, and on the other, to substitute another sort of teacher-made test for essay tests. This countermovement gave rise to what are known as new-type or objective tests. An objective test is one that can be scored so mechanically that two persons scoring the same test ought to assign the same score. Instead of using essays, these new-type tests were constructed so that students merely underlined, or checked, or numbered, or matched correct responses. If written answers were requested, the responses were kept to a few words. Here are some examples of new-type, or objective, test items:

1. Encircle the correct answer:
   TRUE   FALSE   Written tests are older than oral tests.
2. Underline the correct alternative:
   Written tests were used first in the state of:
   (a) California
   (b) Hawaii
   (c) North Dakota
   (d) Massachusetts
3. Fill in the blank:
   New-type tests are called also _____ tests.

The "objectivity" of objective tests versus the "subjectivity" of essay tests, the ease of scoring objective tests versus the hours required to score essay tests, the increased quantities of pupils attending school, and the desire of teachers to be considered scientific have been factors contributing to the popularity of new-type tests. These tests continue to be used widely at the present time.

But within the last third of a century, a counter-countermovement has begun. Exponents of this movement suggest that new-type tests have their limitations, too. For one thing, they measure perceptual learning much better than they measure conceptual learning. Also, a lazy student who is clever at guessing could get a high score on an objective test without deserving such a score. And an objective test that is really an excellent test is extremely time-consuming to construct.

These exponents have pointed out, further, that some of the principles used in constructing and scoring new-type tests can be used in constructing and scoring essay tests, making essay tests less subjective. They have pointed out also that a teacher's goals in his courses should affect the choice of tests. If his goals center around having pupils learn facts, new-type tests should be used. If they center around the use of conceptual reason, essay tests measure more accurately. They have pointed out, finally, that no one test ever measures everything that teachers should know in order to evaluate pupil progress.

As the teacher-made test movement, and the new-type test counter-movement, and the counter-countermovement have developed, educational psychologists have become increasingly sophisticated about the measurement and evaluation of pupil progress. They have learned a great deal. Usually college departments of education offer separate courses in tests and measurements built around the sophisticated educational-psychological insights now available.

Standardized Tests

Standardized tests are different from teacher-made tests. While the questions used may be identical, standardized tests are constructed with more care. Each question is chosen for its ability to differentiate among children. Only those items that measure what that test attempts to measure are included. The test, when finally constructed, is given to a carefully selected group of children in order to establish levels of achievement known as norms. These norms are then used for interpreting scores that other children attain on the test. Standardized tests are checked also for validity and reliability. Validity refers to whether or not a test really measures what it claims to measure; reliability refers to whether or not the same individual taking the test again would receive the same score—assuming that no learning had occurred in the intervening time.

Standardized tests are a new phenomenon, a product of modern science. They were not developed before the last two decades of the nineteenth century. During the 1880's and 1890's, feeble and crude efforts were made to construct scientific measurements of mental and academic achievements. For example, in the early 1890's, an American by the name of Joseph Rice put together a rough, semi-standardized test of achievement in spelling, and shocked an unbelieving nation with findings gained from it.

It was not until the first decade of the twentieth century, however, that full-fledged standardized tests appeared. From that time on, the growth in the number of standardized tests has been stupendous. Today the market is filled with thousands of standardized tests of almost every conceivable variety and quality.

Standardized tests do not serve the same purpose as teacher-made tests. The latter are designed to measure how well the students have learned what their teacher has taught them in the light of his teaching emphases and objectives. Standardized tests are designed for broader and different uses, such as comparing a given pupil with other pupils in the school, state, region, and nation for the purpose of understanding the pupil more fully. Standardized tests can be used to diagnose a student's difficulties and strengths, to foretell a student's probable behavior or achievement, or to ascertain how much a student knows about a given topic. They can be used as a clue to the educational needs of a student. They can be used to suggest the ratio of a student's achievement to his abilities. With much caution, they can be used sometimes as a clue to how well a teacher teaches. They can be used to ascertain the special interests (such as vocational interest), aptitudes (such as intelligence), and problems (such as psychiatric disorders) that a student might have. Standardized tests are especially useful for guidance purposes and in order to understand pupils more fully. The construction, use, and interpretation of standardized tests has become a field of its own within the larger field of educational psychology.

Evaluating Pupil Progress and the Transfer of Training

One of the most perplexing problems faced by teachers is that of measuring not only their pupils' learning but also the probability of a transfer of that learning. When a child receives an "A" on a test, does this mark mean that the child will make use of what he has learned later in his life? Is the "A" student most likely to transfer his training, and is the "F" student least likely to transfer the modicum of learning that he has received? Remember our discussion early in this chapter of the patrioteer, the white-collar criminal, and the religious bigot. Apparently all of these sorts of people have done some learning, but they have failed to transfer adequately what they have learned.

How does one measure future transfer? Some teachers, rather hopelessly, suggest that pupils should not be evaluated until a lapse of a quarter of a century in order to find out whether or not the pupils actually can use, do use, and have used the knowledge to which they were exposed as youths. This suggestion is not realistic, of course, but it does point to a real problem —that of testing for transfer.

While there is no ready answer, the situation is far from unpromising.

There is an old maxim that states, "The boy I am today is the man I will become tomorrow." There is some continuity to an individual's behavior, although the maxim is too simply put to be accurate. The person who, as a child, displays an unusual degree of intelligence probably will continue to be above average in intelligence for the rest of his life. The person who, as a child, displays an ability to apply universals to specific situations or to generalize from a series of related specific situations probably will continue to do so easily for the rest of his life. The person who, as a child, is able to verbalize a concept quickly probably will be able to do so for the rest of his life. This, in fact, is one of the reasons why standardized tests are useful. They can be used as instruments for predicting future behavior. Experienced teachers know also that pupils tend to be fairly consistent in the marks they receive in various courses from one grade level to the next. The child who does poorly in arithmetic in the third grade probably will do poorly in arithmetic in the fifth grade and in the seventh grade and in the ninth grade. Thus, both from teacher-made tests and from standardized tests, there is some basis for predicting the future behavior of pupils.

But the basic questions remain unanswered still. How does a teacher actually test future transfer of training? Some very consicentious educationists suggest that the teacher should take time to write down all of the course objectives before preparing his test. These objectives would include societal aims, educational aims, and, to the extent that he is aware of them, the aims of his pupils. Then, as he writes each test item, he should ask himself, "How does this test item contribute to the realization of these aims?" Only those test items that are consistent with these aims and that contribute to the realization of these aims should be included in the test. Further, every test should include within it enough items so that all of the aims of the course are represented in the test. It is hoped that through this process the scores made by the pupils on such a test will represent their progress toward a realization of the above aims. The assumption underlying this practice is that if progress is made toward these aims, transfer of training must surely occur.

Other teachers suggest that no test question should ever solicit mere memorized information. Every test question should force the student to apply what he has learned. This means that test questions should be worded in such a way that students are forced to make use of conceptual learning and to reorganize and transfer their learning. This approach, it is thought, helps to establish in the student the habit of transferring his knowledge. Thus, Earl H. Bell, a sociologist, in the test-question manual that accompanies his college-level textbook in general sociology, encourages teachers of sociology to use questions that call upon the students to interpret material and to apply their knowledge. He offers this example of one such question.

A friend wants to adopt an infant; a little girl approximately two weeks old is available. She is normal to above normal in intelligence. While the parents and grandparents are healthy and of long-lived stock, the antecedents on both sides have a history of immorality and crime for two generations. The child is the illegitimate child of a mother 14 years old. The maternal grandmother was a prostitute. The child's father, 30 years of age, is serving a prison sentence for bank robbery. Its paternal grandfather was a gangster bootlegger during prohibition.

Your friend consults with you regarding the advisability of adopting this child. What sociological principles will you point out to him? [6]

In order to answer this question, one must apply various sorts of previous learning. The assumption is that if students can answer thought questions ably, they will continue to apply their learning later. Thus, transfer is tested.

Still other teachers, unconvinced of the ability of any test to measure future transfer of training, suggest that the greatest utility of a test (teacher-made or standardized) is that of understanding the pupils more thoroughly. This deepened understanding of the pupils may be used, then, to make the educational experience more meaningful to the students. A more meaningful educational experience, in turn, can contribute to the pupil's ability to transfer his training to life beyond the confines of the classroom.

In Summary

Psychology, perhaps the most forceful of the social sciences affecting educational practices, has given rise to that foundational field of education known as educational psychology. This chapter has taken a few swatches from the bolts of psychology's materials in order to suggest the kinds of contributions that psychology makes to that elaborate garment, education. The student who plans to teach will have occasion to study educational psychology with considerable depth.

The crucial question of educational psychology is transfer of training. While no foolproof recipes yet exist for developing transfer of training, prudent teachers, through their understanding of pupils, of learning, of motivation, and of pupil evaluation, seek means to make educational ex-

[6] "Instructor's Manual for Earl H. Bell's *Social Foundations of Human Behavior.*" (New York: Harper & Brothers, n. d.), p. 1.

periences so rewarding that their pupils will remember, use, and apply what they have learned.[7]

The Chapter in Capsule Form

1. It is thought generally that no social science holds a more important foundational place in the structure of education than psychology.

2. Educational psychology contains a selection of those materials of a psychological nature that are useful to educationists for accomplishing the goals of education and of society.

3. If educationists expect to achieve a transfer of learning on the part of their pupils, they must:

3.1 understand children.

3.2 understand learning.

3.3 understand desirable motivation.

3.4 understand measurement and evaluation of pupil progress.

4. In order to understand children, educationists may:

4.1 learn about children from studies of child growth and development.

4.2 become sensitive to the similarities and differences of the children within their classes in order to accommodate the individual differences of their pupils.

4.3 utilize the guidance services of the school.

5. In their understanding of learning, educationists have identified two significant types of learning:

5.1 perceptual learning—appropriate especially for learning skills, data, tasks, and the like.

5.2 conceptual learning—appropriate especially for solving problems.

6. In order to motivate students in a desirable fashion, educationists might use such techniques as these:

6.1 create a democratic atmosphere.

[7] If you are wondering still about Joe Doodlebug, here is the answer. Joe does not have to jump forward; he can jump sideways and backward, as well. Joe had made one sideways jump to the east just before the food was put down. Thus, he had to make three more sideways jumps east before he could make one sideways jump west and land on the food.

6.2 present materials vividly in terms that the pupils comprehend.

6.3 attempt to utilize the self-motivation of pupils.

6.4 offer tuition to the pupils as they learn—including the recent tuitional technique of programmed instruction.

7. In order to understand pupil progress, educationists may use one or both of two kinds of tests:

7.1 teacher-made tests—designed to measure how well the student has grasped the materials in some course in which he has been enrolled.

7.2 standardized tests—which have broader uses such as diagnosis, prognosis, or motivation.

8. Students planning to become teachers will have occasion to study the psychology of education in advanced courses.

For Supplementary Reading

BUROS, OSCAR K., ed., *Mental Measurements Yearbook.* Highland Park, N. J.: The Gryphon Press, various years.

This is the basic reference volume with regard to standardized tests.

HARRIS, CHESTER W., ed., *Encyclopedia of Educational Research,* 3rd ed. New York: The Macmillan Co., 1960.

This is an important reference work for educationists. See especially the articles on adolescence, childhood and pre-adolescence, counseling theory, educational psychology, evaluation, learning, measurement and scaling, mental development, motivation, student personnel work, student records and reports, tests and examinations, and transfer of learning.

JENKINS, GLADYS GARDNER; SHACTER, HELEN; and BAUER, WILLIAM W., *These Are Your Children,* expanded ed. Chicago: Scott, Foresman and Co., 1953.

Here is an amply illustrated, easy-to-read account of child development.

ROSENBLITH, JUDY F., and ALLINSMITH, WESLEY, eds., *The Causes of Behavior.* Boston: Allyn and Bacon, 1962.

This book of readings has valuable selections from many sources. Some of the selections may prove difficult to read.

ROSS, CLAY C., *Measurement in Today's Schools,* rev. by Julian C. Stanley, 3rd ed. New York: Prentice-Hall, 1954.

Since its first edition in 1941, this has been a widely used introductory volume on the subject of tests and measurements.

SAWREY, JAMES M., and TELFORD, CHARLES W., *Educational Psychology.* Boston: Allyn and Bacon, 1958.

Part I of this book has an extensive description of motivation and learning.

The entire book amplifies materials discussed in the present chapter.

Trow, William Clark, *Psychology in Teaching and Learning*. Boston: Houghton Mifflin Co., 1960.

This is one of several standard textbooks in educational psychology. It will give the reader an idea of the general topics treated by educational psychologists.

Your Child from 6 to 12. Washington: Children's Bureau, U. S. Dept. of Health, Education and Welfare, 1949.

This is one of the most widely distributed publications in the world with regard to the elementary-school child.

8

A Philosophical Approach to Education

> *Every year if not every day we have to wager our salva-*
> *tion upon some prophecy based upon imperfect knowl-*
> *edge.*
>
> from Mr. Justice Holmes' dissenting opinion in *Abrams*
> *et al.* v. *United States,* 250 U. S. 616 (1919).

Thinking It Over Beforehand

1. Why must a teacher have a philosophy of education?

2. From the educational standpoint, is the material to be learned or the learner himself the center of the educational processes?

3. When is a person fully educated?

4. Should courses such as folk dancing, cooking, driver training, or leathercraft be taught at school?

5. Can schools prepare students adequately to face a future way of life that will probably be very different from the present way of life?

Philosophies and Education

Twentieth-century American education has provided the arena for a lengthy battle among strikingly different points of view, strikingly different orientations, and strikingly different philosophies of education. The number of children pounding at the doors of the nation's schools has grown enormously. Educational laws force schools, except in extreme circumstances, to accept all members of this heterogeneous throng, regardless of the psychological or sociological or anthropological backgrounds of the pupils. Under these circumstances, questions arise as to the role of the schools in our society and as to the prime objective to which American education should be dedicated.

But there is no time to wait until ultimate answers have been collected. Children are in school *now*. They must be taught *now*. This means that educationists must use partial, inadequate, tentative, fractional social-scientific findings upon which to base their actions. Educationists must use their judgment as to what is best in a given situation when many of the facts are unknown to them or perhaps not even available. They have to guess what to do. They must improvise when no music is at hand. This is where philosophy enters.

Some shallow educationists, posing as high priests of education and surrounding themselves with fistfuls of statistical sigmas, chi squares, and medians, insist that education is completely a science and that, in a science, everything can be reduced to black or white. Thus, there is a right way to teach and a wrong way to teach. There is a right objective for education and a wrong objective for education. There is a right emphasis in education and a wrong emphasis in education. There is a right viewpoint in education and a wrong viewpoint in education. There is a right orientation in education and a wrong orientation in education.

Maybe someday the answers will become so fixed and the evidence so indisputable that one will be able to put the "do's" and the "don't's" in opposite columns. But we are still a long way from that point. Scientific materials about education certainly do exist, and some of them are very valuable. Most of these materials, however, are not entirely complete. We could know a great deal more about education than we do now. Furthermore, even when the scientific materials are reasonably available, there is still the question of the relative importance of each scientific item. Also, there is the question of what each scientific datum *really* means. There is much room for sincere, honest differences in interpretation, in point of view, in values. Scientific facts are weighed, measured, and catalogued differently by different people because of value differences, because of differences in orientation, because of differences in points of view—in other words, because of philosophical differences. Philosophical differences affect how and what a teacher teaches, what goes into the entire curriculum, what kind of educative work the school performs in its community.

Twentieth-century American education has been an arena. Two extreme philosophies, in particular, have been vying with each other for control of the schools. One of these basic philosophies insists that the *center* of the educative processes must be subject matter. If children are to become adequate citizens of tomorrow, they must know about the cultural heritage of mankind. They must know about the ways of citizens who went before

Courtesy of United Air Lines

SHOULD SUBJECT MATTER OR THE CHILD BE THE CENTER OF EDUCATION?

them. Only when they know the best of the accumulated intellectual legacy of mankind will there be direction in their lives.

The other extreme philosophy is just as insistent that the *center* of the educative processes must be the learner himself. The hopes, the still embryonic dreams, the needs, the wants of this potential citizen of tomorrow must be the focal point for education. Unless the learner can discover how to make his dreams come true, unless the learner can satisfy his innermost longings, there will be no tomorrow worth worrying about.

Almost overnight, America has been plunged from a sleepy, simple, neolithic, agricultural way of life into a busy, swift-moving, complex, atomic age of machines. How can we best educate for these, our giddy and intricate times? On this topic, too, the vying philosophies have had their say. One of them insists that only by clinging to the living truth that has survived the years can we know how to cope with the basic problems of life itself. The best way to plan for the future is to know the past—the rich, hoary knowledge that has survived the furnaces of time without the smell

[257]

of fire. Know the truth and it will liberate you. The rival philosophy states that new occasions teach new duties. The waltz steps that satisfied people in the past are not necessarily satisfactory in these, the new contrapuntal, polyphonic times. Turn not to the records of the past for the key; turn rather to the learner himself and the needs that beset him from day to day. Teach not subjects—teach pupils.

Each of these two philosophies of education has a career that we shall examine hastily. First, however, a word of caution is necessary to prepare the reader for the inevitable distortion that occurs when one selects a few facts in a rather hurried manner. The scores of each of these rival philosophies can be found in that vibrant symphony which is the history of education in the Western World. In the following paragraphs, a few bars from the main theme of each of these scores will be played by itself. Be aware of the fact that the score for a single instrument will not give a very good idea of the depth and flow of an entire symphony. The violent blast of the trombone or the nasal whine of the clarinet is hardly an adequate representation of Beethoven's Fifth. Recognize that the description of each of these philosophies omits the parts that other instruments of education have played. Do not expect these excerpts to sound highly sonorous under the circumstances. With this warning in mind, we turn first to the concept of the subject-centered school.

Greeks Bearing Gifts

Many of our educational practices can be traced to Grecian taproots. Among these practices is that of the subject-centered curriculum.

Plato

The idea of a subject-centered, rather than child-centered, curriculum can be perceived readily in the thinking of that fourth-century Grecian giant, Plato. In an earlier chapter, mention was made that Plato had founded a college at Athens—the Academy. This broad-shouldered Greek, whom we know by the descriptive nickname Plato, has left us the legacy of his philosophical writings. In his monumental book, the *Republic,* we have his dream of the ideal educational system—a dream stimulated by the perplexing political upheavals of Athens at the close of the Hellenic period.

Plato, fully aware that people differ from one another in capability, envisioned a utopian society in which every child, whether boy or girl, would have the opportunity to go to school. Who knows if genius lies hidden in the child until he has an opportunity to develop his potential? The education that Plato outlined for all children resembles very much the traditional elementary education offered to the boys of wealthy citizens in Hellenic Athens. The children would study gymnastics, music, and letters. He suggested further that religion should be included in the curriculum. He saw religion somewhat as a Marxian opiate to keep people content with their lot. Plato made no apologies whatsoever for suggesting that all materials taught to the young must be highly edited. It is more important, he thought, for students to *know* "correct" answers than to *understand* the reasons behind them, especially when some children cannot understand in any event.

After the pupils attained the age of twenty in this utopia, there would be a relentless culling process. They would be examined vigorously. The examinations would be both theoretical and practical in nature, and the questions and tasks would be made very difficult. Many students would fail because of their lack of necessary intellectual powers. Failing students would drop out and would become business people, artisans, or farmers who, according to Plato, need not possess much intelligence to perform their lowly tasks.

The remaining students would continue as a group for another ten years. They would receive moral, mental, and muscular training of an advanced nature. When the ten-year period had expired, there would be a second comprehensive examination more difficult by far than the first. Most students would fail. Those who failed would become military and governmental workers, career soldiers and civil-service personnel, guardians and aides for the utopia.

The few students who remained—the highly select brain-power elite— would study for another five years. They would go beyond the myths and catchwords taught to the populace and would examine the philosophical answers to life and the universe. In so doing, they would become philosopher kings. After the completion of this final period of study, these geniuses would face a third test. The test would last fifteen years and be of an apprenticeship nature. The students would attempt to apply what they had learned. Finally, at the age of fifty, those who had survived would become the rulers of Plato's utopia.

Even though Plato recognized three distinct levels of mental ability, his primary emphasis was not on how to make the child into a self-realized individual, but on the subject matter to be learned. Plato's dreamings are categorized, therefore, as subject-centered rather than child-centered. He listed subjects that were both worth learning and essential for the person to know in order to function well in the society. If the student could master them, he would be elevated to the next stage. If not, out he would go. The child was to be tailored to the curriculum, rather than the curriculum to the child.

Hellenistic Athens

When Athens became a part of Alexander's empire, the educative system begun by the Hellenic Greeks went into a period of decline and change. The old Hellenic educational system was of a practical nature. Some of its former meaning departed when the Athenian city-state was gone. Once boys were prepared for their role as citizens by training in literary studies, in music, and in physical prowess. After 300 B.C. this sort of education no longer had a practical outlet. Athenian music changed in quality and became somewhat similar to our own contemporary mass music. The words were fatuous, the tunes were of the ditty variety, and elite people found the study of this sort of music distasteful. Music schools disappeared. Athletics underwent professionalization, somewhat as intercollegiate sports at their worst have done in our colleges and universities. People of quality considered association with this type of athletics to be unsavory. The demand for physical-education schools slackened, and the schools sank into oblivion. On the higher level of education, military training was unnecessary after Athens as a separate city-state had ceased to exist.

All that remained educationally of the old school system were the schools of a strictly academic variety. But even in those schools the curriculum did not offer the practical, semi-vocational training that had been offered in earlier times. Education moved in the direction of becoming an end in itself. A person studied oratory or the persuasive use of words not to sway political gatherings, but for the aesthetic value of being able to put together well-constructed phrases. Higher education of the sort initiated by men such as Plato and Aristotle became absorbed in metaphysical speculations. The ability to cleverly bat ideas about like pingpong balls became the objective.

The final result was that the original marriage of education and practical affairs ended in divorce. Education was separated from the routine processes of everyday life, and was expected to train the mind through mastery of subject matter. The objective of education became education. It was an end in itself.

The Latin Lamp of Learning

Grecian education was in this emasculated condition when the Romans became acquainted with it. The Romans, somewhat like the Americans, were doers more than thinkers. Also, they were adept at borrowing. Impressed by the seemingly advanced nature of Grecian education, the Romans appropriated a modified form of the sort of Grecian education just described.

The Roman elementary school copied the Grecian literary school—not the worn-out music school or gymnastic school. The Greeks had forgotten the well-rounded person. The Romans probably were unaware of this earlier Hellenic ideal, or else were not impressed by it. The Roman elementary school emphasized training in the three R's for the children of the elite.

The Bettmann Archive

EDUCATION IN ANCIENT ROME WAS SUBJECT CENTERED.

The Roman secondary school had a narrow curriculum, too. The Romans thought so little of their own language that their first secondary schools were Greek grammar schools. Students studied the Greek language and its literature. Only later did native-language secondary schools develop. The parallel in our early American educational scene is striking. Our first secondary schools were foreign-language schools. Only later were native-language secondary schools promoted in America.

In the early days, a Roman who wanted a higher education had to go to Greece or to some Grecian-influenced area to study. When the Roman Republic was on the point of expiring, Roman rhetorical schools began to crop up. These rhetorical schools were aimed at preparing students for political careers. But vocational outlets narrowed when the republic disappeared. Thus, the rhetorical schools offered students the opportunity of studying oratory as an end in itself. The ability to express something sparklingly became the objective.

In the waning years of the Roman Empire, the contents of advanced formal education began to be packaged neatly into what came to be known as the seven liberal arts. Capella, a pagan Latin, wrote an educational allegory concerning a heavenly wedding between philology and Mercury. Seven angelic bridesmaids attended the bride, philology. These seven bridesmaids represented the most important subjects that the Romans had borrowed from Greece. Since the heavenly bridesmaids were celestial, ethereal creatures, they could represent only those Grecian studies that were also out of this world—those studies that were basically mental or spiritual, not physical. Thus the seven liberal arts were born. These seven liberal arts can be remembered by means of a convenient mnemonic device: *G(i)RL GAMA*.

> *G*rammar
> *R*hetoric
> *L*ogic
>
> *G*eometry
> *A*rithmetic
> *M*usic
> *A*stronomy

Capella's list in time became the basis for the curriculum of generation after generation of scholars. He who was conversant with the subject matter of the seven liberal arts was thought to be a learned man. The essence of education was the knowledge of this spiritual subject matter.

Enter the Church

In the meantime, Christianity began to crystallize and assume a fixed shape. As it did so, there came into existence *right* Christian ideals, *right* Christian beliefs, *right* Christian creeds, and *right* Christian practices. In order to make sure that communicants would know these right ways, the Church entered the educational scene during the decadent years of the Roman Empire. At first instruction was scant—hardly more than a catechism-like class for prospective members. Eventually, however, by the time the empire which was Rome lay in ruins, the Church became the dominant educative force in Western Europe.

As the Church took a greater part in the task of formal education, the curriculum expanded to include not only catechizing but also the training of personnel for the priesthood and, to some extent, the educating of noblemen. For prospective priests, years and years of formal training were needed so that a man might have both a scholarly education and vocational proficiency.

The question of how to educate a scholar posed a problem for the Church. A man named Cassiodorus, however, helped to find a satisfactory answer. Cassiodorus had resented the fact that the unbaptized, heathen

Capella had organized the seven liberal arts; yet, at the same time, he found it difficult to reject the seven liberal arts as marks of the learned man. In his own mind he reached a compromise: he Christianized the seven liberal arts. By poring over the Bible, Cassiodorus came upon a verse that proved to his satisfaction that the seven liberal arts were gifts from God Himself. Proverbs 9:1 reads, "Wisdom has built her mansion, and set up her seven pillars. . . ." [1] Cassiodorus believed that the verse referred to those seven pillars of wisdom, the seven liberal arts. The seven liberal arts became the core of the secondary and collegiate curriculums of medieval Europe. To know the seven pillars of wisdom was to be liberally educated. Both priests and noblemen began to study these arts, and again subject matter stood at the heart of the curriculum.

Several centuries later, at the end of the Dark Ages, another churchman continued the Christianizing of pagan writings. Western Europe had stumbled upon the works of the ancient Greek, Aristotle. Thomas Aquinas converted heathen Aristotelian writings to Christianity in a skillfully developed synthetic philosophy of theology known as Scholasticism. Aristotle's works, having received a Christian blessing, were added to the seven liberal arts. The learned man was the man who knew the liberal arts and who was conversant with Aristotle as filtered through Scholasticism. Mastery of these subjects was the mark of the educated person.

The Rebirth of Secularism

Fourteenth-century Europe was marked by a rebirth or renaissance of learning. Secular Grecian and Roman literature was reintroduced into the scholarly world. A renewed interest in earthly scientific pursuits developed. The intent of the intellectual leaders of the Renaissance was to augment learning, to liberalize the liberal arts by emphasizing secular studies, to free men's minds from the strait jacket of traditionalism.

From the educational standpoint, the liberalizing of learning was incomplete. Two reasons are especially significant. First, the study of the classics, which began as a way to escape from narrowness of thought, became a prevalent enterprise of the intelligentsia. Educated people were supposed to pore over the classics. A perusing of the classics became an end in itself, not a means to freedom of thought. Into the curriculum came the study of the classics, the badge of intellectualism. Knowledge of the classics overshadowed freedom through the classics. Mastery of subject matter predominated.

Second, the Renaissance was marked by the rise of a wealthy middle-

[1] James Moffatt translation.

class merchant group often referred to as the bourgeoisie. The bourgeoisie, wanting to think itself the equal of the nobility, demanded for its sons the same sort of education that noblemen were receiving. No substitutes. No diluted instruction. This meant that the bourgeoisie clamored for the aging pillars of wisdom veneered with a layer of Aristotelianism, for this was the traditional curriculum that gentlemen studied. The bourgeoisie defined the educated person as one who has been exposed to a particular body of information.

Thus it was that educational systems during the Renaissance continued the seven liberal arts, plus Aristotle, adding to this a study of the classics, including the study of classical languages as such. Thus it was, also, that the subject-centered curriculum continued.

Ecclesiastical and Nationalistic Surges

Two significant upheavals occurred in Europe in the sixteenth and seventeenth centuries. The Western church was split into Catholic and Protestant sectors, and the Protestant sector was splintered in matchwood fashion into a series of sects. Accompanying the religious upheaval was a governmental upheaval, as powerful states began to develop in Europe. These twin movements added, at least in embryonic form, two new considerations: education for salvation and education for citizenship. In both cases *correct* ideas were looked upon as being more important than freedom of thought. The soul, to be saved from damnation, needed to know correct answers. The citizen, to be loyal, needed to know the correct version of patriotism.

The wealthy, both bourgeois and noble, demanded a continuation of the aging curriculum designed to produce gentility—the seven liberal arts, Aristotle, and the classics based on a thorough study of ancient languages. But, particularly in Protestant countries, lower schools for the masses began to take shape. The beginnings of the modern public school can be found here. The lowly masses needed the rudiments of education, too—for their souls' sakes, if not to increase their patriotism. The curriculum for the children of commoners was the time-honored three R's, together with a sizable dose of a fourth R: religion. These subjects were taught in the pupils' native language. To be an educated member of the masses meant to be able to read Scripture and recite dogma, both pious and patriotic. This called for a subject-centered curriculum.

It was during this period that colonists sailed from Europe to America. American educational systems took shape, bearing European labels and formed from European subject-dominated molds. The European subject-

Courtesy of St. Augustine and St. Johns County
Chamber of Commerce, St. Augustine, Florida

COLONIAL AMERICAN EDUCATION WAS SUBJECT CENTERED. THIS IS A PICTURE
OF THE OLDEST WOODEN SCHOOLHOUSE IN THE UNITED STATES.

centered approach fitted neatly into the Puritan philosophy of childhood.
The chapter herein devoted to the history of education emphasized the
early interest of New England Puritans in education. The Puritans saw
children as ignorant, evil creatures who, at the same time, had the ability
to become partly rational. Instruction and discipline were necessary, however, for encouraging the child to use his reason and for suppressing his
untoward nature. Instruction meant putting into the child something that
he did not possess originally. It meant filling an empty vessel, substituting
desirable qualities for depraved ones. All of this, of course, called for in-
stilling subject matter derived from sources outside the child. On this
European and Puritan base the current American educational system has
been constructed. Traditionally, the American school system has been built
around a core of academically oriented subjects. (The reader is referred
again to Chapter 3 for a description of the development of American education.)

[265]

And Today

Today there are sincere, well-informed, dedicated people in America who are convinced that whatever else is done in the schools, the supreme immediate objective of education is to expose students to a particular body of subject matter. They are convinced that a school must be evaluated in terms of the subject-matter contents of its courses. They are convinced that a pupil's progress in school must be measured in terms of the mastery of subject matter. These people are highly displeased to find that rival educational philosophies have so invaded all levels of American education that the quality of curricular offerings is being jeopardized and our schools are being turned into "educational wastelands." [2] They believe beyond doubt that America's civilization is in real danger of being subverted because the schools and colleges fail to emphasize intellectual content in their classrooms. There must be a "restoration of learning." [2]

The Council for Basic Education is representative of vociferous groups of contemporary Americans who are genuinely troubled by what they see as the unscholarly status of American education. In the Council's volume, *The Case for Basic Education,* Clifton Fadiman, author, entertainer, and humanist, clearly states the case for basic education and for the subject-centered philosophy of education when he writes:

. . . apparently men desire to know and transmit all kinds of matters, from how to tie a four-in-hand to the attributes of the Godhead.

Obviously this chaos cannot be taught. Hence in the past men have imposed upon it form, order, and hierarchy. They have selected certain areas of knowledge as the ones that, to the exclusion of others, both *can* and *should* be taught.

The structure of this hierarchy is not a matter of accident. Nor is it a matter of preference. . . . Basic education concerns itself with those matters which, once learned, enable the student to learn all the other matters, whether trivial or complex, that cannot properly be the subjects of elementary and secondary schooling. In other words, both logic and experience suggest that certain subjects have generative power and others do not have generative power. When we have learned to tie a four-in-hand, the subject is exhausted. It is self-terminating. Our knowledge is of no value for the acquisition of further knowledge. But once we have learned to read we can decipher instructions for the tieing of a four-in-hand. Once we have learned to listen and observe, we can learn from someone else how to tie a four-in-hand.

[2] Both of these expressions are from the titles of books written by Arthur Bestor, a leading critic of American education.

It has, up to our time, been the general experience of men that certain subjects and not others possess this generative power.

. . . .

. . . however their forms may be modified, a core of basic or generative subjects exists. This core is not lightly to be abandoned, for once it is abandoned we have lost the primary tools which enable us to make any kind of machine we wish. Other subjects may seem transiently attractive or of obvious utility. It is pleasant to square-dance, for instance, and it is useful to know how to cook. Yet we cannot afford to be seduced by such "subjects." Hard though it may be, we must jettison them in favor of the basic subject matters. And there is no time for an eclectic mixture: only a few years are available in which to educe, to educate the rational soul. We cannot afford bypaths.[3]

Arthur Bestor, a college professor and vehement exponent of the subject-centered school, describes the sorts of basic courses needed in American schools.

A simple glance at two or three of the most obvious developments in the life and thought of the twentieth century will show the direction in which the school curriculum ought to be developing. So far as the experience of the ordinary man is concerned, the most spectacular development has been the application of advanced scientific knowledge to the things of everyday life. Electronics (that is to say, advanced physics) has entered the living-room with radio and television. Chemistry has become part of the household with detergents and synthetic fibers and plastics. Biochemistry and physiology are affecting the daily regimen of all persons who make use of vitamins and antibiotics. None of these matters can be understood except in terms of concepts vastly more complicated and abstract than those required to explain the operation of the devices with which our grandfathers were familiar. If present-day scientific and technological developments mean anything for the public-school curriculum, they mean that an intensified emphasis upon the theoretical principles embodied in the basic sciences is essential in a modern school.

Equally significant in the twentieth century has been the application of precise quantitative thinking to an ever wider range of human affairs. From the Bureau of the Budget to the Bureau of Standards, mathematics and statistics have entered more pervasively than ever before into practical life. The implication for the school is that the simple-minded conception of mathematics as primarily a matter of making change and figuring how many cups of punch can be dipped from a gallon bowl is completely outmoded, and that algebra, trigonometry, and calculus have now become essential elements in the education of any citizen who expects to be well-informed in the modern world.

It is a truism, finally, that modern communications have thrown the various peoples of the world, willy-nilly, into more intimate contact with one another

---

[3] Clifton Fadiman, "The Case for Basic Education," *The Case for Basic Education*, ed. by J. D. Koerner. Boston: Little, Brown and Co., 1959, pp. 5–8. Copyright, ©, 1959, by Council for Basic Education.

than ever before. A knowledge of foreign languages can no longer be looked upon simply as an ornament. For an ever-increasing proportion of the residents of our once-isolated continent, such knowledge has become for the first time an extremely practical need. The implication for the public-school curriculum is obvious.[4]

Pupils in the Limelight

We turn now to the opposing extreme philosophy of education, which is advocated with equal integrity and genuineness. The idea of the pupil-centered curriculum has grown out of a spirit of revolt against traditionalism. This same spirit of revolt has been largely responsible for bringing into being the democratic way of life as interpreted in the modern world. It has been a humanitarian movement that has placed human values above all other values. The history of the pupil-centered curriculum and its philosophy are best appreciated through a study of the ideas of its major exponents. The views of three of them will be examined in the following sections of the chapter.

Rousseau: Education Within Nature

One of the most important forerunners in the development of the idea of a child-centered school was the French author, Jean Jacques Rousseau (1712–1778). He was not a teacher, but a writer of essays on social issues. When the student turns to Rousseau, he turns to one of the strangest men ever to affect human history. Rousseau's critics can readily point out that his life was one of paradox, instability, and frustration. They can point out that he was undisciplined in his behavior, neurotic, and out of joint with life. But after his many flaws have been identified, it is difficult to find any other one man who has lived during the past third of a millenium who has more deeply influenced human thought and institutions than Rousseau. His political philosophy anticipated modern democracy as we understand that term today. This philosophy certainly is echoed in American Jacksonian democracy and in the reliance on the dictum of *vox populi, vox Dei*. Likewise, contemporary educational practices mirror Rousseau's ideas about education, even though no important group has ever seriously tried to follow his educational suggestions word for word.

[4] Arthur Bestor, *The Restoration of Learning*. (New York: Alfred A. Knopf, 1955), pp. 41–42.

Rousseau, like most people, was a child of his age. In fact, his bitterest critics accuse him of plagiarism. Yet, while he borrowed liberally from his times, his particular statements of these views had an effect that few other writings have had. His unique contribution was, perhaps, not so much *what* he said as *how* he said it. Rousseau's ideas sprang largely from that intellectual movement of the eighteenth century known as the Enlightenment. The philosophy of the Enlightenment, in turn, was to extend Newtonian physics to all branches of knowledge—especially to those dealing with human affairs.

There is an order in nature, thought the philosophers of the Enlightenment, that applies as much to the apple falling from the tree as to the behavior of human beings. When the natural order is followed and respected, all is well. When this order is interrupted or violated, trouble occurs. Thus it is with gravity: respect gravity, and you will be happy; defy gravity, and you will be harmed. Thus it is, too, with man's social ways. Man as a natural being has been created to live a particular way of life, just as chickens are created to live like chickens and bobcats to live like bobcats. When people follow the sort of life that nature has designed for them, all is well. When people molest nature's patterns, they suffer from corrupt governments, inane customs, and superficial social ways. Society should be made for man, not man for society. Those clerics who insist that man's original nature is sinful are wrong. Man is not born depraved; he is born good and is capable of perfection. He becomes depraved only through the corrupting influences of an unnatural environment imposed upon him by people who themselves have become corrupt. Thus, if man is immoral, it is an immoral society that has made him so.

Most of the philosophers of the Enlightenment placed heavy emphasis on human reason as the means whereby mankind can discover what nature intends. Rousseau parted from their company on this point. He placed his emphasis, instead, on feeling or emotion and on what contemporary behavioral scientists would call inner tendencies (what earlier generations would have called instinct). Man instinctively senses what is good because he is born good.

Rousseau, like Plato centuries before him, longed for an ideal society. For Rousseau the ideal society was one that would conform to nature. Several of his writings were addressed to this subject. In time he pondered a question that Plato had also pondered. How best can one educate a person to take his place in the ideal society? Rousseau's basic answer can be found in a novel entitled *Émile, ou De l'Éducation*. With the brush strokes of an artist, Rousseau detailed the sort of education that would prepare a person to become an ideal citizen in an ideal society in which justice, brotherhood, and equality would flourish, in which man's inhumanity to man would be unknown, and in which spearshafts could be beaten in to drive shafts.

The ideal education must conform to nature. "All things are good as they came out of the hands of their Creator," are Rousseau's opening words, "but every thing degenerates in the hands of man." For this reason, the ideal education must not be contaminated by preconceived notions about how or what to teach. Nature itself will determine the pattern of education. To a great extent the ideal education must be a negative one. It concerns what *not* to teach. Introduce nothing to the pupil until nature offers cues for its introduction.

The role of the teacher in this sort of educational setting is very different from his role as conceived traditionally. It is not the teacher's function to decide on his own what subjects should be taught. It is not the teacher's function to present materials that require parroting or rote memorization because they lack meaning for the learner. It is not the teacher's function to be the active agent of education while the child sits passively. Rather, the teacher must do what the roots of the word "education" imply. Education comes from two Latin words, $\bar{e}$ and *ducere,* meaning to draw from within. In other words, the teacher must pull out of the child what is already in him. This means that the teacher must actually be the student— the student of the child. When the child indicates that he is prepared to learn a certain subject, the teacher must then offer (or, if necessary, create) situations in which the subject can be learned most readily and meaningfully. Since the learning comes from within, the so-called "telling" method of teaching must be pushed aside. Instead, the child should be his own teacher, as he experiences for himself, guided by his tutor, those things that he is prepared naturally to learn. Learning is active, not passive. The instructor merely sets the scene when the time is ripe, and the child finds out for himself by doing and by undergoing. Learning, then, is discovery. The teacher must be careful not to short-circuit the learning process by offering the child prefabricated answers. The child should find the answers for himself with only minimal coaching from the tutor.

Children go through four quite abrupt stages of educational development, according to Rousseau. Each stage is sufficiently different from the others to warrant a different sort of curriculum. At the same time, each stage, when treated educationally as nature intends, prepares the child for the succeeding stages. The story of *Émile* is the story of the four stages of educational development through which the hero of nature's education, a lad named Émile, goes. Emile intuitively knows what he needs to learn at each stage, and his tutor merely assists him in taking full advantage of nature's wishes in the matter.

The first stage (until age five) is infancy. During infancy, nature's education centers around acquainting the child with the functions of his body and with the unavoidable inconveniences that the body must endure, such as changes in the weather, fatigue, and hunger. The child during this stage of his education should have no habits or routines thrust upon him by outsiders. Rousseau went so far as to suggest that the child's own routines, such as sleep, be interrupted in order to condition Émile early to the inconveniences to which he must soon adjust.

The second stage (age five to twelve) is early childhood. During early childhood, nature's education centers around training the child in the use of his senses and in simple lessons concerning morality. Sensory training will lead him to study geometry and drawing. For example, if Émile wants to pick cherries, he must procure a ladder of the right height, and this calls for a knowledge of measurement. Moral training should be negative. The child learns the consequences of untoward acts by having to suffer them. For example, little Émile, interested in plants, sows seeds in a bed already planted by another gardener. The gardener uproots Émile's seedlings, much to the boy's sorrow. But Émile learns through this experience a respect for the property of others.

His senses now attuned, the child is ready for the third stage (age twelve to fifteen), that of reasoning. Learning at this stage, as in the previous stages, will be based on what the child is desirous of knowing and on what he feels the need to learn. He is now ready to read, to find out about the physical sciences, and to develop a trade. He will learn to read almost automatically, because he is ready to read. His reading materials will be limited to books that come closest to depicting nature as it actually is, such as *Robinson Crusoe,* because this is where his interests lie and this is what his previous training has prepared him to understand. In his study of the sciences, he will construct his own equipment, because, in so doing, he will comprehend more fully the principles he is studying. Trade training is included because the child has begun to sense the need of man to be independent economically of other men.

The fourth stage (age fifteen to twenty) is adolescence. During this stage, nature's education centers around the emotions. With the dawn of Émile's sexual powers comes a broader interest in all human interpersonal relationships. This is the time to introduce those courses that we today call the social studies. Through direct observation and travel, Émile will become sensitive to social problems, to comparative governments, and to the wide range of vocations that exist. Sex education will be introduced and will be treated in a straightforward manner. Religious instruction of a highly naturalistic nature will be introduced also during adolescence, now that the youth has a feeling for life.

At last the boy, trained by nature, is ready to be a man—a "noble citizen of nature" for a nobler society.

Rousseau's ideas are extravagant and are at best semi-truths. Yet these ideas, as seed blown by the wind, fell on fertile minds. Later thinkers, stimulated by Rousseau's heresies, were challenged to revise their own deliberations about education. Perhaps there actually is a developmental pattern within the child. Perhaps teachers ought to study children in order to find in them the clue regarding what and when to teach them. Perhaps it is better to wait until a child is ready to learn a subject before introducing it to him. Perhaps education should be tailored to the child, rather than the child forced in Procrustean fashion into some prefabricated educational scheme.

Pestalozzi: Education Through Child Growth

Johann Heinrich Pestalozzi (1746–1827) was a Swiss teacher who possessed far greater insight into teaching than Rousseau. Pestalozzi, deeply moved by Rousseau's thinking, challenged the subject-centered approach to teaching that prevailed in Europe. Where Rousseau was a marginal man, Pestalozzi was a warm, sensitive, discerning reformer. Where Rousseau was a dreamer, Pestalozzi was a doer.

Pestalozzi's chief concern was that of developing an adequate elementary education for the common man. During a part of his life he was an elementary-school teacher. He turned later to training would-be teachers in his "new" method of teaching. Pestalozzi's influence extended to various parts of Western Europe, such as Prussia, and thence indirectly to the United States. Horace Mann, among others, came under Pestalozzi's influence.

Starting from premises similar to Rousseau's, Pestalozzi recognized within the child a native developmental pattern from which teachers should take their cue. It is easy to understand Pestalozzi's views if one compares a child to a rosebush. The rosebush has within itself the potentials to grow into a beautiful plant with clusters of pointed leaves. It has the potentials to produce buds, which, in turn, have the potentials to become charming many-petaled flowers. All of these potentials are within the rosebush. The bush can grow and bloom if it is given the opportunity. But if one disturbs it, if one tries to make it into a geranium or a petunia or an oak tree, he will cause far more harm than good; he will abuse the rosebush. There is another consideration regarding the rosebush. The bush has the potentials to grow and bloom, but it must be cared for if these potentials are to be realized. For a fine bush full of perfect flowers, one must plant the bush in the right kind of soil, fertilize the bush, prune it, water it, and keep the myriads of pests from devouring or mutilating it. Thus, growing a perfect rosebush requires a twofold process. First, one must have the sort of plant that has the potentials to produce roses, and second, one must care for it. From within, the bush grows according to its own patterns, *provided that it has an appropriate environment in which to grow.*

Interpreted pedagogically, this allegory of the rosebush comes close to the core of Pestalozzi's beliefs. The child has within him his own pattern of development. To teach him effectively, one must know him, understand him, respect him, love him for what he is. The child is the center of his own education; an education that will benefit him most must conform to him, not him to the education. The school becomes the environment in which the child grows toward his own potentials. The school must be rich in those items that nourish the child. Start with the simple and the concrete, said Pestalozzi. Rely heavily on the child's own powers of observation. Place him in those learning situations that are so alive with interest *to him* that he will react with heart, mind, soul, and spirit. Pestalozzi was suspicious of materials that came only from books in the elementary school. Instead of reading or talking about something the child does not understand, let him see it for himself. Later, when he is ready, he can go from the concrete to the abstract.

In summary, Pestalozzi stimulated in teachers an interest in studying children. Today a person who plans to teach at the elementary-school level usually is required to take course work in child growth and development or some similar work of a genetic-psychological nature. This is a Pestalozzian influence. Pestalozzi also helped to develop courses in education. Before a person teaches, he should know how to teach. Another of Pestalozzi's contributions was his emphasis on the use of concrete objects to illustrate what is being learned. Filmstrips, motion pictures, sand tables, and the host of other aural and visual aids found in today's classrooms are traceable, at least in part, to Pestalozzi.

Froebel: Education of the Whole Child

A third European contributor to the concept of a child-centered school was the Germanic educator, Friedrich Froebel (1782–1852). Froebel was an associate of Pestalozzi and thus, rather obviously, came under the influence of Pestalozzian educative methods. Froebel is remembered chiefly as the founder of the kindergarten movement, but he was by no means the first person to see the importance of pre-primary education. He did, however, coin the word "kindergarten," a garden in which the tender child-

Courtesy of L. M. Cox Manufacturing Company, Inc.

CHILDREN ARE EAGER TO LEARN ABOUT THOSE THINGS WHICH INTEREST THEM.

rosebush could begin to develop. His prime interest was in the very young learner. His views about how to educate are focused upon the preschool child.

Froebel used a somewhat different base from those of Rousseau or Pestalozzi for developing his philosophy of education. In the technical language of the philosopher, Froebel would be classified as an absolute idealist. To Froebel the world and all in it, the universe and all in it, were parts of a greater encompassing unity. Each item is part of a larger item, which is part of a larger item, which is part of a larger item, which is part of a larger item, until, finally, one comes to the all-inclusive item, the Mind of God Himself. A clue to this wheel-within-wheel approach to the universe and its contents can be seen in the following address on a letter to one of the characters in Thornton Wilder's *Our Town:*

>   Jane Crofut
>   The Crofut Farm
>   Grover's Corners
>   Sutton County
>   New Hampshire
>   United States of America
>   Continent of North America
>   Western Hemisphere
>   The Earth
>   The Solar System
>   The Universe
>   The Mind of God.[5]

Froebel believed that each part was created for the purpose of serving the larger unities. And surrounding and embracing everything was God, who also has purposes. Everything that happens is involved in larger purposes, which ultimately lead to God's purposes.

Froebel wove his educational ideas within this elaborate framework. Each child is a creation of God. God has purposes, some of which have been placed within the child. The child should be given every opportunity for these God-given purposes to realize themselves through him. If someone else were to *tell* the child what to do or not to do, God's purposes might be thwarted. It is imperative that the child's behavior be self-directed, thus God-directed. The teacher must adjust education to the child, not the child to education. Everything the child does has purpose behind it. Education should not be viewed primarily as a preparation for something in the future, but rather as a means to the achievement of a current purpose of the child. Thus, education should not be thought of as a preparation for life, but as life itself.

If one watches the young child, he will find that the child is obsessed with play. Play is to the child as an occupation is to the adult. Education should center around play—supervised, directed, meaningful play. Education, if it really serves the purposes of the child, should be fun. Through

[5] See Burns Mantle, ed., *The Best Plays of 1937–38.* (New York: Dodd, Mead & Co., 1938), p. 75.

activities such as bouncing a ball and piling blocks and smearing papers with paint and molding snakes from clay and dancing and swinging and playing make-believe, the purposes of the child are realized.

The child himself, like God, is a unity of parts. If the purposes of the child are to be served, he must be thought of as a unity. Education cannot serve the child fully if it is aimed at the brain only. The *whole child* must be educated—his senses, his feelings, his emotions, his muscles, his mind. Here, too, play is relevant. The child exuberantly gives his energies completely to play. He trains muscles. He develops his senses. He exercises his emotions. He thinks. All education should be like this.

But the child himself is part of a greater unity: the group of his classmates. Education must involve him in the group, for his purposes and God's purposes intend that he be a functioning member of human associations. Unless the child's education assists him in learning how to participate in groups, God's purposes (through the child) will be thwarted. Education, then, must be socialized as well as individualized.

Froebel's ideas on education have been largely shorn of their pious-sounding metaphysics by his followers. When Froebel's thoughts about God are ignored, two sorts of educational emphases remain. The first concerns pre-primary education and how it should be approached. The second gives one of the bases for many of the popular catchwords that have become shibboleths in education. "We teach children, not subjects." "Educate the whole child." "Provide for individual differences." "Education is life, not merely preparation for life." "Learn by doing." "Start where the child is." "The best motivation is self-motivation." "The school is a society." "Don't teach about democracy—teach through democracy." "The curriculum includes everything that happens at the school."

A Fable for Our Times

Here is a fable written by a twentieth-century American psychologist. It illustrates effectively the impact of educational philosophers such as Rousseau, Pestalozzi, and Froebel on current educational thought in the United States. It gives a taste of what contemporary child-centered educationists have in mind when they insist that the child—not the subject—is their central concern.[6]

Once upon a time there was a man who had a son. He loved his son dearly and believed that he should provide for his child the best education of which he knew. He gave much thought to the matter and decided what he considered

[6] Florence M. Teagarden, "The Man Who Would Educate His Son: A Fable," © *School and Society*, LX (November 25, 1944), pp. 347–349. Used by permission of the publishers.

the purpose and the aim of education to be, and what administrative devices and principles should be employed to bring it about. To this end he planned carefully for the education of his child. After considerable investigation he chose for his son a consolidated school which provided adequate transportation facilities. The building was scientifically heated, lighted, and ventilated. Architectural design was of the most approved type. School physicians, he ascertained, administered an up-to-date medical program of inspection and prevention. Trained dietitians planned noon lunches, and rest periods were a part of the day's curriculum. Recreational activities were carefully supervised, and playground and gymnasium projects were outlined in the course of study. The library of the school contained the best of the heritage of the past, together with the best of current science and literature. Above all, he assured himself, each teacher had been chosen because he or she was a specialist and a master in his own field. Reading was not taught as it had been when the father was a boy, but rather as the experimentalists said it should be taught. Visual and auditory aids were provided without stint. Social studies, the language arts, science, project activities, and units of work, he was told, were according to the best of current educational thinking.

Day after day and night after night, the man thought of little else than the education of his son. In his quiet meditation at eventide he was wont to say, "I thank whatever gods there be that my son is not being educated as some children are."

THE CHILD'S WORLD ENGAGES MORE THAN THE BRAIN ALONE.

In time the father came to be known throughout the land as the man who *studied* education, the man who acquainted himself with the best administrative and supervisory principles and who studied school law. No one in the countryside thought more or knew more about best practices in education, and so it is small wonder that eventually he was sent for to attend a meeting.

The presiding officer of the meeting addressed him thus: "We bow before your knowledge of education. We respect your thinking and your erudition, and we beg leave to ask you a few questions. We should like to inquire in the first place if your son enjoys school and is eager every morning to be off to the school."

The man looked bewildered as he replied, "I cannot answer that question. I do not know whether my son *likes* school or not."

"Well, then," the interrogator continued, "does your son like his teachers? Is he fond of them?"

To this the man made answer: "I am sure I cannot say. However, I might add, I did not choose my son's tutors with any regard to whether they were individuals whom he would *like*. They were chosen because they know how to *teach*."

"Yes, of course," answered the president. "I can see that you might not know these things, but perhaps you *can* tell us whether your son studies and learns because he is obliged to or because he loves to."

"No," said the father, "I do not know that, but I know that he *does* study."

"Well, with your indulgence, we shall ask you questions along a somewhat different line. How does your child get along with other children of his own age? Does he adjust better to them, or to younger children, or does he get along only with his elders?"

"I cannot tell you how my son gets along with children. How should I know that? I can tell you, however, that in my presence or the presence of his teachers his behavior is exemplary."

"I see," said the president. "Perhaps you have observed how your son responds to people from other nations and races. How does he feel about having Negro children or Japanese children in his activity groups and does he object if the Mexican child goes to the school party?"

"No, I do not know these things."

"Well, of course, it *is* hard for an educator to know *everything* about a child. May we ask you some further questions? How does your son feel when the other team wins the game? Perhaps you can tell us that."

"No, I am sorry. I do not know that."

"All right then. Maybe you will be so good as to tell us how your son feels about home, and marriage, and children. Does he understand how to get along well in the family? Do you know what his attitudes are toward his parents?"

"I am sorry, sir, I have never gone into that. I have concerned myself about my son's *education*."

The president paused. He turned to the secretary and the vice-president and conferred with them for a time. Finally, he said in a quiet voice: "We must not allow our meeting to fail. We shall proceed. Sir, will you tell us what your son would do if he saw an opportunity to get into the movies for less admission than his actual age requires? Would he pay the honest admission or would he decive and thereby save some of his allowance?"

"I do not know that about my son, sir. As I have told you I have devoted my interest and concern to my son's *education*."

"Well, maybe that *is* being rather minute. But you can tell us, of course, whether your son is honest because he wants to be, or because he is afraid to be otherwise, or because he thinks that in the long run it would not pay not to be honest."

"No, sir, I do not know how my son feels about the principles of honesty nor do I know whether they are being taught in his curriculum."

"I see. You do not know about your son's feelings in regard to honesty. With your permission then we shall go into a somewhat different field. Do you know whether your son assumes and maintains responsibility?"

"Responsibility? No, I do not know. I have told you that it is my son's *education* in which I am interested. I know nothing as to whether he concerns himself about taking responsibility."

"Yes, yes, yes, but if your son makes a promise or a commitment does he carry through faithfully in its execution?"

"I cannot tell you that. Not many persons seem to regard promises seriously today—either individuals or nations—so how should I know whether my son does? But, by the gods, *should* I know that? I am truly sorry, gentlemen, that I do *not* know," and he bowed his head slightly.

"Well, then, sir, let me ask you further. Does your son have any worries that he carries to school with him and that may hinder his learning?"

"Worries? Worries? Do children have worries? I do not believe they do. If my child has any, I certainly do not know what they are."

"How about fears? Is he afraid of anything? Is he afraid of people or of social situations or afraid of trying new things? Has your child any fears?"

The father hesitated, and then slowly he replied: "I shall have to admit I know nothing about any fears my child may have—I suppose he *may* have some.—I remember—I remember—Oh! how *well* I remember some of the fears that almost crushed my childish heart when I was my son's age! Do you suppose he does have fears and I have never helped him about them?"

"Well, well," said the president. "I did not intend to hurt you. Perhaps even a more important thing to know is whether your son has some one to whom he can *talk* about his fears, his worries, his doubts, his questions, and his hopes and aspirations. Is he a child who talks freely about such things or does he keep them all inside himself? Do you know what or whom your son uses for his emotional outpourings?"

At this the father hesitatingly rose from his chair. His shoulders drooped and his eyes were downcast. He stood thus for a time and then slowly he straightened, raised his head, and looked directly at those before him. Warm, vigorous life seemed to have begun pulsating throughout his body. "Gentlemen," he said, "I have had a rebirth. It is as if suddenly I were seeing with new eyes. It has never been so clear before. I see it now as if it were written out there before me. I have not been *educating* my son. All I know is that he has been exposed to the learning of the academicians. Oh, I see it! I see it! I see it! That isn't education, that *isn't* education. My son's heart, and his soul, and his feelings must be educated, and I have been thinking only of the education of his mind, and that is not *education*. My child may have had no real education, for aught that I know about it. Gentlemen, until this moment I have never known the meaning of Education."

Battles and Armistices

The battle has raged between the educationists who insist that *subject matter* is the center of education and those who insist that the *learner* is the center of education. These two views represent extremes of thought. Most teachers try to make some sort of compromise between the two. One group of compromisers feels that both viewpoints need refinements to allow room for other significant considerations. Another group of compromisers feels that the subject-centered viewpoint is vital, but that the learner is deserving of equal consideration. We shall examine some of the views of these compromisers in order to illustrate some of the compromise philosophies prevalent today. The first group will be referred to as the experimentalists, the second as the popular compromisers.

The Experimentalist Compromise

One of the twentieth-century philosophies of education which is neither subject-centered nor child-centered, strictly speaking, is the one usually known as experimentalism. Experimentalism has had a deep effect on educational thought in America. Numerous educationists who have held strategic positions in teacher-education programs have been followers of experimentalism and have shared their views with thousands upon thousands of people preparing to become schoolteachers. Experimentalism as a philosophy of education in America was strongest during the period between the two world wars. Its immediate influence has been on the decline since mid-century.

Few people would disagree with the statement that the undisputed leader of experimentalism was John Dewey (1859–1952). Likewise, few people would disagree with the statement that Dewey was by far America's greatest educational philosopher. Dewey was a college professor and a prolific writer; during a lifetime of almost a century, he produced so many books and other writings that it would take another person half a lifetime to read and assimilate them. Although his training was in the field of philosophy, Dewey became very interested in the vocational field of education. He worked closely with educationists in applying his philosophical ideals.

Frequently, experimentalism is confused with child-centered progressive educational philosophies such as those described earlier. There is some justification for this, because experimentalists lean closer toward the child-centered than the subject-centered point of view. For the sake of accuracy, however, it is better to classify this philosophy as a compromise that leans toward the child-centered approach.

Dewey's philosophy and that of the experimentalists who follow in his wake evidence a decidedly American flavor. Will Durant compares Dewey with Walt Whitman in this regard. The American culture is relatively lacking in traditions. Americans take pride in the changes—the constant changes—that have been and are being wrought in their land. Americans are wont to attribute these changes to the intelligent experimental way in which the people have adapted themselves and their circumstances to unprecedented events. Americans have the reputation for being practical people. They want to be known and judged by their accomplishments. This sort of folk spirit is captured and elaborated in the philosophy of experimentalism.

Most philosophies, whether child-centered or subject-centered, accept stability in the universe as one of their basic assumptions. Plato, for example, was convinced that there are unchanged and unchanging principles that undergird and sustain the universe. Rousseau and the philosophers of the Enlightenment built their philosophies around immutable natural laws. Experimentalists refuse to accept this static point of view. The universe, if indeed there is a *uni*verse, is marked by fluidity and change. As the ancient Greek philosopher, Heraclitus, observed poetically, "One cannot step twice into the same river." You are not now exactly the same person you were when you began to read this book. No matter what your reactions to the book—favorable, unfavorable, or neutral—you are different now because of these reactions. You know something now about a book in education that you did not know before. You are different as a result, and the book is different, too. Before you began to read the book, it held a different place in your life than it holds now. Thus, the book has changed. This, according to experimentalists, is true of all our experiences. We are changed by an experience, and the other ingredients of the experience are changed as well. We are changed because our understandings, attitudes, or reactions are changed. The other components of the experience are changed because they are viewed differently before and after we have been involved in the experience. Nothing, then, is static or constant. Everything changes.

Everything that a person knows for certain is based ultimately on experience. Until a person has experienced something for himself, he can only speculate about it. Experiences themselves change as they are repeated. "One cannot step twice into the same river." Knowledge, therefore, is no more static than any other component. Before a person has driven an automobile, he cannot know fully what it is like to be in command of a ton of moving machinery on a roadway. He can only theorize. But subsequent

Leland Harriman

KNOWLEDGE COMES FROM EXPERIENCE.

experiences behind the wheel of an automobile are never identical to that first experience of releasing the clutch, stepping on the gas pedal, and having a bulky automobile move. Knowledge is relative to what has gone before, to the situation in which it was gained, and to situations that follow. We gain knowledge (we learn) from the experiences in which we are involved. Learning cannot be divorced from life, because learning occurs as we face and live through our life's experiences.

We learn from situations that are meaningful to us. Something is meaningful when it is challenging. And something is most challenging to us when it confronts us as a genuine, real-life problem. Learning is most likely to occur in a practical setting. When confronted with a practical, genuine problem, the best approach for a person to take is the scientific one. The scientific way to meet a problem involves appraising the problem, hypothesizing, gathering data, and experimentally applying hypotheses and the data until the problem is resolved. The scientific approach is an experiential and experimental adaptation to problems. One finds out by trying out.

Some of the genuine problems that beset us and through which we learn are personal problems. Very frequently, however, the problems we face are also faced by other people at the same time. This means that sometimes an individual struggles alone with a problem, and that at other times he works with several people toward solving a mutual problem. When a problem is of a group nature, there is an adjunct to the scientific method that is of great significance to experimentalists. All of the people who face a common problem should become involved in the experience of solving that problem for two reasons. First, since we grow in knowledge and since we learn through experiences, the more people participating in solving the problem, the more learning done and the more knowledge gained. Second, each person brings to the solution of a problem a different background of experiences and insights from those of everyone else. These experiential backgrounds and insights can be shared with the other people. Individual differences among people can be exploited to the benefit of everyone concerned. The more people involved, the greater the chances of finding a highly satisfactory solution to the problem. Experimentalists are deeply committed to a Jacksonian variety of democracy that emphasizes the worth and value and importance and dignity of everyone.

In applying this philosophy of experimentalism to the school, one can readily see how it departs from both the subject-centered and the child-centered philosophies of education. The latter are based on concepts of permanence and stability in the universe. The subject-centered view assumes that the catalogued heritage of the past is sufficiently changeless to be applicable to the present and the future. Subject-centered educationists can speak authoritatively about what a person *must* know. The child-centered view assumes that the inner nature of the child is so dependable that a curriculum can be built around it. Experimentalists, with their fluid universe, can speak neither of timeless truths to be learned nor of constancy and reliability in nature. It is absurd for a group of experts to set up a rigid curriculum and impose it upon students when experience and knowledge are not rigid. It is equally absurd for children to determine through the magic of their inner tendencies their own curriculum when there is no guarantee that inner tendencies are immutable.

A curriculum is situational. It develops and changes, as does all else.

Courtesy of the Aerospace Corporation

WHAT MAKES THE TIN CAN TALK? HERE IS A PROBLEM WHICH COULD LEAD THE CHILD INTO LEARNING A GREAT DEAL ABOUT BOTH PHYSICS AND COMMUNICATION.

Children learn by meeting the problems that beset them. The curriculum should be viewed as a series of problems so genuine and so real to the pupils that they become involved in them. This does not mean that the curriculum is haphazard, unplanned, or chaotic. Far from it. The teacher is a guide who purposely directs his students into situations in which there will be genuine problems of a sort which, in all probability, the students can meet, face, and resolve satisfactorily. The curriculum is not separate from life outside the ivied walls of the school. Schoolwork is a microcosm of the macrocosm that confronts people in real life.

Pupils at school are taught how to solve their problems intelligently by using a scientific and experimental approach. In so doing, they experience how knowledge is gained, and how knowledge from former experiences is applied in the solution of new problems. The education they receive is highly practical, because it springs from experiences that are real to the students.

Experimentalists distrust the use of mere verbalization as a way of teaching. When children are forced to memorize materials that have no meaning in their lives (because they have not experienced them), they really have not learned the materials. Teaching cut-and-dried subjects from a textbook is impractical and a waste of time, because children and adults alike learn from being involved in experiences. All teaching, therefore, should be experiential. Meaningless materials, when memorized, may soon be forgotten and will probably not be used. Materials discovered through living in a real-life situation probably will be remembered without being memorized, because they have made a difference in the lives of the learners.

The commitment of the experimentalists to democratic processes leads them to emphasize the use of democracy within the classroom and within the entire administrative structure of the school. Within the classroom the children should be given a chance to experience democracy by living democratically. The teacher should not be a boss; instead, he should be a friend, guide, counselor, and older sibling, as he assists his students in meeting satisfactorily the problems they encounter at school. The children should be given every opportunity to work cooperatively with their peers in resolving their mutual problems.

From the administrative standpoint, the superintendent and the principal cannot afford to be bosses; they are teachers also. If they deny their staffs and their public an opportunity to participate in decision-making, the school is failing in a part of its mission. Administrative problems should be shared widely so that as many people as possible can bring their unique personalities to bear on the problems, and so that as many as possible can grow in knowledge by experiencing these problems. Happy solutions to administrative problems are most likely to be found when a large number of people aid in the solutions.

The point of view of the experimentalists is neither child-centered nor subject-centered. It is a problem-centered approach, in which, through intelligent experiencing and experimenting, people and subject matter are brought together in meaningful real-life situations.

The Popular Compromise

The popular compromisers are the more prevalent of the educational compromisers in America today. They attempt to effect some sort of reconciliation between two contradictory social forces that they consider significant. One of these is the shared heritage, which is a homogenizing force. As mentioned in Chapter 2, people who share a culture tend to be similar in their behavior and outlook. The common learnings offered by an established series of school subjects, contribute to this sort of similarity. At the same time, people differ psychologically and sociologically even though they may practice the same culture in some respects. People are not completely interchangeable; each person is unique. The popular compromisers attempt to harmonize the individual differences of the learners and the standardization that accompanies a predetermined curriculum.

They are convinced that there are some subjects in the curriculum that are essential, but that children need to be respected, too. One cannot say that either the subject matter or the pupil is the center of education; they are both at the center of education. If one were to step into the average American classroom today, one would find probably that the teacher subscribes to this middle-of-the-road position.

Adults, through a variety of techniques, work out a course of study for each school grade. They decide which arithmetical concepts are appropriate for grade three, and which for grade six. They decide which grammar lessons shall be taught in grade four, and which in grade seven. They decide which social-studies materials shall be covered in grade five, and which ones shall be covered in grade eight. They decide which books shall be used. They decide what courses must be taken if the pupil is to graduate from high school. They determine the courses that must be taken by a student in order to graduate from college. All of this is quite obviously subject-centered and belongs with the subject-matter-dominated point of view. The approach, however, is tempered by considerations for the learners also.

From current educational practices several examples of this reconciliation of individual differences and the homogenizing effects of essential learnings can be cited. Here are three present-day illustrations.

Team Teaching

Team teaching, a plan of organizing subject matter, classes, teachers, and pupils, has become popularized during the last decade. In some circles team teaching is thought to be an innovation and even a fad. Those people who are grounded thoroughly in the history of American education realize that team teaching as an idea is by no means neoteric. Its roots can be found in such diverse practices as, for example, the monitorial system, with its use of a master teacher and subordinate teachers as well as varying sizes of study groups; and, for example, the survey courses that were common on the collegiate level some years ago with their crews of teachers; and, for example, the use of specialists on the elementary level who teach cooperatively with the regular teachers in the classroom.

Team teaching can be entirely subject-centered. It can also be rather child-centered. As popularly conceived at the present time, however, team teaching is a flexible coalition of students and teaching talent which adapts the learning processes to the students, the teachers, and the materials to be learned.

In the traditional, large elementary school there will be, let us say, four or five third grades, each having a separate teacher and a separate group of pupils. In the traditional, large secondary school there will be, let us say, four or five sections of a class in the same subject, meeting during the same period. Each section will have a separate teacher and a separate group of pupils. In either case, the teachers actually are not interchangeable, even though their assignments suggest that they are. The backgrounds, the preparation, the interests, the talents, and the abilities of the teachers will vary. Likewise, the students are far from interchangeable, and they will bring to the school their sociological and psychological differences. Team teaching is a means whereby the differences both in teachers and in pupils can be used to educational advantage, by bringing together as a block the separate classes studying the same materials at the same time, and by pooling the teachers and the pupils.

Several teachers in one school who teach the same grade, or who teach the same subject at the same time, join together as a team. They combine their separate classes into a single corps. The teachers determine in concert how best to bring subject matter and students together while, at the same time, exploiting most fully the differences among the teachers themselves. Instead of each teacher being responsible for his own class only, he shares his students with the other teachers on the team, and assumes part of the responsibility for the students assigned to the other members of the team. For example, let us say that four high-school teachers are assigned to tenth-grade English classes composed of thirty pupils each during Period Three of the school day. These teachers decide to use the team approach. The 120 students are combined into a single block, each teacher having responsibilities for all of the students. The four teachers plan how, daily, weekly, and monthly, to teach the students in the best possible fashion, recognizing that both the teachers and the students possess individual differences. Because team teaching is marked by flexibility, it is difficult to state categorically how they might proceed from this point. Occasionally all of the students might meet together as a single class to be instructed by the member of the teaching team who is best able to present a particular body of material to a large group. Occasionally one teacher might take half of the students, while each of the other three handle only one-sixth of the students. Or any other combination of students with teachers could be possible. The students are brought together, or divided, as the subject matter and the talents of teachers and students dictate. Large lecture sessions, individual conferences, supervised study for slow or fast learners, individual or group work on projects or problems, seminars, informal discussion groups, individual or group research—all of these become possible when the teachers can readily shift the size of the groups with which they are working.

The flexibility of team teaching makes it possible for all of the pupils to be exposed to a variety of teaching situations and the best abilities of several teachers. It makes it possible for teachers to have some spare time occasionally for pupil conferences, and to prepare better for their classes provided that the school administrators will cooperate with them in this regard. It makes it possible for teachers to give more individualized attention to all of the pupils. It makes it possible for students of similar abilities to be grouped together without feeling alienated from the other students. Team teaching combines, thus, a commitment to subject matter and a deep interest in the human side of the educative process as it relates both to teachers and students.

The Education of Students Who Are Divergent Intellectually

Most people are rather average when it comes to most human characteristics. Human traits tend to be so distributed that few people within a society are so different from their fellows that they appear odd or aberrant. Regarding intelligence (as we are able at present to measure it), the vast majority of people are close to average. If one accepts at face value the arbitrary intelligence quotient of one hundred as the average, almost 90 per cent of the American people have intelligence quotients which fall

"The Oregon Statesman," Salem

TEAM TEACHING PERMITS FLEXIBILITY IN THE USE OF TEACHER TALENT AND IN
THE GROUPING OF PUPILS.

within twenty points of that score. Only a scant handful of people possess
I. Q.'s above one hundred and twenty. Another scant handful of people
possess I. Q.'s below eighty.

There has been a tendency—probably a growing tendency since the
introduction of compulsory attendance laws—for teachers in traditional,
subject-centered educational settings to address their teaching to those
"average" students whose intellectual endowments fall within the usual
limits. If all factors except intelligence are totally disregarded,[7] almost all
students in the typical class are able to understand the presentation, complete the standard assignments, and make minimum acceptable scores on

[7] This discussion is purposely so oriented.

whatever tests or other measurements of attainment are used. A few pupils are too slow-witted to respond acceptably or to comprehend the lessons as presented.

In the days when school attendance was not obligatory, the question of dealing with mentally inept pupils was not critical. Today it is. As they are identified, the most extreme cases of mental retardation become segregated commonly in special establishments. This means that, for practical purposes, the most extreme cases will be rapidly weeded out and rarely found in the upper grades of the elementary school or in a high school. These most exceptional cases, therefore, need not concern us here. It is the borderline cases that are most often present in the schools, and there are enough of them to create a problem.

Humanitarian and egalitarian impulses on the part of parents and public, as well as the enlightened understandings on the part of educationists, have pushed for an adaptation of curricular materials when dealing with mentally retarded children. Compulsory education laws insist that slow learners attend school with the same regularity as average and fast learners. It seems to be a sacrifice of human dignity to force slow learners into situations in which almost constantly they must be frustrated by failure and must be made to feel inferior. Human compassion and a realization derived from scientific research dictate that slow learners cannot be treated in precisely the same fashion as the others. Special provisions are needed if these children are to reap the benefits from education that the society wants them to have.

During much of the twentieth century, both formal and informal attempts have been made to modify the presentation of subject matter for subnormal learners. An early technique, still fairly prevalent, has been to offer individualized tutorial help to slow learners. This subject-centered method has assumed that the crucial factor is the amount of time spent in learning an idea—that slow learners can learn the same materials that other pupils can grasp if given more time. Teachers have tutored retarded children before school convenes in the morning, or after school in the afternoon, or during time assigned to recess or lunch. Though based on a half-truth, this practice is also based on a half-lie. Something meaningless when heard once may remain meaningless when heard a hundred times. Merely lengthening the lesson time for slow learners may not in itself resolve their intellectual shortcomings.

More recently, middle-of-the-road educationists have come to the realization that increasing the amount of subject-matter instruction is not the panacea for mental retardation. Subject-centered curriculums, and their consequent administrative procedures, need to be recast in order to meet squarely the individual differences presented by subnormal learners. Reshaping educational procedures has given rise to practices such as the following for dealing with slow learners. First, special classes for slow learners can be found at all three levels of education, from separate grades based on ability at the elementary level, to general survey courses at the secondary level, to noncredit make-up courses such as "bonehead" English at the collegiate level. Second, on the junior- and senior-high-school level especially, there has been a trend toward broadening the required courses and enlarging the scope of the electives. This has been done to accommodate differences in pupils, including those of retarded students. For example, the required courses in mathematics need not be limited to algebra and geometry only. A student might select, instead, as his required courses business mathematics or general mathematics. And public speaking or drama might be substituted for part of the required course work in English. Broadened required courses and broadened electives make it possible for the slow learner to find some material that will be rewarding to him as well as within his limited grasp. A third procedure is to center instruction around projects and problems, rather than around the mastery of bookish materials. Slow learners can feel that they are making a contribution to the class when they become engaged in studies that they can manage successfully. For instance, if a class is studying the westward movement of American history, a slow learner might find out about the typical diet on a wagon train. He might even prepare a meal in the manner of the pioneers. Or perhaps he could draw authentic pictures of Conestoga wagons if he is artistically inclined. These practices stem from the point of view that education is more than the mastery of subject matter. Education includes also the most favorable development of the individual's own unique traits for the benefit of himself and society.

At the other end of the intellectual scale are the fast learners. Their proportionate size in the student body increases as they reach more advanced grade levels because of the identification and segregation of the extremely dull children and the dropping out of pupils with meager amounts of intellectual ability. Theoretically, at least, the graduate school of a university should be expected to contain only mentally able students. Fast learners have tended to receive less attention than slow learners during the past half-century, partly because they have not usually been looked upon as aberrant, even though they are abnormally adept at learning abstract materials. The lack of attention directed toward gifted children is relative, however, as the above comments suggest. Universities have been oriented far more in terms of students who are above average in intelligence than in terms of those who are below average. But in the schools there has been less regard for gifted students than for subnormal children. One educational psychologist has stated the matter in these words.

There has persisted a belief that the dull should be pushed and helped more than the bright. It has even been argued that the bright must not be pushed or urged along because their minds would be injured, the assumption being that such rushing would not injure the dull mind. We wonder if a mechanic would reason thus about the differences between speeding a small, four-cylinder automobile and a high-powered, twelve-cylinder one! [8]

The means of dealing with gifted students has changed over the years from an emphasis on acceleration to an emphasis on enrichment. Acceleration has tended to accompany a subject-centered approach, and is based on the idea that the mastery of a certain quantity of subject matter is the criterion to be used in determining when a child should be promoted and eventually graduated from school. The normal child is expected to master a given quantity of subject matter in a school year. If a gifted child can accomplish the feat in less time, he should be advanced to the next grade. As early as the Civil War decade, elementary schools in St. Louis were using this method of handling gifted students, and as late as the World War II decade, the University of Chicago had a program whereby, in theory, a student could receive the baccalaureate degree in one year, or even less, if he could successfully pass subject-centered examinations in that time.

Recently the emphasis has shifted from acceleration to enrichment. Middle-of-the-road educationists have felt that individual growth is fully as important as exposure to subject matter. Merely pushing a child through school in a minimum amount of time does not guarantee the fullest educational development of the child. Enrichment has been used as a compromise between providing for individual differences and presenting subject-matter content. Enrichment involves enlarging the materials presented each year to the gifted students. These students may take as long to complete their schooling as the more average students, but they are fed a specially improved intellectual diet devised specifically for their interests, talents, and capacities.

Since World War II, there has been a growing interest in providing an adequate education for fast learners. The interest has been stimulated partly by the writings and findings of respected men and committees, and partly by international politics. In the race for control of the skies, the Russians took the Americans by surprise with their scientific achievements. Suddenly the hue and cry arose across the land that the American schools and colleges were not doing enough to challenge and capture the ablest talent. Almost in bandwagon style, schools and colleges have been rushing to establish or advertise already existent special programs for gifted students—programs that reflect not only an interest in teaching subject matter

[8] H. C. Witherington, *Educational Psychology,* rev. ed.; (Boston: Ginn and Co., 1952), p. 129.

but also an interest in tailoring education to the capabilities of the students. Colleges throughout the country have instituted honors courses and even honors curriculums designed to enlarge the mental powers of the ablest students. In the schools, both elementary and secondary, numerous procedures have been adopted. Able students are placed in enriched programs or advanced sections of classes, or are assigned special projects geared to their talents. New courses, open especially to gifted students, have been introduced. For example, foreign-language classes, for years sorely neglected and slightingly taught, have been vitalized on the elementary level. Even remedial classes for capable students having difficulty with such essentials as mathematics, composition, or reading, have been set up. On the secondary level, cooperative work with colleges is now common. Sometimes gifted students are enrolled in enriched high-school courses that carry college credit, or they are permitted to attend, on a part-time basis, a neighboring college while completing their regular high-school work, or, in a few cases, they are enrolled full time in college without being required to complete high school. In each of these instances there is an attempt to adapt subject matter to the unique qualities of the students.

Some people—educationists and others—would hope that this current trend in recognizing the educational needs of superior students is neither a cycle nor a fad that is running its course. They would hope, instead, that it reflects a basic philosophical viewpoint that both subject matter and a cherishing of the precious differences among individuals must be at the heart of all educational enterprises.

The Nongraded School

A third example of the middle-of-the-road point of view can be found in a contemporary movement that seeks to abandon grade levels. Since the movement has centered around elementary education, we shall confine our description of it to the elementary school. Perhaps the quickest way to understand and appreciate the nongraded elementary school is through analogy.

Imagine a woodland area with a footpath winding through it. Groups of children with adult leaders walk from one end of the path to the other and absorb the scenery. There are several groups at varying intervals along the path. Some children walk very slowly. They linger behind and find themselves encompassed by children in the group behind them, who come upon the laggards. Other children race forward and catch up to the group ahead. Each child, however, moves at his own pace. In so doing, he finds himself at most times in one or another of the clusters of children who are walking along the path. Let the woodland area represent the elementary school. Let the path represent the essential subject matter found in the curriculum. Let the groups of children represent classes in a nongraded school.

In the traditional, graded elementary school, each class is kept separate from the one ahead and the one behind it. All children are expected to walk at the same speed. Also, each year the children are forbidden to go beyond a certain arbitrary point staked out on the path. Thus, even though a child in the second grade is ready to begin his study of materials at the third-grade level, he must wait and mark time until the current school year is over and the next one begins. The laggard, on the other hand, who cannot keep pace with the rest of the class, is faced with two alternatives at the end of the school year. He must either go back to where he started a year ago in the hope that he will be able to walk faster next time, or be catapulted into the next grade. If he goes back, he sees again just what he has seen already. If he stays with the class, he misses some scenery that he can ill afford to miss.

There are no separate grades, nor is there a strictly prescribed amount of subject matter that must be taught yearly in the nongraded school. Certain subject matter is presented by the school as a whole. Every pupil is expected to cover all of the essential material to be learned, but each child is given the opportunity to set his own pace for learning. The pace he sets probably will vary from time to time and from subject to subject. If the child's gait is too different from those of the children with whom he started, the school may move him from learning group to learning group and from teacher to teacher in order to adjust learner and materials.

Often the curriculum in the nongraded elementary school is divided into a series of learning experiences. As soon as a child completes one set, he goes on to the next, regardless of whether some arbitrary calendar says that it is promotion time or not. For example, when a child can read at the traditional third-grade level, he is introduced to materials appropriate to that level whether he has been in school one year or four. The child is introduced to materials when he is ready for them. An ignoring of the rigid grade-level categories makes this approach possible. Each child can be grouped with students who are working at his level, regardless of age differences. If capabilities change, the children can be reshuffled.

Advocates of the nongraded elementary school insist that grade levels must be forgotten completely. We must cease to think in terms of either a particular body of subject matter belonging to a certain grade, or a child of a certain chronological age belonging to a certain grade. The elementary curriculum consists of a series of learning experiences that each child should undertake at his own rate of speed. In a six-year elementary school, most children will need approximately six years to complete the series, although their paces probably will not be steady *during* the six years. Some may move rapidly at first and slow down later; others may do the opposite. Whatever the exact pattern, it probably will show spurts. Some children need longer or shorter periods to complete the entire series of learning experiences in the elementary school. But if one thinks in terms of continual growth rather than grade level, the amount of time involved for these experiences is inconsequential.

The concept of the nongraded elementary school is based on several fundamental assumptions. First, there are some materials that ought to be learned by all children in the elementary school—a subject-centered belief. Second, children are so variable that forcing all of them to learn at the same speed is unrealistic. Children should learn at their own gait—a child-centered belief. Third, the organization of learning experiences into grade levels is unsound, because it is based on fictitious averages that ignore differences both among pupils and within pupils. It is by no means unusual to find in an average grade a variation among pupils of four to six years in mental age. And a child may vary just as greatly within himself in his ability to handle various subjects. Fourth, able students should not be denied exposure to certain essential subjects by being skipped from one grade to another, nor should they be held back arbitrarily. They should work at their own rate. Fifth, slow learners should not be made to repeat studies that they have learned already, nor should they be denied the chance to learn some materials by being shoved beyond their limits into the next grade. Sixth, education should be thought of as the continual intellectual progress of the individual. No artificial time barriers should be erected to hold back this process. As each school year starts, the child should begin where he left off the previous year. The concept of the nongraded elementary school combines in these six assumptions a concern for subject matter as well as a concern for the uniqueness of the learner.

Team teaching, special provisions for slow and fast learners, and the nongraded school are three illustrations of the moderate approach of the popular compromisers. Not every person who accepts this middle-of-the-road viewpoint would advocate all of these practices. But common to this mid-course point of view is the desire to combine an emphasis on subject matter with an emphasis on the individuality of each learner, to the enhancement of both.

Summary Statement

Here, then, are four philosophies of education prevalent in contemporary America: a subject-centered philosophy, a child-centered philosophy, a problem-solving philosophy of experimental adaptation, and a modified subject-centered and child-centered philosophy. Each philosophy accepts whatever facts of education are available and can be identified; however, each philosophy interprets these facts in a different way. Each philosophy, therefore, has a different point of view, a different outlook, a different emphasis.

Every conscientious teacher must do the same thing. Every conscientious teacher must learn all that he can about education. Then he must interpret, evaluate, and appraise what he has learned. Through this process he will develop a philosophy of education that will guide him and direct him as he enters the classroom and as he offers his pupils the finest instruction he can.

The Chapter in Capsule Form

1. Teachers as applied social scientists must use incomplete educational facts as they teach their classes.

2. This forces teachers to make value judgments, which are philosophical judgments.

3. Two extreme philosophies of education vie with each other today in the American educational arena:

    3.1 The subject-centered philosophy

    3.2 The child-centered philosophy.

4. The subject-centered philosophy is ancient and can be traced to the classical civilizations of Greece and Rome. It is based on the point of view that an education consists *primarily* of inculcating a particular predetermined body of knowledge.

5. The child-centered philosophy is more modern. It is based on the point of view that education consists *primarily* of helping the students grow and develop in such a way that their potentials become realized.

6. Most teachers effect a compromise between these two extremes.

7. One fairly widespread compromise is that of the experimentalists. This compromise views education as a cooperative enterprise that strives toward experimental adaptation through problem-solving.

8. Another compromise that is popular nowadays is neither child-centered nor subject-centered, but a combination of both. Education, according to this view, consists of teaching pupils subjects. Some contemporary illustrations of this view are team teaching, the provision of

special techniques for handling fast and slow learners, and the nongraded school.

9. A conscientious teacher cannot escape developing a philosophy of education for himself to guide him and direct him in the classroom.

For Supplementary Reading

ASHTON-WARNER, SYLVIA, *Teacher*. New York: Simon & Schuster, 1963.
A fascinating account of the use of utterly unorthodox methods of teaching Maori children in New Zealand which illustrates the application of a compromise philosophy of education.

BRACKENBURY, ROBERT L., *Getting Down to Cases*. New York: G. P. Putnam's Sons, 1959.
This book is a gem. Its heuristic style plunges the reader into the philosophy of education and makes him enjoy every minute of the experience.

BRAMELD, THEODORE, *Philosophies of Education in Cultural Perspective*. New York: The Dryden Press, 1955.
There are numerous introductory textbooks in the philosophy of education, but none is more provocative than Brameld's, which uses a comparative approach couched in political terms.

BRUBACHER, JOHN S., ed., *Eclectic Philosophy of Education*. New York: Prentice-Hall, Inc., 1951.
Many collections of readings in the philosophy of education are available. This is one of the best, and it has been compiled by one of the outstanding interpreters of educational philosophy.

DEWEY, JOHN, *Democracy and Education*. New York: The Macmillan Co., 1961.
Published originally in 1916, this book is probably Dewey's greatest. Copies are available now in paperback edition. The book is not easy reading, but it is one of the most influential works in philosophy written in the twentieth century.

INLOW, GAIL M., *Maturity in High School Teaching*. Englewood Cliffs, N. J.: Prentice-Hall, 1963.
There are hundreds of books about methods of teaching. Each one reflects philosophical views of education. Inlow's book represents one of the more readable current books dealing with methods of teaching on the secondary level.

MULHERN, JAMES, *A History of Education*. New York: The Ronald Press Co., 1946.
For the person who wishes to view the philosophies of education in historic perspective, this is one of the best treatments. Consult the index for references to specific philosophers and movements.

TRUMP, J. LLOYD, and BAYNHAM, DORSEY, *Guide to Better Schools, Focus on Change*. Chicago: Rand, McNally & Co., 1961.

This book reflects the practical application of philosophy to the schools as it describes what our schools might become.

ULICH, ROBERT, *History of Educational Thought*. New York: American Book Co., 1950, 1945.

This is a most useful and well-written source for sketches of several of the philosophers mentioned in the present chapter.

9

Approaches to Teaching as a Profession

I have not been able to accept the recent doctrine that a citizen who enters the public service can be forced to sacrifice his civil rights. I cannot for example find in our constitutional scheme the power of a state to place its employees in the category of second-class citizens by denying them freedom of thought and expression. The Constitution guarantees fredom of thought and expression to everyone in our society. All are entitled to it; and none needs it more than the teacher.

from Mr. Justice Douglas' dissenting opinion in *Adler* v. *Board of Education of New York*, 342 U. S. 485 (1952).

Thinking It Over Beforehand

What makes a profession professional?

Is teaching a profession?

How and why did the vocational education of teachers develop in America?

What is the National Education Association, and what are its functions?

Should teachers belong to a labor union?

Is Teaching a Profession?

Ranking educationists, professors of education, and college students who are preparing to enter the vocation of teaching have a deep-seated interest in the status of the occupation of schoolteaching. They wonder whether or not teaching can be classified as a profession. They wonder what can be done to enhance schoolteaching's status.

Because this issue is live, because the topic is discussed to a considerable extent, because people who are concerned for education need to assess the matter carefully, this final chapter will be devoted to an investigation of the status of teaching. Four approaches to the professionalization of schoolteaching will be examined: professionalization through debate, through education, and through two kinds of organization.

Through Debate

In the tradition of the medieval scholastics, there are those who believe that the professional status of teaching can be determined effectively through disputation. This is the route taken by many introductory books in education. It is based on the assumption that the side with the stronger argument has the correct answer, regardless of the issue being debated. This procedure ignores the power of forensics. The clever debater who has learned some of the stratagems can make black look green and white look purple—which may prove nothing but that he is a clever debater. While disputations have their place, some questions are far from resolved by debate alone. The ailment of the physician's patient is not cured adequately by energetic argumentation. Nor is the validity of religious dogma settled finally through discussion. Nor is the professional status of education determined by lists of pros and cons weighed in some arbitrary balance.

Even though the attempt to ascertain the professional standing of education through debate is of little value, it warrants an examination because of its popularity. The technique involves identifying characteristics of a profession and then amassing evidence from the occupation of teaching that either illustrates or fails to illustrate these characteristics. If, somehow, one can amass an abundance of positive evidence, teaching becomes a profession. If the negative evidence is more ponderous than the positive evidence, teaching is not a profession. Zeal and prejudice have their influence on the choice of characteristics and the illustrations used.

Witness a demonstration of the disputational approach. We select, somewhat at random, four of the many characteristics of a profession. We then indicate how materials from the vocation of education either display these characteristics or do not display these characteristics. The following characteristics of a profession will be used for the demonstration: prestige, control over entry into the occupation, responsibility for making decisions vested in the practitioner himself, and service as the practitioner's motive.

A Case for Schoolteaching as a Profession

Prestige

Professions can be characterized as the choicest occupations. They are ranked high in desirability, which has the effect of giving them prestige. The public admires the higher-court justice or the surgeon. Parents brag that their sons are priests or dentists and that their daughters are lawyers or pediatricians. Professions are respected occupations.

Does teaching meet this test? On the typical liberal-arts college campus more students will list schoolteaching as their prospective occupation than any other single occupation. Here are our college-educated (thus, our best-educated) youths who want to enter upon a career of teaching. This speaks well for the respectability of teaching. Nationwide studies of how people rank occupations indicate that the public rates schoolteaching well above average. Many parents are proud of their children who are teachers, and they boast of the fact. Numerous young people use entry into schoolteaching as a means of social mobility—of raising their socio-economic status—because of the esteem and prestige that surrounds teaching.

Control Over Entry into the Field

In order to become a physician, a dentist, or a lawyer, it is necessary not only for a person to be trained vocationally, but also to be licensed by the state in which he intends to practice, States have licensing boards that are empowered to sift applicants who seek admission into numerous professional areas. Sometimes an organ of the profession itself, acting on its own rather than under state auspices, imposes winnowing devices upon applicants. The ministry offers an example of the latter. Aspiring divines are given admittance into the clergy of their denomination by ecclesiastical rather than state agencies.

How does teaching meet this criterion? If a person wants to become a public-school teacher, he must be certified in accordance with state regulations. Certification will be denied unless the person has met the minimum standards. Teaching, then, is comparable to other professions in regard to the criterion of control over entry into the vocation.

Individual Responsibility for Decision-Making

One of the often listed characteristics of a profession is autonomy. The practitioner has a great amount of freedom as well as responsibility;

he alone is responsible for his actions. The physician illustrates this well. The physician is given, for example, the freedom to administer deadly poisons and pernicious concoctions because he is expected to use these carefully as agents of healing, not as instruments of destruction. The physician has the freedom to decide when an operation is in order, because he is expected to use his freedom responsibly and to operate only to the extent that an operation is called for in order to save or restore the patient's health. The physician has much autonomy.

Teachers also have autonomy in conducting their classes. They have jurisdiction over the children under their care. They are responsible for the learning that occurs in the classroom. They have freedom coupled with responsibility for deciding such things as the assignments from day to day, the strictness of discipline employed within the classroom, the motivating devices used to stimulate learning, or the amount of recognition that each child shall receive in the classroom. The criterion of autonomy, then, is descriptive of teaching—suggesting once more that teaching qualifies as a profession.

Service as the Motive

The financial rewards for professional work may or may not be above average, although they frequently are so. The pay itself is thought to be secondary to the opportunity the professional work affords for service to humanity, or to some cause such as *ars gratia artis*. Professional people are deemed to be dedicated people. Their monetary remuneration is supposed to be simply a mundane necessity for sustaining them so that they might continue their missions. Professions, by and large, are occupations that the society identifies as indispensable to its welfare. The society wants only dedicated people to occupy professional positions. People risk their lives when they place themselves under the surgeon's knife, so they want the surgeon to cast aside all thought of anything except the well-being of his patients. People risk their immortal souls when they call upon a clergyman, so they want the clergyman to push aside all other interests when he ministers to his parishioners. People risk their fortunes and reputations when they place themselves at the mercy of the lawyer, so they want him to erase from his mind his own problems when he pleads their case. One can jest about the "service" station operator who is not really interested in service but is eager to have profits. It would not be at all amusing if a doctor, a priest, or a lawyer were to have a five-day, cut-rate, bargain-basement sale on operations or on salvation or on lawsuits. These professionals are expected to put service first.

And what about teaching? Teachers, on the whole, are considered dedicated people. They are expected to fit fairly well the television or motion-picture stereotype of the present-day scientist who becomes so engrossed in his work that he does not know what time it is or that he should go home for dinner. Teacher after teacher exerts himself far beyond the call of duty because he wants to and because it is a thrilling experience to watch young minds come into flower. The public looks upon teachers as pivotal people in the society who perform indispensable work. Teachers are molders and shapers of tomorrow as they instruct the youths who will be the future take-over generation and who are the next link in the society's chain of cultural immortality. Remember that one of the universal purposes of education is to guarantee the survival of the group. Thus, the society expects its teachers to be high-minded, devoted people who place dedication to teaching above all other considerations.

On the basis of the four criteria which have been discussed, one may conclude that teaching is a profession.

A Case Against Schoolteaching as a Profession

But there is another side to be heard. Using the same four criteria, one can demonstrate that schoolteaching is still a far cry from a profession.

Prestige

Anyone using the panoramic historical approach to the vocation of teaching will find that schoolteachers have been held in miserably low esteem. In the classical Mediterranean world it was not unusual to assign the work of teaching children to slaves. The ancient attitude was one of paradox. On the one hand, the learned man was glorified. On the other, the instructor of children (embryonic learned men of the future) was relegated to a menial status. Lucian's words are again relevant: ". . . whom the Gods hate they make schoolmasters."

The schoolteacher in America has not escaped the ancient stereotype. One need not go back to the colonies and to Ichabod Crane in order to find evidence regarding the humble status of the schoolteacher. Within the memory of some living Americans, the schoolmistress was a semi-charity case. She was boarded and lodged month by month by the families within the school district. She received a beggar's pay.

To be sure, when a random sample of Americans rates the various occupations, public-school teachers are given an above-average rank, but in contrast to venerable professions, they are rated rather low. Moreover, numerous occupations that are not professions are rated well above schoolteaching.

As for quantities of college students giving teaching as their occupational choice, several studies have demonstrated that usually the most scholarly students do not want to be schoolteachers. It is the mediocre students, or less than mediocre, who are most likely to select education as their major in college. Only such collegiate majors as home economics and physical education attract less capable students, on the average. Furthermore, other studies have demonstrated, with regard to advanced college degrees, that students who earn vocational masters' or doctors' degrees in education have lower intelligence, on the average, than do the students who earn the time-honored arts and philosophy degrees. These facts do not speak well for the prestige of teaching.

Control Over Entry into the Field

States do regulate the licensing of many professionals (and others who are not professionals). They regulate the licensing of teachers, too. Look more closely at how the licensing is done. Concerning doctors, lawyers, veterinarians, and even barbers, the board that does the actual licensing is composed mainly, if not exclusively, of practitioners of the fields for which the licenses are granted. Physicians license physicians, dentists license dentists, pharmacists license pharmacists. Yes, and barbers license barbers.

But regarding schoolteachers—and this is true in virtually all of the states—the majority of the licensing board (if not the entire board) is made up of people who are *NOT* teachers. While optometrists license optometrists, butchers, bakers, and candlestick makers license teachers. Stated in different terms, while such professionals as lawyers and physicians can themselves control the conditions under which a person may enter their fields, the schoolteachers have little or no control whatever over entry into or expulsion from their vocation. They are mainly at the mercy of outsiders. Barbers, beauticians, and certified public accountants have more control over admission into their callings than teachers have. This does not speak well for the professional status of teaching.

Individual Responsibility for Decision-Making

Review the power structure of a public-school district. It is arranged somewhat like a corporation. The school board is like a corporation's board of directors; the superintendent of schools is like the corporation's president; the principals are like branch managers; the supervisors are like section or department managers; the teachers are like the workers. If there is anyone in this structure who comes close to being as autonomous as a physician or a lawyer, it is the superintendent of schools. But he, too, is limited because he is a hireling also. The principals are expected to perform the work delegated to them by the superintendent, the supervisors are expected to perform the work delegated to them by the principal or by

the superintendent, and the teachers are expected to perform the work delegated to them by all of the above administrators. Even the superintendent is expected to execute policies formulated by the directorate (or board) to which he is responsible and which he represents.

Certainly from the standpoint of the schoolteachers, there is little room for genuine autonomy regarding *consequential* decisions, because major education decisions are not placed in their hands. The conduct of the teachers, the definition of the role of the teachers, the quality of the teachers are responsibilities of the superintendent (and behind him the school board), not the teachers themselves. Teachers are not autonomous. They are workers who must watch their step and comply with the bidding of their superiors, or they may be dismissed. Teachers, in this sense, are not free moral agents. They merely carry out policy decided by others. Thus, they are not given freedom and responsibility for their own actions, because they do what other people tell them to do.

When one adds to the local picture the complicating factors of state-level pressures and special-interest-group pressures, the schoolteacher can be seen as little more than a pawn as far as autonomy is concerned. An earlier chapter delineated the state-level public-school power structure, which actually comes closest to being the seat of responsibility and autonomy in school matters. Pressure groups made up of hyperactive people, who all too frequently display more fervor than common sense, limit the autonomy of teachers, too. Schoolteaching holds a low position when measured by the criterion of individual responsibility for action.

Service as the Motive

Why do people become schoolteachers? There are many reasons, of course. Among them, however, several are repeated often enough to be typical. One reason is that teaching is a stopgap before marriage, or before some "better" situation becomes available. Another is that teaching affords a means of social mobility. A third reason given often—especially by women—is that it supplements the family income.

Commonly in the past, and to some extent today, there have been people who have become teachers in order to earn enough money to continue their education or to have a reserve for some new venture. In either case, teaching is a way station. It is viewed as a temporary expedient to be exploited until the expense of a start in some more desirable vocation can be afforded. Numerous women training for schoolteaching want really to be wives and mothers. They teach only until they are married and become housewives. As we suggested in an earlier chapter, sizable numbers of schoolteachers are recruited from an upper segment of the lower class. They, as well as their parents, see schoolteaching as an escalator, a device for moving themselves into a higher occupational category than their parents, a means to social mobility. Numerous schoolteachers, both young and old, are married women. Their husbands work. The women supplement their husbands' earnings by teaching school in order, among other purposes, to give their families a higher standard of living.

All of the foregoing are important reasons why people become schoolteachers. Many teachers, when pressed, will offer one or more of these reasons. Notice that each of these stated reasons is a selfish one. The person wants to advance himself; is whiling away the hours until the right man proposes; wants to lift himself a social step or two; wants a higher standard of living. Notice also that service to mankind is not present among these motives. If these are important reasons why people enter teaching—and they are—schoolteaching rates low with regard to the criterion of service, too.

On the basis of the four criteria, one may conclude, therefore, that teaching is by no means a profession.

Semantic Roulette

Which side is correct? This discussion has been a game of semantic roulette that has employed the disputational approach in order to determine whether or not teaching is a profession. This approach depends less on facts than on the ability to present a case adroitly. It probably depends also on who has the last word. In the preceding debate, the negative side may seem to have scored a victory partly because it was assigned the last word and there was no opportunity for rebuttal. All of this discussion merely underlines the earlier contention that the attempt to make teaching into a profession by debate is too superficial.

Now we shall turn to more fruitful attempts to promote the vocation of teaching and to increase its respectability through deeds rather than words alone.

Teaching Elementary-School Teachers to Teach

A second means of increasing the status of teaching has been to improve the education of teachers. Passing reference was made to this movement in Chapter 3. By no stretch of the imagination can one label elementary-school teaching a profession before the nineteenth century in America. That century witnessed a major educational battle to improve the caliber of schoolteaching. A principal weapon used in the fray was that of developing specialized training for teachers.

The idea of teaching teachers to teach developed first in Europe. Later it infiltrated American educational thought. In the late eighteenth and early nineteenth centuries, a concerted movement to establish teacher-education facilities had begun in Europe. Prussia led the way. Then came France. In both countries, efforts were initiated to erect governmentally approved schools designed especially for the training of teachers. In Prussia the interest in educating teachers was confined in the early days to elementary-level teachers. People wanting to teach in elementary schools were encouraged to attend a special three-year, secondary-level course of study in separately instituted teachers' seminaries. In France the preparation of teachers was aimed first at the secondary school. Napoleon Bonaparte, as a phase of his program to organize a nationalistic system of education in France, created a new school to prepare people to teach on the secondary level. He called it the Superior Normal School. Prussian concepts of teacher education and the French name "normal" were brought to America. However, they did not come to an educational wilderness. Already Americans were beginning to show concern for teacher education. The European notions quickened this development.

The first school actually to be established in America for the specific purpose of educating elementary-school teachers was opened in 1823 at Concord, Vermont. It was a private school. Before 1823, however, there were two movements that had in them the seeds of an interest in educating people for the occupation of schoolteaching. One was an unfledged attempt to offer education for teachers. Franklin, when he started his academy at Philadelphia in the eighteenth century, hinted that it might be wise to include training for teachers in the curriculum of the academy. Later, when the monitorial (Lancasterian) system of education hit America full force in the early nineteenth century, there was a recognition that teachers using the method needed to be instructed in its procedures.

The other movement that demonstrated a growing concern for teacher education was a crusade supported by a vociferous avant-garde. Its purpose was to kindle an interest in establishing normal schools. During the second and third decades of the nineteenth century, both articles and lectures were used to awaken the Americans to the need for specialized education for teachers. The proponents pointed out that elementary-school teaching was wretchedly performed by incompetent teachers. The way to have competent elementary-school teachers was to offer them specialized training in how to teach. These advocates suggested that each state should have a public normal school for the express purpose of teaching teachers to teach.

As has been indicated, normal schools began as private schools in America. It was not until 1839 that a public normal school for educating

Courtesy of the Educational Media Center, Oregon College of Education

"WHO DARES TO TEACH MUST NEVER CEASE TO LEARN."

elementary-school teachers, located at the historic town of Lexington, Massachusetts, opened its doors. The state-sponsored, public-normal-school movement started at a snail's pace. States were painfully slow to respond and very reluctant to invest public money in normal schools. This hesitancy of the states encouraged two other sorts of sponsorship for normal school. One was private; by the year 1900, approximately half of the normal schools in the United States were private schools. The other was municipal; several municipalities, such as New York, Baltimore, and Philadelphia, created their own normal schools, rather than waiting for the states to organize them in these cities.

It was the trans-Appalachian West that was most responsive to state-nurtured normal schools. The West has been the center of the public-education idea in America, even though many aspects of the movement had their start in the East. In the West, public education has been received, and continues to be received, with greater enthusiasm than private education. The reverse tends to be the case in the Atlantic States. (Notice, for example, that with few outstanding exceptions, the most noteworthy western universities are public universities. Notice, too, that the greatest eastern universities are private.) After 1850, state-supported normal schools developed in fair numbers in western states, and were accepted by a citizenry that was conditioned favorably toward public education.

Before normal schools were instituted, a few academies, apparently taking the clue from Franklin, experimented with course work for students interested in becoming elementary-school teachers. For example, it appears that the Zion Parnassus Academy of Salisbury, North Carolina, had a minimum curriculum for prospective elementary-school teachers as early as 1785. One of the first state-sponsored moves to promote teacher education occurred in New York. A state law in 1827 ruled that the State of New York should pay private academies to include teacher-education programs in their curriculums.

The fact that academies offered courses for the preparation of elementary-school teachers was very significant. This helped to determine at what level the normal school belonged in the American educational hierarchy. The normal school was identified as a *secondary* school, on a par (from the standpoint of grade level) with academies and emerging high schools. This meant, further, that scholastic requirements for admission to a normal school were comparable to those for entry into an academy or a high school. This, of course, was in line with the early Prussian practice.

The normal-school curriculum consisted of three segments: course work in disciplines taught in the elementary school (arithmetic, spelling, geography, etc.), course work in educational methodology, and supervised teaching in an elementary-level laboratory school attached usually to the normal school. The work in educational methodology, particularly during the second half of the nineteenth century, was influenced deeply by European thought. By the time public normal schools appeared in America, European philosophical ideas on education were being brought to the United States. Under this European influence, students were taught to go beyond the centuries-old practice of teaching directly from a book. For ages the standard method of teaching little children was through memorization, drill, and cat-and-mouse questioning to find out if the pupils had studied their lessons diligently. Advanced European thought suggested that this approach should be supplemented in order to enliven and vitalize the lessons. This marked the beginning of progressive education in the United States, as prospective elementary-school teachers were taught to be more than taskmasters and lesson hearers.

By the outbreak of the Civil War, normal schools for the training of elementary-school teachers had become established in America, although their position was still somewhat unstable. Most of the elementary-school teachers had never attended a normal school. And die-hards were sure then (as they are today) that the most effective means of educating a would-be teacher was to prepare him in subject matter only. They believed that methods would take care of themselves if a person had a clear understanding of the subject that he was assigned to teach.

From Normal Schools to Teachers' Colleges

The period following the Civil War was one in which public elementary-school education won an indisputable place in American life. It was a time when the significance of educating people to staff elementary schools began to be recognized widely. It was a time, too, when high schools began to be prevalent and to enroll sizable numbers of youths.

The popularity of high schools had the effect of raising several questions about both normal schools in particular and the teacher education movement in general. First, with high schools more available, people in some circles began to wonder if it might not be advisable to require applicants to normal schools to attend high school first. When secondary schools were uncommon, and when only a small fraction of the population had a secondary-school education, it would have been unrealistic to have required graduation from a secondary school as a prerequisite for entry into a normal school. But times were changing. Both high schools and high-school graduates were more numerous.

Second, if normal schools were to offer post-high-school education, should they not, then, be thought of as colleges rather than schools? And if normal schools were to become colleges, should they not, then, grant

college degrees to their graduates? Further, if normal schools were to become colleges, should their course offerings not be modified to include
collegiate-level liberal-arts courses?

Third, if training improves the caliber of elementary-school teachers,
would not comparable training to teach on the secondary level improve
the caliber of high-school teachers? Should special training, then, be offered
for high-school teachers as well as for elementary-school teachers?

Fourth, if normal schools were to prepare teachers for secondary-
school teaching, should normal schools be secondary schools themselves?
Should a person be expected to attend secondary school twice in order to
teach in a secondary school (assuming that he would have attended the
sort of school in which he intended to teach)?

Questions such as these fomented change in the education of teachers
during the latter years of the nineteenth century and during the twentieth.
Some normal schools remained secondary schools, and at the same time
began to offer an education for prospective high-school teachers. These
schools were not in the ascendency, however. Most normal schools began
to include graduation from high school as a prerequisite for entry, regardless of whether one wanted to be an elementary- or secondary-school
teacher. By the end of the nineteenth century a new trend became obvious.
Normal schools were becoming post-secondary schools. But at the same
time, people planning to become secondary-school teachers were very
reluctant to enroll in a normal school, whether secondary or post-secondary
in status. There was a strong feeling that a person ought to go to college
if he intended to teach in a high school. Normal schools, even post-secondary ones, were *not at that time* degree-granting colleges.

The next logical step in the development of teacher education is not
hard to foresee. If secondary-school teachers were to be educated in normal schools, there would have to be a metamorphosis of the normal school;
it would have to become a college. And that is what came to pass. The
old normal schools of the nineteenth century became teachers' colleges or
colleges of education in the twentieth century. As they did so, the percentage of their enrollees planning to teach in secondary education increased. Also, the curriculum of the normal school became broadened to
include many of the venerable liberal-arts courses as well as vocationally
oriented courses of a teacher-education variety.

Collegiate Departments of Education

A movement parallel to the change from normal schools to teachers'
colleges also occurred in the latter part of the nineteenth century and in
the twentieth. This second movement was a gesture on the part of colleges

and universities to extend their curriculums to include specialized education for elementary- and secondary-level teachers. This movement can be traced to several causes.

First, Senator Morrill's Land Grant College Act of 1862 had opened colleges to the newer professional fields. As long as colleges were enrolling agriculturists, engineers, and career military people, it was not illogical for them to extend the hand of fellowship to schoolteachers as well. The Land Grant College Act paved the way for collegiate-level education in teaching, because it set the precedent of including vocational training for newer occupations in college curriculums.

Second, after normal schools began to become teachers' colleges and to offer courses in the liberal arts, they began, in effect, to compete with the nonteachers' colleges. It is very revealing today to go to a so-called "average" liberal-arts college and discover the proportion of the student body that plans to teach in the public schools. Usually, as described earlier, more college students expect to teach school than to enter any other single occupation. Many liberal-arts colleges have felt themselves forced to offer instruction in teacher education in order to compete effectively for students.

Third, as mentioned earlier, by the end of the nineteenth century there was a growing feeling that high-school teachers should have a college education. At the same time, there was a growing feeling that high-school teachers should also be trained to teach before entering their careers. Colleges are by no means immune to public pressures, especially publicly supported colleges. It is not surprising to find that the first higher-educational establishment to institute a separate department of education was the western, state-supported University of Iowa, in the year 1873. By the turn of the century, an impressively large minority of the colleges and universities in the United States had facilities for offering course work in education.

Fourth, the growth of the social sciences during the nineteenth century helped to develop academic content for the courses taught by collegiate departments of education. When the education of teachers began in America, the course work was offered in lower than collegiate-level normal schools. This set a precedent, the end results of which are still to be witnessed. Many colleges were reluctant to teach methodology courses in education because those courses were associated with secondary-level normal schools. But when the courses in education were seen to be applied courses in the social sciences, they were classified as being appropriate for a higher-educational establishment to offer without bemeaning itself.

By way of an aside, notice how one still finds on college campuses (both teachers' college campuses and liberal-arts college campuses) a feeling that education courses are not on a par with other courses in the curriculum. This feeling is a residue from the past, when courses in education were not college-level courses. But notice, too, that when the merits of specific courses in education are discussed by noneducationists, these people are less vitriolic in their condemnation of courses in the history, psychology, sociology, or anthropology of education than they are in their condemnation of methods courses. The foundational courses in education are looked upon as specialized courses in the social sciences and, thus, more appropriate college-level courses.

For reasons such as the above, colleges and universities began in the latter part of the nineteenth century to offer training for prospective elementary- and secondary-school teachers. Thus, teachers-to-be could choose between two sorts of higher-educational establishments in which to prepare for a career in teaching. They might attend a teachers' college or an academically oriented college or university.

Two other trends in teacher education deserve identification. First, as research into education and knowledge about teaching have multiplied, universities have set up graduate curriculums in education leading to master's and doctor's degrees. This has brought a certain amount of prestige to the occupation of teaching and has helped to define teaching as a learned occupation. Just as one can receive a doctorate in medicine or dentistry or law, one can also receive a doctorate in education.

Second, as liberal-arts colleges have introduced work in education into their curriculums, and as teachers' colleges have introduced liberal-arts

Courtesy of Southern Oregon College

YESTERDAY'S NORMAL SCHOOL IS BECOMING A GENERAL-ARTS COLLEGE WITH TEACHER-EDUCATION FACILITIES.

studies into theirs, the distinctions between liberal-arts colleges and teachers' colleges have blurred. Along with this blurring process, there has been a noticeable trend among teachers' colleges, particularly since the 1930's, to drop their distinctive label and to become general-arts colleges. For example, in 1930 in California there were several state teachers' colleges, including Fresno State Teachers College, San Francisco State Teachers College, and San Jose State Teachers College. Today these colleges are regional general-arts colleges, and they have dropped the term "teachers" from their titles. This trend has occurred throughout the United States.

The Professionalization of Schoolteaching Through Education

Here, then, is another way to advance the status of schoolteaching. This method, instead of using debate, attempts to improve teaching by refining the competency of teachers and by transforming teaching into a learned occupation. This method is designed to make the shoddy, under-educated person less and less able to be accepted as a teacher. Schoolteaching is becoming one of the learned vocational studies for which training is obtained in higher-educational establishments. Schoolteaching is taking its place beside engineering, social work, and business administration as a learned occupation. It does not remain outside the higher-educational fold, as barbering, cosmetology, and stenography still do, with their noncollegiate, post-secondary trade schools.

The dreams of the avant-garde of a century and a half ago that pressed for the establishment of teacher-education facilities in America are being re-enforced in our day by a new avant-garde. The new avant-garde, building on the progress made in the education of teachers, seeks to improve the status of teaching even more. It wants schoolteachers to be as cultured as the best-trained professionals in law, medicine, or theology. The new avant-garde seeks to enhance the respectability of teacher preparation and, thus, of schoolteaching through such means as increasing the academic ruggedness of the work taken in college by prospective teachers, reorganizing the collegiate course offerings in education, and pruning out education courses that still smack of the secondary-level normal schools of the past. The very desire of the new avant-garde to foster the finest possible education for teachers bespeaks the success of the nineteenth-century normal-school movement, which aimed to increase the status of schoolteachers and of schoolteaching through education. We turn now to a third method of bettering the position of teaching.

The Professionalization of Schoolteaching
Through Circumspect Organization

It is exceedingly difficult to raise the quality of work in an occupation if each worker in that occupation is a free lance. It is exceedingly difficult to improve the public's respect for an occupation if each worker in that occupation goes his own direction. Without organization, consistent standards would be impossible. Without organization, the interchange and interplay of ideas among co-workers would be minimal. Without organization, the publicizing of improved techniques would be unlikely. Without organization, the effective investigation of weaknesses in the occupation and concerted action to obliterate the difficulties would be visionary. Without organization, the strength to insulate the occupation from excessive interference from outside would be improbable.

Because of these facts, many leaders in the occupation of teaching are convinced that the best method for professionalizing teaching is through a nationwide organization that can speak for the teachers, encourage the qualitative growth of teachers, be an effective cushion between the public and the teachers, delve into research activities the results of which will improve the educative processes, define standards of ethics for teachers, keep the teachers informed concerning their occupation, and lobby in behalf of education. Such an organization is the National Education Association of the United States, known familiarly among teachers as the NEA.

The NEA was originated in 1857. Before that time a few states had teachers' associations. Some of the people belonging to these associations held a national meeting at Philadelphia for the purpose of launching the National Teachers' Association. Only men were permitted to belong to the National Teachers' Association during its first nine years of existence. In 1866, women were permitted to join also. Four years later (1870) the scope of the National Teachers' Association was enlarged. The National Association of School Superintendents and the American Normal School Association combined with the National Teachers' Association to form the National Education Association. This merger was of deep significance, because it has become the basis of a major source of conflict among those who are vitally concerned about the status of schoolteaching. The merger brought school administrators and teachers into the same organization.

Some people are convinced that a national organization for teachers is sapped from within when administrators are included in the membership. They feel that this makes the national organization a company union, which

is illegal in private industry. They point out that the presence of administrators stifles the teachers and keeps them from being entirely candid, frank,
or straightforward in their organizational deliberations—just as took place
in industry when the company union approach was used. They believe
teachers have reason to doubt that administrators (those managerial hire-
lings of school boards) are on their side. They assume, therefore, that the
presence of administrators in the NEA retards the genuine professionalization of teaching, especially when it has been school administrators who
have tended to hold the strategic offices in the organization.

National Education Association, photo by Carl Purcell

HEADQUARTERS OF THE NATIONAL EDUCATION ASSOCIATION OF THE UNITED
STATES, 1201 SIXTEENTH STREET, N. W., WASHINGTON, D. C.

Other people are convinced that only when there is a single organization—as monolithic as the American Medical Association—that can be
the representative for all educational personnel, can there be an effective,
unified, professional voice. The alternative of splitting the educators into
a series of splintered organizations is said to weaken professionalization,
particularly when all educational personnel have much in common. There is
a common cause: that of developing an admirable profession. This cause
is said to transcend differences in the specific job situations that various
educational personnel might hold. It is with this common cause that the
national organization of education is concerned. In fact, the NEA adver-

tises itself as "the only organization that represents or has the possibility of representing the great body of teachers in the United States."

In 1906 another very significant event in the career of the NEA occurred. The Congress of the United States offered a charter to the organization. The offer was accepted in the following year (1907), and the association changed its name to its present one, the National Education Association *of the United States*. The congressional chartering of the organization is another major source of conflict among people who are vitally concerned about the status of schoolteaching.

Some people point out that this congressional chartering sold the teachers' birthright. The NEA, as an organization created by Congress, is responsible in its actions to a nonteaching organization, the Congress of the United States. It is impossible for members of the NEA to change their charter—and thus the character of their organization—without an act of Congress. This hamstrings the NEA by vesting the final power of decision (of what might be crucial issues) in the hands of politicians, not educationists.

Other people suggest that this seeming disadvantage is more than offset by the prestige, renown, and publicity that is brought to the organization by being one of the very few in the United States to have a congressional charter.

The NEA is rather complex. A clue to its many-faceted educational interests is found in Diagram V. Notice in particular the list of departments and the list of commissions and committees. The departments are somewhat akin to the organizations for specialists in the subfields of medicine. The NEA has specialized organizations in social studies, music, audio-visual instruction, and the like. Membership in the NEA does not make one automatically a member of these departments. Typically, there are separate dues for membership in a department. Typically, also, each department has its own publications, which are circulated among the members of that department. Among the commissions and committees, the National Commission on Teacher Education and Professional Standards (or TEPS Commission) is identified by numerous concerned educationists as the major agency of the NEA for professionalizing schoolteaching. Begun in 1946, this commission is charged with the leadership role in improving the preparation, recruitment, certification, and advancement of teachers. The TEPS Commission is in a position to change markedly the caliber of the teaching vocation and perhaps to genuinely professionalize it. Its activities bear watching, even though they have not been earth-shaking to date.

Separate from, but linked to, the NEA are state and local education associations which, as indicated above, actually preceded the national organization in origin. The state and local organizations vary to a consider-

ORGANIZATION CHART

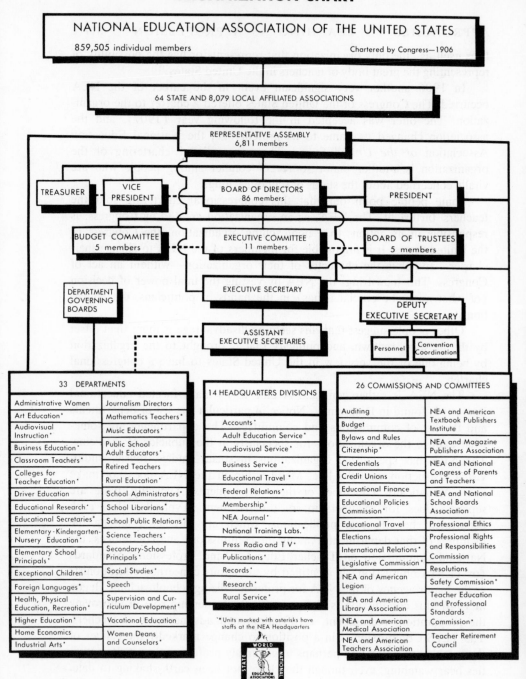

NATIONAL EDUCATION ASSOCIATION OF THE UNITED STATES

859,505 individual members

Chartered by Congress—1906

64 STATE AND 8,079 LOCAL AFFILIATED ASSOCIATIONS

REPRESENTATIVE ASSEMBLY
6,811 members

| TREASURER | VICE PRESIDENT | BOARD OF DIRECTORS 86 members | PRESIDENT |

| BUDGET COMMITTEE 5 members | EXECUTIVE COMMITTEE 11 members | BOARD OF TRUSTEES 5 members |

DEPARTMENT GOVERNING BOARDS

EXECUTIVE SECRETARY

DEPUTY EXECUTIVE SECRETARY

ASSISTANT EXECUTIVE SECRETARIES

Personnel | Convention Coordination

33 DEPARTMENTS

Administrative Women	Journalism Directors
Art Education*	Mathematics Teachers*
Audiovisual Instruction*	Music Educators*
Business Education*	Public School Adult Educators*
Classroom Teachers*	Retired Teachers
Colleges for Teacher Education*	Rural Education*
Driver Education	School Administrators*
Educational Research*	School Librarians*
Educational Secretaries*	School Public Relations*
Elementary-Kindergarten-Nursery Education*	Science Teachers*
Elementary School Principals*	Secondary-School Principals*
Exceptional Children*	Social Studies*
Foreign Languages*	Speech
Health, Physical Education, Recreation*	Supervision and Curriculum Development*
Higher Education*	Vocational Education
Home Economics	Women Deans and Counselors*
Industrial Arts*	

14 HEADQUARTERS DIVISIONS

Accounts*
Adult Education Service*
Audiovisual Service*
Business Service *
Educational Travel *
Federal Relations*
Membership*
NEA Journal*
National Training Labs.*
Press Radio and T V*
Publications*
Records*
Research*
Rural Service*

*Units marked with asterisks have staffs at the NEA Headquarters

JULY 1963

26 COMMISSIONS AND COMMITTEES

Auditing	NEA and American Textbook Publishers Institute
Budget	
Bylaws and Rules	NEA and Magazine Publishers Association
Citizenship*	
Credentials	NEA and National Congress of Parents and Teachers
Credit Unions	
Educational Finance	NEA and National School Boards Association
Educational Policies Commission*	
Educational Travel	Professional Ethics
Elections	Professional Rights and Responsibilities Commission
International Relations*	
Legislative Commission*	
NEA and American Legion	Resolutions
	Safety Commission*
NEA and American Library Association	Teacher Education and Professional Standards Commission*
NEA and American Medical Association	
NEA and American Teachers Association	Teacher Retirement Council

Courtesy of the NEA

DIAGRAM V. ORGANIZATIONAL STRUCTURE OF THE NATIONAL EDUCATION ASSOCIATION.

[318]

able degree in structural details. These organizations are the source of elective leadership in the NEA. Since 1920, the controlling body of the NEA has been the Representative Assembly. State and, under certain circumstances, local organizations are permitted to send delegates to the ponderous Representative Assembly, which is composed of almost seven thousand members. These delegates, in turn, plan policy for the NEA. On the local and state levels there are also youth organizations to encourage an interest in schoolteaching among high-school and college students.

The NEA has done much to stimulate a consciousness of profesisonalism in education. It holds annual conventions, bringing teachers and administrators together from all parts of the United States to share interests, ideas, and ideals. It publishes copious quantities of materials, thus helping teachers keep abreast of developments in their fields. It has more members than any other profession-like organization in the world. Over 50 per cent of all public-school teachers and administrators in the United States belong to the NEA. It is the most important voice of the schoolteaching vocation in the world.

National Education Association, photo by Oscar of Detroit, Inc.

THE NATIONAL EDUCATION ASSOCIATION CONVENTION AT DETROIT, MICHIGAN, IN 1963 BROUGHT EDUCATIONAL PERSONNEL TOGETHER FROM THE ENTIRE NATION.

The NEA has developed the reputation of being a conservative organization, more interested in slow, gradual, moderate improvement of teaching than in swift, cataclysmic, sudden change. It is interested in dignity at all times, eschewing those actions or activities that might bring more notoriety than respect to teaching. It is a proud organization that holds a high opinion of itself and its field.

Some ardent members of the NEA, and of its state and local affiliates, are of the persuasion that the professional status of teaching depends upon having all educational personnel enrolled in the NEA. Thus Cressman and Benda write:

> While the percentage of teachers belonging is now over 50, it is far short of what it ought to be and is nothing short of a disgrace. We will never attain complete professional status until a much greater number of those engaged in teaching belong to the largest of all professional organizations in the world.

Again they write:

> It is the strong feeling of the authors that it should very soon be unthinkable that any teacher should fail to join his National Education Association and become *actively* interested in it. That will be a major step toward true professional status and toward a better tomorrow for education in America.[9]

People with little zeal wonder why an organization that enrolls at present so great a body of teachers must wait until it becomes a monopoly before it can professionalize schoolteaching. A more moderate position is that the NEA certainly has aided the cause of schoolteaching (for which it deserves much credit), that its progress in this direction has been slower than some of its partisans would lead one to believe, and that the enrollment of larger percentages of teachers will not in itself resolve all issues impeding professionalization.

Improving the Status of Schoolteaching Through Assertive Organization

An alternative type of organization to that of the slow-moving NEA is the intense type of organization, such as the American Federation of Teachers (known among educationists as the AFT). It is a labor union for teachers and the second most important national teachers' organization in America, although it is much smaller than the NEA. Even though the AFT is only about one-eleventh the size of the NEA, its influence on the status of teaching has been too weighty to ignore.

[9] G. R. Cressman and H. W. Benda, *Public Education in America*. New York: Appleton-Century-Crofts, 1956, pp. 193, 196.

The AFT is built on several assumptions. It is based, first, on the assumption that workers in the same endeavor have enough in common with one another that an organization in which their ideas may be discussed is beneficial to them. It is based, second, on the assumption that the status of an occupation depends to a considerable extent on the ability of the workers in that occupation to have a voice in determining the conditions of work. It is based, third, on the assumption that one person stands little chance to improve the status of his occupation by himself. On the other hand, if that individual joins forces with other like-minded individuals, the ideas of each are more apt to be heard and heeded. It is based, fourth, on the assumption that morale and output are appreciably improved when workers are respected by their employers. Thus, everyone benefits through such an organization: teachers, administrators, children, school boards, other educational agencies, parents, the general public.

The American Federation of Teachers began officially as a national organization in 1916. Before that time there had been a few teachers' unions, but there was no single federation of teachers that was national in scope. The AFT became affiliated with the American Federation of Labor. The teachers'-union movement grew fantastically during its early years. The NEA, seeing the AFT as a threat to its own existence, became antagonistic toward the unionization of teachers. This hostility of the NEA toward the AFT continues to the present time, despite several incongruities: First, the AFT was not organized as a rival of the NEA. Its founders believed that both organizations were needed. The NEA was needed to better the "professional" side of teaching, and the AFT was needed to ameliorate the working conditions of teachers. Second, numerous teachers belong to both organizations. Third, the AFT has indeed contributed to the well-being of schoolteachers.

By 1925, campaigns against the AFT were so successful that its membership had been reduced to only a small fraction of its size in 1920. Since 1925, the AFT has rallied slowly. Today there are some teachers' unions that are not associated with the AFT and the AFL–CIO. Most teachers' unions hold membership in these larger bodies, however.

The AFT has a simpler, and in some respects more democratic, organization than the NEA. (See Diagram VI.) Nationally, the policymaking body is the Annual Convention, a smaller and hence more wieldy body than the Representative Assembly of the NEA. There is also an executive committee, composed of a president and a series of vice-presidents elected by the Annual Convention. The executives of the AFT are more directly responsible to its members than is true with the host of national officeholders who decide policy for the NEA. As with many of the delegates to the

Courtesy of the American Federation of Teachers

HEADQUARTERS OF THE AMERICAN FEDERATION OF TEACHERS, 716 NORTH RUSH
STREET, CHICAGO, ILLINOIS.

[322]

NEA's Representative Assembly, the delegates to the Annual Convention of the AFT come from local organizations.

States are permitted to have state-level federations if they so desire. The heart, however, of the AFT is the local. The structural details of locals vary, just as the local organizations connected with the NEA vary. Membership in the AFT local is more limited than in the NEA. Superintendents of schools cannot belong, inasmuch as they are representatives of

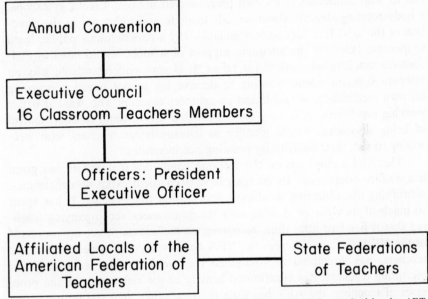

Redrawn from materials supplied by the AFT

DIAGRAM VI. ORGANIZATIONAL CHART SHOWING THE STRUCTURE OF THE AMERICAN FEDERATION OF TEACHERS.

school boards and possibly hostile to the best interests of teachers. Lesser administrators and supervisors are permitted membership in a local. They may belong to the same local as the teachers if the majority of teachers in the local are willing to accept them. Otherwise they must form their own local if they want affiliation with the AFT. Another stipulation regarding membership is that there can be no discriminatory practices based on race or religion in accepting members if the local wishes affiliation with the AFT.

Locals of the AFT have flourished in those school districts in which the surroundings have demeaned teachers. They have bloomed in teacher morasses and quagmires. They have thrived when the working conditions of teachers have been offensive. In these untoward circumstances, teachers have organized, voiced their grievances, exerted pressure, and frequently improved their positions appreciably. As a result, the AFT has become associated with insurgency in the minds of the public, the school administrators, and some teachers. In fact, this has led to the rash conclusion that teachers who belong to the AFT are contumacious.

Since the accusation is made frequently, it deserves further comment. Who is rebellious? Who is insurgent? Often these labels are used as a name-calling device to describe anyone who is opposed to maintaining the status quo or who challenges one's own preconceived notions. Like a gyroscope, a body rotating steadily about an axis tends to resist changes in the direction of the axis. It is very understandable why a parsimonious public, loath to increase taxes for the adequate support of schools, would label as malcontents teachers who asked for raises. It is very understandable why an insecure superintendent, wanting to deceive his school board concerning his own inefficiency, would brand as agitators teachers who wanted better working conditions. It is very understandable why a timid teacher, fearful of being dismissed, would identify as irreconcilables teachers who were willing to risk their security by pointing out inequities.

The AFT's emphasis on the working conditions of teachers has given it a welfare orientation. Its energies have been spent exposing deficiencies, identifying ills, objecting to abuses, and erasing harassments. It has spent so much of its vigor on dealing with the annoyances accompanying teaching that it has had little time, resources, or inclination to set up programs of the NEA variety. Whereas the NEA has developed a code of ethics for teachers, has attempted to strengthen the procedures for educating and recruiting teachers, has contributed heavily to the refinement of the processes of teaching, the AFT has little to show other than the improvement of teacher welfare. Even the basic publication of the AFT, *The American Teacher,* is far too often less scholarly than the *NEA Journal* and reflects the welfare emphasis of the AFT.

One further point deserves comment. Antilabor groups, eager to muffle the AFT, feel that the desirability of having *professional* public employees belong to labor unions is dubious. Three of their reasons are these:

First, the legal status of teachers' unions is in dispute. Teachers, for the most part, are public employees. Does a public employee have the right to belong to a union? This question has been settled fairly well at the federal level. Since 1912, the federal government has recognized the right of public employees to unionize. But most teachers are employees of state or lesser levels of government. State laws and state court decisions are vague and conflicting with regard to the right of a public employee to join a union. Because of the inconsistencies in state policy, some people believe that if a teacher affiliates with a union, he might be committing an illegal act. Thus, he should not join a union. Other people point out that teachers *do* belong to unions. Teachers have done so for years without seriously being challenged. A cautious conjecture would be, therefore, that unions of public employees are here to stay and that state action inimical to teachers' unions, as such, will not withstand the test of time.

A second argument against teachers belonging to unions is that labor unions get what they want through the strike. Striking is thought to be utterly unbecoming a teacher who holds a public trust. While it is true that teachers' unions have been involved in strikes, the AFT has had an official "no-strike" policy to which it has adhered fairly well. Strikes have been a last resort only—not the principal weapon. On this point the late Eleanor Roosevelt, for many years America's first lady, has suggested that the community, not the teachers, deserves the blame if teachers are forced to strike in order to procure the attention they deserves: ". . . if we pay so little attention to their interests that they are obliged to strike, it is the fault of the community and not the teacher." [10]

A third argument against having teachers belong to a union is that the association of teachers with the AFL–CIO undermines the well-being of teaching as an occupation because it identifies teaching as a job, not a profession; it predisposes teachers favorably to labor; and it destroys the autonomy of the teachers. Questions such as the following are asked. Can teaching become a profession if it is allied, in the minds of the public, with day labor? Can teachers be objective in their teaching if they belong to a *labor* union? Is not the AFT really a puppet of organized labor since it is federated with the monolithic AFL–CIO? The anticipated anti-union answer to each of these questions is expected to cast serious doubt on the wisdom of employing teachers who hold membership in a labor organization.

Those who favor having teachers belong to unions point out that this line of questioning is based far more on emotion than on fact. They argue as follows. First, the AFL–CIO numbers among its affiliates people who belong to high-status occupations as well as people who belong to humble-status occupations. Symphony-orchestra conductors, legitimate actors, engineers (of the Massachusetts Institute of Technology variety), even some physicians belong to unions.

Second, concerning a pro-labor bias of teachers who belong to a union, where is *any* person who has no biases? If a teacher is a Unitarian or a Seventh Day Adventist or a Roman Catholic, he has certain religious biases. If a teacher is a Republican or a Democrat or a Prohibitionist, he has certain political biases. If a teacher is a birdwatcher or a philatelist or

[10] Quoted in *The Nation's Leaders Praise the Program of the American Federation of Teachers* (pamphlet distributed by the AFT, n. d.), p. 2.

a numismatist, he has certain hobby-oriented biases. If he is a lover of Chopin and Haydn and a hater of jazz and rock 'n' roll, he has musical biases. Most teachers are mature enough not to be bigots when they teach their classes. It becomes rather farfetched to think that a Catholic teaching grammar to an Episcopalian will shatter the student's faith, or that an admirer of Debussy who teaches arithmetic to a devotee of popular music will crush the musical taste of the student, or that a labor sympathizer teaching spelling to the child of a plutocrat will destroy the child's appreciation for the privileges of wealth.

Third, concerning the betrayal of teacher autonomy, the AFT, like all other federations of employees that hold membership in the AFL–CIO, is self-governing. The relationship with the higher body is entirely voluntary. There is no obligation to accept or follow the suggestions of other affiliated federations. Labor does not control the AFT. Only the Annual Convention of the AFT establishes basic policies for the AFT.

The actor, Ralph Bellamy, replying to the question of whether or not the professional stature of teaching is damaged when teachers join unions, states:

As an actor, I understand the reluctance of teachers to associate themselves with a labor union. I wish that I had the opportunity of speaking to thousands of teachers so that I could tell them that actors, as professionals, had the same feelings and apprehensions at one time. These feelings are no longer present because through collective bargaining and a strong united professional union, we have been able to achieve that professional status which we could not attain as individuals or through unaffiliated groups.[11]

Zealous members of both the NEA and the AFT may err in the direction of crediting their organizations with more good works than they deserve. At the same time, however, both organizations have played significant roles in bringing schoolteaching to the point of congealing as an estimable vocation.

Toward the Professionalization of Teaching

This chapter has reviewed a few attempts to secure a higher status for schoolteaching. There are several teachers' organizations dedicated to the improvement of teaching. A full account of this topic should include mention of each of them, but our cursory examination has had to omit all but two of them.

[11] Quoted in *ibid.*, p. 4.

Schoolteaching is no longer that baneful occupation that it was in Colonial America. The very debate over the reputation of teaching is sensitizing people to the fact that teachers deserve respect. The pressure to enrich teacher preparation has readied the public to accept the teachers' college or some counterpart as a necessary ingredient of the American educational system. This has resulted in an increased public realization that teaching is a special occupation. The growth, strength, and stature of the NEA are enlarging the appreciation of the public for schoolteaching. The assertiveness of teachers' unions is increasing the public's awareness that the welfare of teachers cannot be ignored.

Even the rivalry between the NEA and the AFT has salutary implications. Where the NEA has been fainthearted, the AFT has been bold in its pronouncements in behalf of teacher welfare. Where the AFT has overlooked some profession-like factors, the NEA has been in the forefront. In actuality, the AFT and the NEA have complemented each other's activities. It is possible that in some future day a new organization, born of Hegelian-like processes, will arise and combine both the courage of the AFT and the stateliness of the NEA. Schoolteaching as an occupation cannot but benefit.

The Chapter in Capsule Form

1. A lively question among people concerned about education is that of the status of schoolteaching. Is teaching a professional occupation?

2. One way to determine whether or not teaching is a profession is to argue the issue. This approach, while common, falls short of settling the issue.

3. A second method of bringing high standing to schoolteaching has been the movement to educate teachers to greater competence. Having begun as normal schools, teacher-education establishments are now fully collegiate. The public views schoolteaching as one of the contemporary learned vocations.

4. A third mode of bettering the status of teaching has been through the development of a profession-like organization for teachers. The NEA is such an organization. It has brought dignity and esteem to schoolteaching.

5. A fourth plan for advancing the position of teaching has been through unionization. The union movement has been correcting some serious shortcomings of the teaching vocation.

6. These several approaches are helping to lift the status of teaching to that of a profession.

For Supplementary Reading

CONANT, JAMES B., *The Education of American Teachers.* New York: McGraw-Hill Book Co., 1963.

Conant is a moderate, friendly critic of American education. His book places him in the camp of the new avant-garde that seeks to improve the preparation of schoolteachers. This is an important book.

Education for the Professions, Sixty-first Yearbook of the National Society for the Study of Education, Part II. Chicago: University of Chicago Press, 1962.

This book contains a series of articles concerning the education of professional people. Chapter 7 is addressed specifically to the education of teachers.

EDWARDS, NEWTON, and RICHEY, HERMAN G., *The School in the American Social Order,* 2nd ed. Boston: Houghton Mifflin Co., 1963, Ch. 16.

A brief historical account of the development of educational facilities for teachers since 1860. Numerous books dealing with the history of American education contain similar materials.

HALL, CLIFTON L., *et al.,* eds., *Readings in American Education.* Chicago: Scott, Foresman and Co., 1963, Part IV.

A series of well-selected readings from historical and contemporary sources which investigate several aspects of the vocational side of teaching.

STINNETT, T. M., and HUGGETT, ALBERT J., *Professional Problems of Teachers,* 2nd ed. New York: The Macmillan Co., 1963.

As the title suggests, this book introduces the reader to several of the significant vocational problems that confront teachers, such as tenure, working conditions, and ethics.

KOERNER, JAMES D., *The Miseducation of American Teachers.* Boston: Houghton Mifflin Co., 1963.

Mr. Koerner seeks improvement in the methods of preparing teachers and in the caliber of student who chooses teaching as a career. While the author writes with a bitter pen, his words carry too much truth to be cast aside easily. The book is provocative, even if somewhat visionary.

LIEBERMAN, MYRON, *Education as a Profession.* Englewood Cliffs, N. J.: Prentice-Hall, 1956.

A penetrating, sometimes unpleasant analysis of the occupation of teaching, this is the outstanding book on the subject.

N. E. A. Handbook. Washington: National Education Association, published yearly.

This useful reference book gives a concise, yet encompassing sketch of an important organization.

Index